INSTINCTUAL INTELLIGENCE

THE PRIMAL WISDOM OF THE NERVOUS SYSTEM
AND THE
EVOLUTION OF HUMAN NATURE

Theodore J. Usatynski

FLYING CEDAR PRESS
WORLEY, ID
2009

This publication is designed to educate and provide general information regarding the subject matter. It is not intended to replace the professional advice of physicians, psychologists, or other trained specialists. The author has taken reasonable precautions in the preparation of this book and believes the information presented to be accurate. However, neither the publisher nor the author assumes any responsibility for errors or omissions presented herein. The publisher and the author specifically disclaim any liability resulting from the use or application of the information presented in this book. The information in this book is not intended to serve as professional or therapeutic advice related to any specific individual situations.

For information, contact the publisher:
Flying Cedar Press
Flyingcedar@msn.com

Printed In United States of America on acid-free paper

Publisher's Cataloging-In-Publication Data
(Prepared by The Donohue Group, Inc.)

Usatynski, Theodore J.
  Instinctual intelligence : the primal wisdom of the nervous system and the evolution of human nature / Theodore J. Usatynski

  p. ; cm.

  Includes bibliographical references and index.

  ISBN: 978-0-9818167-2-2

  1. Intellect. 2. Instinct. 3. Evolutionary psychology. 4. Human behavior. I. Title.

  BF685 .U83 2009

2009906168

Dedication

This book would not be possible without the love, sacrifice, guidance, and patience of many individuals. To each and every being who has shown me kindness or helped me along the way, I am profoundly thankful;

To My Mother and Father, *whose support for my education and growth has been steadfast, I am deeply grateful;*

To My Teachers, *whose guidance and wisdom nurtured my soul. I am eternally grateful. For those that have supported me directly- Rennie Moran, John Davis, Linda Krier, Morton Letofsky, Deborah Ussery Letofsky, and Hameed Ali- I can only express my gratitude by serving others;*

To Nicholas, *who sweated with me in uncovering the living source of instinctual wisdom- may the blood of rhythm and brotherhood surge on;*

To Dag, *my fellow Norwegian explorer, for deepening my understanding of masculine instinctuality at more and more refined levels;*

To Alison, *for the editing and support in an ever growing friendship;*

To Milia, *for grounding me in the fertile fields of divine feminine love;*

And finally…

To my Sister, Joan Usatynski, *whose courage in the face of profound challenges remains a source of inspiration- your presence continues to touch my soul.*

TABLE OF CONTENTS

Preface:

What Is Instinctual Intelligence and Why Do We Need It?.................vii

Introduction:

The Miracle of Human Instincts...xiii

The Basic Systems..xiv

Learning and Adaptation xv

The Evolution of Instinctual Intelligence...........................xvi

The Convergence of Knowledge......................................xv11

I. The Instinctual Basis of Life

1. Fight or Flight 3

2. What Draws Us Together 11

3. Getting After It 21

4. What Happens in Vegas 29

5. At the Edge of Life and Death 41

II. The Limitations of Adaptive Intelligence

6. The Seeds of Stress 51

7. What Holds Us Back?...59

8. The Price of Rationality..67

9. Facing the Facts...79

III. The Next Phase of Human Evolution

10. The Spectrum of Human Potential................................89

11. Surrendering to a Deeper Wisdom 103

12. Stepping Outside the Box..113

IV: The Alignment of Body and Soul

13. Assertive Strength 127

14. Real Connection.. 137

15. Determination 153

16. Passionate Creativity 165

17. Peaceful Power.. 179

18. Contentment.. 191

Notes 211

Index 225

What is Instictual Intelligence, and Why Do We Need It?

As we face into the daunting challenges and breathtaking opportunities of this new millennium, instinctual intelligence is emerging as one of the most valuable of all our human resources. As of yet, only a handful of individuals have realized the extraordinary potentials that reside in our instinctual heritage. But that is about to change.

The Discovery of Instinctual Intelligence

Recent discoveries in the fields of evolutionary science, psychology, and neurobiology are radically transforming our understanding of the human instincts. Across the globe, there is a new interest in the healthy expression of the natural energy of life. Modern researchers are unlocking the secrets of the emotional and instinctive systems of the human body. This state-of-the-art research has revealed the sophisticated capacities of the nervous system to adapt to the infinite challenges and opportunities that life has to offer. This research has shown us that we are born with specific instinctual programs, gifts of every ancestor who survived to reproduce another generation. These basic instinctual programs have an innate intelligence that helps us to survive and thrive in an unpredictable world. Advances in the science of developmental neurobiology have provided insight into how these basic instinctual programs are continuously modified in response to each new experience. We are also learning that our instinctual systems can be healed. In the last few decades, scientists have studied the specific neurobiological mechanisms through which emotionally intense experiences can send the nervous system into a kind of shock. At the same time, therapeutic breakthroughs in the treatment of trauma are enabling psychologists to restore the natural flexibility and intelligent responsiveness of the nervous system with increasing precision.

The basic notion of instinctual intelligence is not just a modern phenomenon. It has its roots in the esoteric teachings of the world's wisdom traditions, where many ancient cultures sought to understand the hidden power of human energy. In recent decades, these secret teachings have been introduced to Western audiences, and are increasingly accepted as valuable sources of human knowledge. The Buddhist and Taoist traditions, for example, developed sophisticated methods for bringing instinctual energy of the body into alignment with the higher aspirations of the human soul. This ancient wisdom has captivated the attention of cutting-edge scientific researchers. In the last decade, scientists have invited spiritual masters from many traditions into their laboratories to study of the neurobiological basis of spiritual transformation. They have discovered that these spiritual traditions also developed extensive knowledge of how to recalibrate the nervous system. This recalibration allows practitioners to transform the functioning of the deepest levels of instinctual consciousness. Through these practices, the most primal impulses are brought into alignment with the most precious of human qualities like compassion, generosity, patience, and intelligence. Modern scientists are finally acknowledging what the ancient mystics have always known: our basic instinctual programming can not only learn and adapt- it can actually evolve.

These ancient and modern streams of knowledge all point toward one indisputable conclusion: Instinctual energy has an inherent intelligence that can optimize the personal and collective evolution of human life. Our instinctual intelligence is the result of 14 billion years of evolution. The universe has given birth to stars, planets, DNA, and a miraculous array of living creatures. Each one of these is a living symphony of inconceivably sophisticated design and complexity. In this light, we can see that human instincts are the repository of a profound self-organizing wisdom. Without our innate instinctual endowment, everything that makes life worth living would be lost. The love of our relationships, the excitement of our careers, and the joy of our creativity are all expressions of this fundamental evolutionary force. Through the emerging paradigm of instinctual intelligence, people all over the world are beginning to recognize this innate wisdom, embrace its healing potentials, and open to its capacity to transform human consciousness.

The Evolution of Instinctual Intelligence

When we are born, nature equips us with a set of basic biological programs to help us survive. As we mature, these basic programs are continuously updated. The modification of this innate intelligence helps us to thrive and find our way as adults. However, the realities of the 21st century present a new challenge. We can no longer rely on the basic programming of our survival-based instincts, which have been shaped by millions of years of evolutionary dynamics to respond to a far more primitive set of environmental and social conditions. Our basic repertoire of emotional and biological responses was not designed to cope with driving in cars, communicating via cell phones, mortgage payments, and the very real demands of virtual realities. Something more is needed. Our instinctual intelligence needs to evolve.

Fortunately, the profound wisdom that will help guide this evolutionary change is encoded deep within our instinctual heritage. Our task is to apply our modern knowledge to unlock this code. This knowledge will help us update our instinctual intelligence, bringing it into alignment with the demands- and exciting possibilities- of modern life. We all need to adapt to our rapidly changing cultures. Whatever we do in this world- managing economic resources, raising families, creating meaningful art, protecting the natural environment, or seeking authentic spiritual realization- a more evolved instinctual intelligence will help us address the critical challenges faced by every member of the human race. It also will provide us with unprecedented opportunities for the realization of human potential. Developing our basic instinctual intelligence can help us meet the basic challenges. Refining our instinctual wisdom will enable us to achieve excellence.

Here are some of the ways that the evolution of instinctual intelligence is changing life in the 21st century:

Optimizing Health. One of the leading trends in the modern world is the desire among educated individuals to expect, demand, and create better health care. The desire for wellness focuses on preventive medicine, improved diet, physical exercise, nutritional supplements, and mind-body healing. The emphasis is on knowledge and education that incorporates the latest scientific discoveries with self-discipline in order to prevent disease and enhance longevity.

Instinctual intelligence is the ultimate form of preventative medicine, and is pivotal in helping humans move from disease to wellness. Emerging knowledge concerning the specific neuro-physiological systems that regulate our instinctual responses is helping medical professionals pinpoint areas of imbalance that contribute to physical disease, mental stress, and professional burnout. For those just beginning to orient themselves towards a healthier lifestyle, instinctual intelligence can help change lifelong habits. Learning to heed the wisdom of our bodies can help bring about disciplined and enriching changes in our diet and exercise. There is tremendous power in the potential to harness our instinctual drives to motivate exercise or guide our dietary choices. Cutting-edge advances in instinctual intelligence are also giving humans the means to reach our optimal physical potential. This knowledge is of vital importance to athletes, performers, global business leaders, and anyone interested in optimal physical well-being and performance.

Emotional and Spiritual Satisfaction. Not only do humans want to live longer, they want to live with more satisfaction. Educated people in all cultures are becoming increasingly knowledgeable about the reality of their inner landscapes. No longer willing to settle for the roles and neurotic conflicts offered by 20th century conventions, there is an increasing emphasis on living life based on one's own authentic values. Humans are increasingly interested in understanding the psychological origins of our motivations and attitudes. This is most evident in the move from dogmatic religion to more personal and eclectic forms of spiritual practice and integrated mind-body healing. Many people simply reject codes of morality that label their natural instinctual energy as evil or sinful. This new generation of independent thinkers is creating an organic spiritual sensibility pervades their lives at every level.

Instinctual intelligence is helping people turn neurotic conflict into spiritual confidence. This knowledge gives us the wisdom to know ourselves as openly and truthfully as possible, free from the outdated concepts of guilt and shame that have restricted the human spirit for centuries. Objective understanding of our innate biological drives and energies means we no longer have to suppress our desires through fear or rigid control. Knowledge of our instinctual heritage is allowing individuals in many cultures to explore the inner workings of their psyches in a way that will lead to real satisfaction and deeper self-acceptance. New methods of recalibrating the nervous system are helping individuals live without fear, control, and repression. Psychologists are using the insights of instinctual intelligence to release the inner conflicts that limit self-confidence, meaningful relationships, and spiritual awakening. This scientific knowledge, combined with the profound insights of the world's wisdom traditions, is making the integration of our physical energy with our deepest spiritual aspirations a realistic possibility.

Embracing Cultural Change. Everyone on the planet is being increasingly impacted by the forces of globalization. The widespread availability of information and knowledge creates opportunities to transform one's inner and outer identity with unprecedented freedom. Who we are- as well as what is uniquely meaningful to us and what kind of communities we participate in- are all in a state of constant flux. Globalization is also affecting how we function in our daily lives. Technological and cultural innovations are changing the tools we use and the speed at which we use them. In an age where everything is available, many of us are perplexed to know what we really want.

Across the globe, instinctual intelligence is helping people overcome the fear of change and allowing them to become global citizens. Without instinctual intelligence, the relentless pressure that demands greater efficiency and integration will be unbearably complex and stressful. Enhanced 24-hour communication within a web-enabled global community can be a profoundly disorienting experience. If we lose touch with our instinctual ground, our sense of self can become fragmented. It will be hard to determine who we are, what we want, and what our priorities are. All of this change can be perceived as overwhelming. However, for individuals who are evolving their instinctual intelligence to adapt to this change, globalization is seen as an avenue for greater connection and support. Leading edge research emerging from the study of instinctive social behaviors is helping individuals take advantage of emerging opportunities for cultural learning and professional development. Pursuing opportunities for excellence will call for novel applications of instinctual intelligence. The dynamic collaboration of today's global business environments requires an instinctually sophisticated form of social intelligence. The global leaders of tomorrow will be those who can best align the wisdom of their human instincts with the values, customs, and technology of global discovery and collaborative innovation. The individuals and companies that thrive will be those that embrace the benefits of sweeping cultural change while enhancing the inherent human qualities of strength, compassion, determination, joyousness, and contentment.

Accelerating Evolution. This is the least obvious but perhaps most pervasive force affecting humans in the modern world. There is an increasing appreciation of the systemic evolutionary forces that created the universe, the stars, the planets, and living beings. These forces are driving the change we see around us. These transformational forces underlie the desire for optimum health, the quest for psychological and spiritual satisfaction, and globalization. The realization that human behaviors, feelings, and thoughts are all directly linked to the universal matrix of evolution brings us into closer contact with our individual, local, and global environments. It is virtually impossible to feel isolated and unconcerned when we realize that we are part of the very fabric of creation.

Everyday in life, we face a basic choice: Stagnation or advancement. We often forget that it is human instinctual energy that drives all the changes we have been discussing. When we lose this perspective, we feel disconnected, as if we are the helpless victims of forces beyond our control. The emerging knowledge of instinctual intelligence reconnects us to the fundamental source of change and transformation.

The modern world offers unprecedented opportunities for the fulfillment of our personal evolution. Never before have we had access to better science, health care, psychological insight, spiritual knowledge, cultural diversity, creative expression, and meaningful career choices. There are less and less barriers to realizing our potential. However, this acceleration of evolutionary potential is not available to everyone. The majority of the world's population still lives in a state of poverty or worse. Advancing the human condition as a whole will require nothing less than a deep transformation of our most self-centered instincts. But this can be done only one person at a time. If each of us accepts this responsibility- and learns to transform our anger into strength, selfishness into compassion, instant gratification into perseverance, and hatred into authentic power- societies as a whole will surely follow.

Not the Problem, but the Solution

For too long, human instincts have been regarded as the cause of the world's most difficult problems. Violence, poverty, political oppression- even the breakdown of the family- are all seen as the result of our ungovernable instinctual impulses. In one sense, this is true. When the blind rage and ignorance of the instincts are unleashed, we cannot help but feel revulsion. The recent genocidal atrocities in Europe and Africa remind us that we have not evolved beyond primitive violence and hatred. However, if we look at the greatest achievements of human history, we must bow to the awesome majesty and nobility of our most refined qualities. The courage that led Moses out of bondage and across the desert, the perseverance of Nelson Mandela's 27 years in jail, and the inexhaustible compassion of Mother Teresa in the slums of Calcutta all speak to the most quintessential of human qualities: the capacity to link the innate biological impulses of our mortal bodies with the most sublime potentials of our souls.

While the achievements of these individuals may seem beyond our reach, it is possible to change the course of our instinctual evolution one small step at a time. I offer this book to those who sincerely want to understand the profound challenges and rewards of accepting this challenge. It is not easy to come to grips with our instinctual heritage in a realistic way. Historically, this is one of the most difficult things for humans to do. No aspect of the human experience has been subject to more self-deception, judgment, misunderstandings, confusion, shame, and conflict than our instincts. Humans have invented laws to suppress them, engaged in wars to express them, and developed disciplines to harness this energy. Each culture has sought to establish a moral code to circumscribe them. However, in the 21st century, we are now in a position to understand our instinctual reality in a uniquely modern perspective. We no longer have to rely on outdated codes of morality or superstition. Nor do we have to hide our instincts through repression. Using the tools of science, we can appreciate the adaptive precision of our instinctual design. Our scientific knowledge also helps us decode the accumulated knowledge of the world's spiritual traditions. Through the integration of science and traditional spiritual wisdom, we can learn to liberate the profound instinctual potentials buried deep within the human body. Instinctual intelligence is something each of us can cultivate and develop throughout our lives.

From my experience, I have come to know with certainty that the most complete path to self-understanding is to dig more deeply into the very substance that makes me human. Stored within the mysterious spiral of our instinctual essence is the fulfillment of our evolutionary promise. I invite you to join me in this journey of discovering the origins of instinctual intelligence and how it can transform our lives. We'll see how the latest breakthroughs in science, psychology, and spirituality are unlocking the innate wisdom encoded within the human body. We'll meet extraordinary individuals working on the leading edge of human development. On this journey, we will wade into streams of knowledge from all over the globe. This adventure will take us from the mysterious Buddhist temples of ancient Tibet, to the frozen tundra of the Arctic Circle, to ultramodern laboratories in New York City. Ultimately, the journey toward instinctual intelligence brings us back to our origins within the cosmos. This life-giving universe has the innate wisdom to weave a human being out of the fundamental particles of matter. The more we open ourselves to this unfathomable creative force, the more we find that each one of us is a unique living expression of its ever-evolving intelligence.

Introduction

You're standing at a busy intersection, anxious to cross the street. The traffic looks clear. You ignore the DO NOT WALK sign, and step into the street, feeling you are safe. Out of nowhere, a horn blares and the whir of an engine grinds toward you. You jump back. The swirl of the speeding car blows through your hair. Within seconds, a prickly heat is boiling up inside your clothes and you feel the sensation of sweat on your face. As you turn your attention back toward the street, you notice that your perception of traffic is more acute. Your vision is sharper. Before you try to cross again, you double check around the corner where the speeding car came from. As you walk, your body feels more alert and alive. A faint smile breaks out on your lips. "Wow, that was close…and it sure feels good to be alive."

The Miracle of Human Instincts

It *is* good to be alive. But how often do we stop to think about the biological systems that keep us alive? Most of us have had the experience of narrowly escaping a dangerous situation like the one described above. In that fleeting second, a complex network of nerves and chemical reactions fire with precision, contracting the muscles in our legs, lifting us out of harm's way. Simultaneously, another cascade of neurochemicals is being released into the bloodstream, accelerating our heart rate, preparing us for more physical exertion. At the same time, deep within the brain, other circuits are being activated that will record the event. While all of this is going on, other areas of our brain monitor the internal action, orchestrating minor neurobiological adjustments in response to the external environment. And all this happens in the time it takes to say "Wow, that was close."

When we actually consider how the instincts function, we cannot help but be amazed. How does a symphony of complex neurobiological processes produce the precise set of responses that will maximize our chances of survival and help us thrive in an uncertain world? This is the question that has drawn scientists all over the globe to probe the secrets of instinctual intelligence. This new field of research is one of the most important and exciting developments taking place in our world today. The more that we learn about this innate intelligence, the more will see that it carries within it a profound wisdom. If we are willing to explore this wisdom, it will lead us back to the early days of our human ancestors and ever further back to the origins of the universe. This book is the story of how modern researchers are decoding the mysteries of our instinctual heritage and how this knowledge is changing people's lives. Above all, it is the story of what it means to be human, to have a consciousness that is an embodied repository of adaptive evolving intelligence that we are just beginning to discover.

Throughout history, instinctual intelligence has always been shrouded in mystery. We have admired individuals who expressed instinctual energy with boldness in the face of danger. We have sung the praises of a wide variety of heroes and heroines- hunters, warriors, seductresses, artists, political leaders- all of whom appealed to our ancestors at a visceral level. This charismatic appeal was, in part, a direct acknowledgment of the power of the human spirit to survive in life-threatening conditions. In modern cultures, we tend to idolize individuals who have the ability to express raw instinctual energy with grace and style. Rock stars, professional athletes, and actors often have the charismatic aura of success. Obviously, there is something compelling about instinctual grace. It's something we all want. But we often believe it is the special endowment of a privileged few. In the 21st century, we now have the opportunity to understand how our instincts function from a scientific perspective. They no longer need to be cloaked in mystery and awe. The emerging knowledge of instinctual intelligence gives each one of us the ability to recognize and develop the extraordinary possibilities encoded within our DNA.

The Basic Systems

First of all, what exactly do we mean by the term *instinct*? The traditional view of the instincts can be summed by the definition of *instinct* offered in *Steadman's Medical Dictionary:*

> *1) An enduring disposition or tendency of an organism to act in an organized and biologically adaptive manner characteristic of the species. 2) An unreasoning impulse to perform some purposeful action without an immediate consciousness of the end to which that action may lead. 3) In psychoanalytic theory, the forces assumed to exist behind the tension caused by the needs of the id.*

This is a good starting point, but throughout this book we will come to discover there is much more that needs to be added to this basic definition. To really appreciate the depth and complexity of our instinctual intelligence, we have to recognize it operates on many levels. In the first part of this book, we are going to explore the basic instinctual systems. These systems are part of our everyday life, usually operating under the radar of our conscious awareness. They help us cross the road safely, make friends, find mates, earn a living, and protect our children. At the beginning of the 20th century, the science of behaviorism sought to reduce the understanding of instinctual behaviors to a few basic principles of survival and reproduction. This worked as an excellent explanatory model, provided that you were studying nothing more complex than slugs. In psychology, this thinking became known as *drive theory*. Freud based his concept of the *id* on the belief that survival and reproduction were the two primary forces that drove instinctual behaviors. The understanding of the instincts has come a long way since then. Today, scientists in the field of *affective neuroscience* have identified a wide variety of core instinctual systems. In Part One of this book, we will explore the unique characteristics of the basic core systems, including self-protection, social bonding, resource gathering, sexual behaviors, and survival responses. We'll also meet the researchers who have uncovered the underlying biological and evolutionary basis of these systems. Their efforts to understand adaptive genius of the human nervous system illuminates the first principle of instinctual intelligence: *There are several neurobiologically distinct instinctual systems that are guided by specialized sets of neural networks. These networks form the basis of the programming that underlies specific cognitive and behavioral instinctual expressions*. Each of these systems is endowed with a sophisticated and unique form of adaptive intelligence.

Once we have a feel for how these basic systems function, we can then begin to investigate the deeper dimensions of instinctual intelligence.

Learning and Adaptation

Back in the dark ages of the late 19th century, scientists and psychologists believed that our instinctual behaviors were immutable. They thought that the basic programs were forever hard-wired into the nervous system and could only be modified by *conditioning*. If you can recall your high school biology, this is the saga of Pavlov and his dogs. Scientists like Pavlov observed that instinctual responses could be elicited by a stimulus that had no direct connection to an instinctual behavior. In his classic experiment, Pavlov would ring a bell just before feeding his dogs. After a few repetitions of this, the dogs would display an instinctual response- salivation- whenever he rang the bell. The salivation would occur whether the food was present or not. In this way, the dogs were *conditioned* to instinctually respond to a stimulus that originally had nothing to do with the food. Over the ensuing decades, scientists discovered that our basic instinctual responses can be modified in many ways besides conditioning. The human brain has extraordinarily *plasticity*. This means that it can reconfigure the architecture of its neuronal connections. Plasticity allows our basic instinctual programs to be constantly updated and revised in the light of new experiences. This capacity to adapt allows us to behave with greater flexibility than our animal cousins. We can think twice before we cross the road. We pay for our food before we eat it. And we quickly recognize when a joker like Pavlov is just yanking our chain, promising us a great meal and then just ringing a bell. This brings us to the second principle of instinctual intelligence: *Human instincts are designed to learn and adapt to changing environmental conditions*.

In recent decades, scientists have discovered that there are a variety of mechanisms though which instinctual responses can be modified. In the second and third parts of this book, we will explore two primary ways in which our basic instinctual programs learn and adapt to changing environmental conditions. The first is the *experience-dependant development* of our instinctual systems that occurs during infancy and childhood. The second is the impact of *emotionally intense traumatic experiences* that can occur at any point in our lives. Research in these fields has yielded important information about the adaptive nature of our instinctual intelligence. These insights are essential for understanding how we can develop and refine our instinctual intelligence.

Experience-Dependent Development

Every interaction between a mother and her infant has consequences for the infant's developing nervous system. Every type of contact- holding, embracing, soothing, cooing- even changing diapers- leaves an imprint on the infant's brain. The mother's smile and playful affection promote the growth of neural circuits that regulate the expression of instinctual behaviors. In Part Two of this book, we will review the latest findings of developmental researchers that demonstrate how these early experiences shape the growth the infant's nervous system. During the first three years of life, the connections between neurons grow at an astonishing rate. This growth is especially intense in the frontal lobes. As the frontal lobes mature, they form connections with deep within the brain regions that regulate the basic instinctual programs like crying and sucking on a nipple. As infants grow, the interaction with their mothers shapes the functioning of the sympathetic and parasympathetic branches of the autonomic nervous system. This directly affects the way the child engages the external world. Their responses to other people, being alone, eating, and exploring their environments are all shaped by the early interactions with the mother. These findings show that once children reach the age of four or five, many of the basic tendencies of each person's unique instinctual disposition are already determined.

The Effects of Trauma

Experiences during early childhood are not the only experiences that can modify the responses of an individual's basic instinctual programs. Emotionally intense experiences such as the death of a loved one, accidents, violence, and abuse also can impact the neural circuits that regulate instinctual responses. The sheer power of traumatic events can reach far and wide. We do not always have to be the direct victims of traumatic experiences to have them impact our nervous system. Thousands of people were vicariously traumatized when they witnessed the violent destruction of the World Trade Center towers on television in 2001. Scientists and psychologists have discovered that intensely stressful experiences alter the functioning in areas of our brain that guide instinctual functioning. These alterations of instinctual functioning can create serious psychological problems and are referred to as *post traumatic stress disorder* (PTSD). The alterations of the nervous system that occur in response to traumatic events are absolutely necessary for our survival. It's the nervous system's way of protecting itself.

However, if we look a little more closely at the capacity of the nervous system to respond to extreme stress, we uncover a deeper layer of our instinctual intelligence. In the process of helping people cope with the effects of PTSD, psychologists discovered something quite remarkable. Part of the natural adaptive capacity of the instinctual nervous system is its ability to recover from extremely adverse experiences. With proper support and guidance, traumatically-altered instinctual programs can be restored to a more optimal level of functioning. In Part Three, we will explore how the new science of *nervous system recalibration* is enhancing the capacity of individuals to heal a variety of nervous system disorders. But that's only part of the story. As it turns out, our knowledge of nervous system recalibration is now emerging as the key to unlocking the deepest evolutionary potentials of instinctual intelligence.

The Evolution of Instinctual Intelligence

By the time we reach adulthood, our basic instinctual programs are pretty much in place. Our childhood experiences- while not perfect- helped us to fashion enough instinctual common sense so we could survive into adulthood. However, as we mature, we may notice something has changed. The gratification of our instinctual desires is not as compelling as it was when we were younger. The desire for sexual satisfaction is complicated by our needs for a realistic and supportive relationship. The craving for sugar-laden treats is now weighed in the light of the impacts on our physical health. Our ability to ignore some of the problematic issues of our lives now takes a back seat to the more pressing need for psychological clarity. Traumatic events, such as accidents or the death of loved ones, leave us feeling tentative about engaging life. Our fondness for drugs and alcohol give way to a quest for a more lasting sense of satisfaction. Even our basic social skills are called into question. We begin to realize the tribal-based modes of communication we learned during adolescence begin to feel obsolete in the new global collaborative networks of the modern world. We discover- sometimes very painfully- that our primal instinctual drives do not always coincide with our adult aspirations. At some critical point, we begin to realize that we need to live a more *mature* life. This brings us face to face with the limitations of our basic instinctual programs. This reveals the third principle of instinctual intelligence: *Most adults living in the modern world live in a frustrating misalignment between the inertia of primitive instinctual habits and a desire to live a mature and genuinely satisfying life.*

The Convergence of Knowledge

In the last part of this book, we will explore how professionals on the cutting-edge of human development are applying the latest discoveries of instinctual intelligence in all areas of life. We'll discover how the emerging knowledge of nervous system recalibration is helping people unlock the power and vitality of their instinctual energy. Developing and refining our instinctual intelligence can help us break out of our inertia and bring us into direct contact with the living wisdom of our bodies. For individuals interested aligning their instinctual energy with a more mature lifestyle in a practical way- grounded in both science and traditional spiritual wisdom- this is an exciting time. Psychological researchers are developing a detailed understanding of how instinctual recalibration works at a neurobiological level. At the same time, experts in the arts of spiritual transformation are turning to science. Spiritual masters like the Dalai Lama are increasingly interested in analyzing the long-secret meditative practices that utilize instinctual energy to catalyze extraordinary levels of spiritual realization. This convergence of knowledge is getting at something very fundamental; it is fostering the development of ever more precise and reliable methods to bring about lasting transformation of our instinctual consciousness.

This convergence is taking place at a critical juncture in our history. People living in the modern world face unprecedented challenges on a global scale. These challenges cannot be confronted in a realistic way if our instinctual intelligence does not evolve. We live in an age where the naïve and immature indulgence of our crude, self-centered impulses is no longer a path to happiness. This immaturity not only creates chaos in our personal lives- but it is also wreaking havoc on the global environment. The questions we face in our interconnected world and our complex responsibilities require sophisticated answers from the collective wisdom of humanity. The precision of modern science helps us identify the adaptive brilliance of our instinctual intelligence with clinical objectivity. The legacy of spiritual insight helps us recognize the profound capacities of our instinctual intelligence to help others with compassion and grace. At this point of convergence, we can fully appreciate the fourth and final principle of instinctual intelligence: *It is possible to harness to the innate energy of our basic programming and the knowledge of the adaptive capacities of our instinctual intelligence to evolve the entire matrix of humanity.*

In the final chapters, we will see how this evolving matrix of intelligence- in all its multiple forms- is emerging in countless ways across the globe. The human matrix includes not only our bodies and our minds- it includes our cultures, our relationships, and our physical environments. This matrix also extends to our virtual communities and the technological infrastructure of our planet and into the spiritual fabric of the human soul. Instinctual intelligence is expressing its evolutionary wisdom through *all* of these living systems. As we explore this matrix, we will come to understand that human instinctual intelligence comes in a wide spectrum of distinct qualities and specific expressions. Using our knowledge developed in earlier chapters, we'll examine the underlying neurobiology of this evolving intelligence to understand exactly how it makes us smarter- and how we can apply this knowledge to our daily lives.

This book is designed to help you understand that something deep in the core of human consciousness is emerging. The ways we love, work, play, and create are changing rapidly. A new instinctual intelligence is emerging in clinics and laboratories all over the world, as researchers investigate the wisdom of the body with modern technology. It is emerging in the global reach of Oprah Winfrey helping adolescent girls deal with the effects of sexual abuse. It is emerging in the powerful competitive drive of Tiger Woods to win golf tournaments and encourage children to change their lives through sports and education. We see it in the small acts of courage and determination we witness everyday. It emerges fresh each moment, every time a child receives nurturing guidance from a loving parent. At times, the development of our collective instinctual intelligence can seem excruciatingly slow, as if humanity can only transform one neuron at a time. But that's OK. Every tiny synapse of progress is better than stagnation or the retrograde of ignorance. Evolutionary change becomes more inexorable as each one of us takes responsibility for our own instinctual intelligence and weaves it into the fabric of our daily lives.

When we begin to notice it, we will see that instinctual intelligence is all around us. If reading this book will bring you anything, I hope that you will begin to appreciate the miracle of human instincts with new eyes. As you begin to understand the mysterious source of our instinctual origins, you might begin to sense a deeper connection to other living beings, as well as to the life-giving cosmos. As these connections are awakened, it is only natural to want to refine this intelligence further. It is my hope that some of you will pursue the exciting new opportunities of human instinctual development described in this book. This doorway of wisdom has so many breathtaking opportunities for adventure and the discovery of human nature. We have reached a point in human evolution where our instinctual heritage will either destroy us or lead us to new levels of cooperation and prosperity.

May this book help to tip the balance.

Instinctual Intelligence

CHAPTER 1

Fight or Flight

It's late at night and you're driving home. The road is deserted, save for the occasional passing headlights. After a long day, your eyes are bleary and all you can think of is how good it will feel to lie down in bed and drift off into oblivion. You notice that your steering is a little shaky. Still twenty minutes to go...a little more speed wouldn't hurt... Suddenly, you see the blinking lights. Right behind you. Where did he come from? The rhythmic strobe of red and blue and blinding white flash in every mirror.

Now you're wide awake. The shock of fear runs through your body. You're the only one on the road. He's after you. You look for a place to pull over. Your thoughts are racing. All you can do is wait for the dark silhouette to walk up to your car. Your body starts to squirm.

You're trapped.

The Protective Instinct

Whether you've ever been pulled over for speeding or not, we have all had experiences like this. It can happen at any time, in any situation. Every time we are frightened or threatened we enter into the world of our instincts. To understand this world- and understand why you're feeling what you're feeling- we need to take a quick step back in time. The primal responses of our instincts are no mere accident. They have evolved over the course of millions of years to insure the survival of our species.

The ancestors of *Homo sapiens* were faced with a constantly changing environment that threatened their survival at every turn. In this cut-throat world, individuals that had the capacity to respond effectively to dangerous situations were able to pass their robust genes on to the next generation. An effective response to dangerous situations requires the immediate arousal of the nervous system. The first and most important component of this arousal is a potent *stress response*. The activation of this response begins in the *amygdala*, the area of the brain that is most centrally involved with the processing of emotional and instinctual reactions. The amygdala is a group of neurons situated deep inside the brain. It has two halves that are symmetrically positioned below the center of the cortex, in the forebrain. When we see the blinking lights of a police car, the amygdala is the first region of the brain to become activated. Neuroscientists have known for years that the neurons in the amygdala respond to threatening stimuli before any other region of the brain. Think of it as an early warning system. Without it, an individual would not last long. Among the first humanoids living in a dangerous environment, a malfunction in this early warning system would have carried the curse of an early death.

One of the most important jobs of the amygdala is to prepare the body for physical responses to potential danger. Depending on the nature of the threat, the amygdala will send out signals to the hypothalamus and the periaqueductal gray (PAG) region of the midbrain. These two areas are responsible for producing the behavioral and neurobiological responses that will defend our bodies or help us escape. The hypothalamus sits in the very center of the human brain. From this central position, it sends out chemical messages to nerves and muscles. The PAG is a very primitive brain structure that responds to basic threats like pain and cold. It is located just above the brainstem. This core amygdala/hypothalamus/PAG network is remarkably similar among all mammals and appears to have its roots in our common evolutionary past. Somewhere deep in the brain cells of even the most primitive animals, there is a basic understanding that abrupt movements, loud noises, and flashes of light usually signal trouble. In most of the animal kingdom, the activation of the amygdala, hypothalamus, and the PAG will instantly produce a response that is anywhere from mildly assertive to aggressively violent. It depends on the animal. A startled deer will bolt through a thicket to avoid a predator. A wolf will growl and prepare for attack.

Adaptive Intelligence

With humans, the situation is a bit more complex. You might feel pissed off that you have been pulled over, but trying to outrun a police car would be futile. And a violent response would be disastrous. This is where a second, more sophisticated component of an effective response to danger is needed. From infancy into adulthood, the human nervous system is constantly recording all types of information relevant to our survival. Certain types of experiences make greater and longer-lasting impressions. Experiences that have a high level of emotional and instinctual intensity are recorded in detail within the brain. Sensations of pain, fear, and nervous system arousal are sharply imprinted on the *limbic system*. The limbic system is a cluster of specific regions in the brain that are responsible for processing and recording emotionally and instinctually significant experiences. The amygdala is one of the primary limbic regions where these intense memories are stored. This recording process insures that when similar dangerous or threatening circumstances are encountered, the entire nervous system is activated in an attempt to avoid or effectively respond to any perceived environmental challenges. Clearly, the capacity to record dangerous experiences is what allowed humans to survive and evolve. If some an early humanoid did not remember that the saber-toothed tiger usually hides behind a large pile of boulders down by the creek…well, let's just say it's more likely that *the tiger* lived to pass on his genes.

Evolutionary neurobiologists have shed a great deal of light on the physical basis of assertive energy. For a long time, this life-protecting energy was primarily associated with aggression and violence. Observing the aggression between competing males in the animal kingdom, as well as our own horrific warfare, might lead us to the conclusion that there is little hope for redemption.

Philosophers, theologians, psychologists, and biologists often saw little but destruction when this energy reared up and took sword. However, this attitude has begun to change. It is now becoming clearer how the basic neurobiological substrates of assertive energy can function as a healthy and adaptive force that supports the evolution of our species.

This new, more enlightened perspective of human instincts has come about thanks to the efforts of neurobiologists like Joseph LeDoux, professor of Neural Science and Psychology at New York University. More than any other researcher, he has helped us understand the design of our assertive neurobiological heritage. He has uncovered the neural substrates that underlie the balanced complexity of our most primal protective responses. In his high-tech New York laboratory, he has conducted numerous scientific studies on neurobiological responses to fear. His early research was instrumental in convincing the scholarly community that the study of emotions and instincts was not only possible, but also *scientifically valuable*. His pioneering work has contributed extensively to the modern understanding of instinctual intelligence.

When LeDoux and his colleagues were finishing graduate school back in the '70s, they never could have imagined how important their discoveries would become. Over time, LeDoux began to focus his research on the amygdala and its associated networks. He became fascinated by how the amygdaloid networks encode memories of emotionally significant experiences. Within the last decade, advances in technology have allowed researchers like LeDoux to understand how the brain records past experiences and then uses this stored information to guide future behaviors, emotions, and thoughts. Among the most important discoveries arising from this research is a detailed understanding of how the amygdala stores impressions of threatening stimuli. But how do these encoding processes help produce more intelligent instinctual responses?

A Balanced Network

The most striking feature of the neuroarchitectural design of the human self-protective system is that it can generate incredibly *flexible* responses to a variety of environmental situations. At the core of this system are the primal structures of brainstem and limbic regions, especially the amygdala/hypothalamus/PAG network. The nervous systems of higher mammals- culminating in the human nervous system- display a complex set of external sensory and internal feedback inputs into the basic core network. This allows our basic instinctual impulses of aggressive energy to be modulated to adapt to an infinite variety of changing environmental conditions and situations. This self-protective system is a marvel of instinctual intelligence. LeDoux's research has demonstrated how the amygdala coordinates a variety of inputs and fashions an appropriate set of neurobiological responses.

The amygdala is very busy while you're in the car waiting for the policeman. As he walks toward you, specific circuits in the brain are frantically assessing the situation. Is he alone? Is he moving quickly? Is he a friend or foe? Is his body preparing for an assault? Is there an indication of hostility in his movements? This flow of sensory information comes in from the visual, auditory, and other sensory channels that flow through the thalamus. The thalamus is the central switching station of sensory inputs, routing incoming information to the appropriate areas of the brain for further processing. Early in his career, LeDoux discovered that the amygdala is at the heart of this information flow. Sensory information that is determined to have any sort of emotional, instinctual, or survival relevance flows directly to the amygdala. The amygdala is the primary junction box within the brain for any information that may influence the nature of our instinctual responses. As soon as the officer reaches our window, the amygdala is busy evaluating everything you perceive. The glare of his pistol, the sound of his footsteps on the pavement, the black stick on his belt all cause the neurons in the amygdala to fire. The amygdala is also responding to any gesture of the policeman's face for clues that might guide an effective response to the situation. All of these potential threats cause the amygdala to become very stimulated.

Instead of compelling our bodies into some immediate aggressive action, another set of inputs quickly begins to modify the amygdala's arousal patterns. While the amygdala is scanning the approaching policeman, networks in the cerebral cortex are calling up memories of similar experiences and situations. The higher regions of the brain have seen enough TV shows to know that attacking the policeman would eventually have very disastrous consequences. Images of high-speed chases and tragic shootouts flicker just below the threshold of consciousness. This cascade of impressions flows down to the amygdala, suppressing a violent response and the urge to flee. The initial activation of the amygdala begins to make you sweat and prepares your muscles for exertion. But further action is held in check- at least for a moment- by the cerebral cortex.

The Assertive Response

How humans respond to threatening situations is also influenced by the intensity of our immediate instinctual needs. Say, for example, you are rushing to the hospital to be with an injured loved one. Your response to being pulled over is probably not one of fear. In this circumstance, you are far more likely to be bold and assertive. Your entire nervous system will convey to the officer the urgency of the situation. The desire get free from this unwanted interruption will activate specific regions of the hypothalamus. With its direct connections to the PAG region of the midbrain, the assertive response is transmitted to the entire nervous system, especially the brainstem regions that control autonomic nervous system responses.

The activation of the PAG region will set in motion specific physiological responses in response to the perceived impingement from the external environment. These responses include the classic *fight or flight sympathetic response* within the brainstem, characterized by an increase in heart rate, activation of sweat glands, dramatic increases in circulating *catecholamines* (dopamine, adrenaline, and norepinephrine) in the nervous system, and a general increase in mobilizing metabolic activity. In other words, you'll be pretty fired up. The fight or flight response has several levels of activation. The first level of activation is the cascade of excitatory effects produced by the sympathetic-adrenomedullary (SAM) axis. The SAM activation will be accompanied by the release of corticotrophin and this will have a direct impact on our cognitive and emotional systems. Under these exhilarating conditions, we are unafraid to assert our needs. If you did indeed need to rush to the hospital, you would have eloquently told the officer that we need to get to the hospital quickly in a confident tone. A balanced SAM activation would help you drive with speed and precision. The activation of the SAM axis enhances the perception of the external environment. If an animal dashed out in front of you on the way to the hospital, we could avoid it with ease and no loss of control. The attentional focus of the SAM response helps to accurately identify, evaluate, and respond to any other potentially threatening situations.

In our example, however, you were not rushing to an emergency. Instead of an assertive response, you'll likely feel afraid and uncertain. In the absence of some urgent motivation behind our actions, humans need more information from the external environment before we can decide on an effective response. You wait for the officer to make his move. "Do you know why I pulled you over?" he asks, while taking your license and registration.

"Well, officer…I may have been going a little fast, but no more than a mile or two per hour over the speed limit" you respond politely.

This seems like a reasonable response. By not being aggressive, you are unlikely to provoke a confrontation that you would surely lose. But by not really admitting any wrongdoing, you are asserting your ability to defend yourself. Your instinctual intelligence is operating in a balanced way, keeping your options open.

The Rage Response

The officer looks into your eyes. "That's right- I had you doing fifty-six in a fifty-five mile an hour zone."

You're stunned. Is he kidding or what? You feel flabbergasted, unable to say anything. You're not sure whether to laugh or cry. You hear a voice in the distance…"Please remain in your car while I do the paperwork." In your mirror, you see a silhouette walking away. You feel hot and sweaty. All of a sudden, a wave of fury boils up. A stream of curse words flies while you pound the seat. You're in the midst of a full-blown sympathetic reaction.

When individuals are in the grasp of an intense sympathetic response, their nervous systems are primed for a natural unrestricted blast of rage and fury through the activation of the hypothalamo-pituitary-adrenocortical (HPA) axis. This is a more intense state of arousal than the SAM activation. The HPA activation is the classic fight or flight sympathetic response. In addition to the arousing SAM responses described above, the HPA also triggers the release of glucocorticoid cortisol- helping the body adapt to the stress of intense metabolic arousal. This aggressive response would be needed if you were truly in danger. Say, for example, you had pulled over to help an innocent-looking young man who appeared stranded due to a flat tire. However, as you pulled your car over and then began walking up to him, he started yelling and trying to hit you. Faced with these circumstances, your first response would likely be to raise your arms to protect yourself. If he looked confused or drunk, you might try to restrain him- especially if you felt he was in danger of running into oncoming traffic. Or if he is dangerously violent, and bigger than you, might run back to your car and call for help from a safe place. Either way, your HPA axis would be in high gear, helping you to fight or flee.

But as you sit, trapped in your car, waiting for the policeman, all you can do is pound the seat. The sophisticated set of inputs into the amygdala, hypothalamus, and the PAG, the arousal level of the HPA axis has been modified to respond intelligently to the situation. The key factor that determines the nature of the assertive response is the degree of *perceived impingement* of instinctual energy from the external environment. These complex modulation circuits helped you wait until the officer returned to his car to fly into a rage. You didn't perceive his actions as an immediate threat to your safety. In this case, an aggressive assertive response was modified via cortical inputs. The activation of various memories stored in various areas of the cortex- the prefrontal cortex, temporal lobes, and the hippocampus- all told the same story. Any kind of violent response would likely result in years of prison and needless suffering. The near-instantaneous analysis of the consequences of our actions is a central feature of our instinctual intelligence. It tells us when the risks of certain actions outweigh the benefits.

Gut Instincts

The reasoning centers of your brain are not the only source of instinctual intelligence keeping you out of prison. Deep inside your stomach and intestines, something began to stir when you first saw the flashing lights. You didn't pay attention to these feelings at the time, but they informed your actions nonetheless. Visceral inputs of the vagus nerve feed back into the assertive instinctual circuits and automatically modify their responses. This *gut instinct* provides us with vital information and is an important source of our instinctual intelligence. Gut instincts tell us how our bodies are responding to perceived threats. All of this happens below the threshold of conscious awareness. Without taking the current status of our bodies into consideration, we might initiate an aggressive response that our bodies cannot sustain. Sometimes we just are too tired or hungry to fight or to flee. In this case, the cramping feeling in your gut was a clear signal that an overly aggressive response would likely result in damage to your body when an angry group of policemen chased you down and forcibly subdued you.

Sometimes it pays just to sit tight.

The Intelligence Behind Aggression

In the most basic sense, anger, aggression, and violence are designed to protect us. These responses are aimed at reducing or eliminating the external impingement that threatens to inhibit our instinctual energy. This response obviously has great survival value and there is enormous intelligence in the complex networks that mediate our protective instinctual responses. As we will see in later chapters, it only becomes twisted into blind anger and violence when it is not allowed to function properly.

The research of LeDoux and his colleagues pinpointed the neurobiological mechanisms behind our more intelligent and adaptive protective responses. In the 21st century, this knowledge is being extended to help us understand the psychological and subjective dimensions of our instinctual experiences. Knowledge of the neural substrates of fear and anxiety is rapidly changing the field of clinical psychology. The treatment approaches to anxiety disorders and post traumatic stress disorder have all been radically transformed by this research. Knowing how the amygdala and its associated networks process sensory data and produce integrated physiological responses allows psychotherapists and clinical psychologists to treat anxiety disorders with unprecedented scientific precision and insight.

In addition to the clinical benefits of this research, LeDoux and his colleagues opened the door to a deeper mystery. The ability of our instinctual systems to encode information is one of the most extraordinary products of our evolutionary history. But as scientists began to probe this intelligent response system, they shed light on a source of wisdom that we are just beginning to understand. The capacity of the nervous system to encode complex neurobiological information has enormous implications for our understanding of the deeper dimensions of human consciousness. LeDoux's findings are just the tip of the iceberg. To really understand those implications, we will need to weave together other lines of research, to see how they contribute to the emerging knowledge of instinctual intelligence. As these strands come together in the following chapters, we can begin to glimpse the outlines of evolutionary path to transform aggression into a *strength* that is far wiser than anger and violence.

It Works Both Ways

After what seems like an interminable wait, the policeman finally returns to your car. Your rage has settled down a bit, and you just cannot resist giving the officer a piece of your mind. "Officer, I was only ONE mile an hour over the speed limit…don't you think you could cut me some slack? I was just trying to get home before I fell asleep." Your heart is pounding, but it feels good to make your case. You take a deep breath. Your protective instincts are working exactly as they should.

He looks at you and suddenly a big smile flashes across his face. "Relax. I had no intention of giving you a ticket. I noticed that you were weaving a bit back there. I thought that if I pulled you over, it would give you a little jolt…you know- wake you up a bit." His smile and warm voice feel comforting. Deep inside your brain, your amygdala is settling down. "Now just be careful gettin' home, alright?"

The tension in your belly melts away and you break into a giggle as he walks back to his car. You realize that your instinctual intelligence, as well as that of others, is at work, all the time, as obvious as that trace of sweat right under your nose.

Instinctual Intelligence

CHAPTER 2

What Draws us Together

Why do humans love their children? Why do we smile with delight when they learn something new? What gives us the strength to go to work each day to support them?

Clearly, the nurturing response we feel for children is more than just an idea or even a powerful emotion. Our need for deep and lasting connections with other human beings is a primal instinct of the human body and the human soul. The capacity to form lasting social bonds is essential for our survival. Infants cannot survive if their instinctual needs for connection, love, nurturance, and empathy are not met. As we grow into mature adults, the capacity to feel love is indispensable for a living a meaningful and satisfying life. To be sure, our adult relationships can be complicated by mixed feelings, sexual tensions, and countless other conflicts. With children, however, it is easier to see the primal instinctual responses of empathy, connection, and nurturance. These social instincts are the glue that holds humanity together.

The Cuteness Factor

Kids can get away with things that no adult ever dreams of. If anyone else came into your bedroom at the break of dawn- full of energy and shaking you awake- to announce that her favorite TV program will be on in TWO hours- what would be your reaction? But when we see their innocent smiles and wide-eyed wonder, all is forgiven. It can sometimes feel like the soft edges of their hair, their toothy grins, and tiny fingers automatically elicit a response of kindness in our hearts. This is no accident. Our instinctual intelligence has evolved over millions of years to soften the emotions of adults in the presence of children. Cuteness goes a long way as far as the instincts are concerned.

The Cry for Help

In a very basic sense, the human instincts cannot be separated from the social contexts in which they operate. The basic needs to avoid pain, to bond with others, and to nourish ourselves are all shaped by the interaction with our parents during infancy. These experiences shape our nervous systems and our personalities. When we look at it in this light, we understand that the expression of our instinctual needs is directly influenced by the interpersonal experiences of infancy and childhood.

The neurobiological substrates of human connection are active right from birth. An infant's cry is a pure instinctual moment for both mother and child. One of the most basic survival mechanisms of infants is to cry out when they feel irritated, frightened, or hungry. When infants feel any of these types of irritation, their nervous systems initially respond in a way similar to the aggressive response described in the last chapter. The amygdala, hypothalamus, and periaqueductal gray (PAG) region are all activated. However, in these situations, infants are rarely responding to an external threat. Thus, the PAG will not activate a full-blown assertive sympathetic response within the brainstem. Instead, the infant's PAG will modulate its response pattern ever so slightly, to produce a more adaptive, socially communicative behavior. The sympathetic activation will be attenuated by a *parasympathetic* outflow from the brainstem. The parasympathetic system consists of various groups of neurons and neurotransmitters throughout the body that produce physiologically calming responses. In infants, the parasympathetic outflow from the brainstem into the PAG will help to reduce the level of arousal by stimulating crying and specific type of instinctual response- *distress vocalizations*.

The PAG is a remarkably versatile region of the midbrain, nestled between the brainstem and the limbic regions of the brain. It has evolved to respond to some of the most basic needs of life, including thermal regulation, environmental recognition and attachment, social contact, and pain avoidance. Infants cannot meet any of these needs on their own. They are totally dependent on adult caregivers to keep them warm, safe, and fed. Therefore, when infants feel distress, and there is no one there to comfort them immediately, they instinctively feel that their survival is at stake. Even as adults, the threat of social abandonment conjures painful emotive and physical sensations of being cold and lost. In infants, this fear of being alone and left to die will gradually escalate activity within the PAG, and the crying will get louder and more intense. This distress vocalization will dissipate some of the stress- but it also does something far more important. It's the infant's primary means of social communication.

Intersubjective Intelligence

Adult mammals are hard-wired to respond empathetically to their offspring. Human adults-especially females- are instinctually responsive to the cries of infants. Its piercing rawness instantly provokes a visceral response. When the mother hears this cry, the infant's desperation is directly palpable. Infants are not only cute, but they are vulnerable. At a very deep level, this vulnerability draws forth an empathetic response in the mother. Within milliseconds of hearing a desperate cry, her nervous system will begin to produce neurobiological responses that are identical to the infant's. This instinctive response is called *limbic resonance*. It doesn't just happen when the infant is screaming. The limbic resonance also occurs when mother and child melt into a pool of relaxation. It also exists in all other types of social contact. We often recognize it with socially attuned animals like dogs, horses, and even dolphins. The nervous systems of the mother and infant are joined with a deep biological alliance that allows them to share the same subjective feelings and physical states with extraordinary precision. Their resonance is a prototype for all other forms of empathy and communication. This neurobiological intersubjectivity is one of the most sophisticated and compassionate expressions of human instinctual intelligence.

While the little baby has an innate proclivity for eliciting social bonds, the mother has the practical intelligence that will ensure the survival of the infant. The mother's brain is full of knowledge of the outside world that the infant does not have. She knows where to get food, diapers, and the location of the pediatrician's office. Beyond that, she also has a more developed intersubjective knowledge. This allows her to "know" what her child needs- and, most importantly- what to do about it. This intuitive knowledge helps her to sense the physical, emotional, and instinctual needs of the infant and respond with appropriate actions. She can tell the difference between a wet diaper cry and cry of hunger. On a more subtle level, she intuitively knows what type of facial gestures can change the inner state of her child and just the right tempo to rock her child into a deep peaceful sleep. The intersubjective limbic resonance allows the mother and infant to share the same physical and emotional states. But it is the development of the mother's cortex, especially the frontal lobes, that supplies this social bond with the practical knowledge of instinctual regulation necessary for the infant's survival.

The Pleasure of Connection

The need for physical and emotional contact runs deep. When the mother picks up a crying infant and begins to sooth it, the physical and emotional fears of abandonment begin to subside. In its place, a new wave of neurophysiological responses begins to flow. Within seconds, the sensation of physical touch will elicit the release of two neuropeptides associated with pain reduction and positive feelings. This occurs within both the mother and child. It begins with a cascade of brain *opioids* that are stimulated by soothing physical touch. Simultaneously, the neuropeptide *oxytocin* is also released in key areas of the brain, further increasing the brain's sensitivity to opioids. This flow of neuropeptides will instantly reduce the feelings of pain, cold, and physical isolation. Soothing physical touch will quickly reduce overcharged parasympathetic activity, bringing it back to a normal range in which it promotes relaxed physiological responses. The crying and other distress vocalizations cease. A mother's worry melts into sweet sounds of cooing and tender smiles.

Nearly inseparable from the basic human needs of touch and warmth is the need for social contact. Being excluded from our social community is one of the deepest and most primal fears etched into our basic instinctual programs. As we have seen, the PAG region that controls our responses to physical pain is also directly involved in responding to the deprivation of social contact. This is true for all mammals. The basic PAG circuits that regulate pain and temperature responses, as well as social interaction, activate neurons in the amygdala. In higher mammals, specific regions in the frontal lobes- especially the *orbitofrontal cortex*- exert strong influences on social behaviors. The neural networks that mediate human experiences of social contact are the most complex of all mammals, due to the larger size and interconnectivity of our orbitofrontal cortex. This mass of socially sensitive neurons sits at the top end of the nervous system, at the bottom of the frontal lobes, just above the eyes. This area of the brain is extremely active during experiences of social bonding. Affectionate social interaction stimulates the production of brain opioids, particularly β-endorphins. Just like soothing touch, social bonding also stimulates oxytocin production. Clearly, instinctual chemistry has evolved in many animals to encourage offspring to bond with their parents. But the sophisticated intelligence behind our human social glue lies in the extensively developed orbitofrontal cortex.

The Instinct for Attachment

Every time you interact with children, their brains change. This may seem a bit troubling at first, given the state of our minds at any particular moment. Every time you come into contact with them- touch them, talk to them, even just look at them- you are shaping their instinctual intelligence. Human beings are born with a brain that is pre-wired to help them orient towards the complex realities of the social world. Researchers in child development have determined that early interpersonal experiences are recorded in specific circuits of the brain. Neuronal connections between the orbitofrontal cortex in the frontal lobes and the amygdala appear to be the primary circuits in which these experiences are recorded. These brain regions begin to associate feelings of discomfort and pain with the responses of the caregivers. When parents help regulate the child's emotional and physical state by changing their diapers, holding them, and feeding them- whatever they may need at any particular moment- the association is made that the pain and irritation will be met with a comforting response. If the infant suffers for a prolonged period of time, or the mother's responses are ineffective at alleviating the infant's distress- the association is made that there will be no comforting response. These associations form the foundations of the child's instinctual responses to pain and discomfort throughout life. They shape our beliefs about the world and our fundamental behavioral and psychological tendencies.

The instinctual responses that promote physical touch and social interaction are at their height during the first three years. Every interaction with parents and other caregivers impacts the emerging instinctual responses of the infant. Forming bonds of social attachment is indispensable for the development of instinctual intelligence. Without the comforting response of the mother, the brain regions that regulate instinctual responses to pain and social contact do not develop properly. Developmental psychologists have determined that infants' brains store impressions of comforting and relaxed interactions in different regions of the brain, but it seems the impressions stored in the orbitofrontal cortex are the most important.

The Center of Social Intelligence

In basic terms, the better parents relate to their children, the more their children will develop a socially competent, instinctually intelligent nervous system. Dan Goleman, one of the leading scholars in this field, refers to this type of interpersonal competence as *social intelligence*. The orbitofrontal cortex is like the command center of this social intelligence. It issues instructions to the rest of the nervous system to help it fashion appropriate and socially nuanced instinctual responses.

According to the latest research in developmental neuropsychology, a lack of soothing responses from parents during infancy is a primary factor in certain types of personality disorders and other forms of mental illness. Neurobiologically, the lack of development within the orbitofrontal cortex impairs the ability of children to modify basic aggressive and motivational impulses. As these children get older, attempts to meet their basic social and physical needs are awkward. They can become overly frustrated or even violent when others do not respond to their wishes. The difficulties faced by these individuals in life stem from an impairment of their ability to modulate autonomic nervous system responses. They simply never got the love and attention they needed to develop an adaptive, socially intelligent nervous system. Their natural instincts for making friends and sharing resources will lack the smooth, relaxed qualities of social competence.

Modern developmental researchers have made enormous progress in identifying the neurobiological basis for social intelligence. One man in particular has made a series of brilliant contributions to our understanding. It is widely acknowledged that his research has helped advance the science of developmental neuropsychology.

Allan Schore is a short, sweet man, with graying hair. While he may not be physically imposing, his eyes shine with a brilliance and a passion that is at once inspiring and a bit intimidating. Within his sharp mind resides a detailed knowledge of every scrap of research relating to infant neuropsychology and the development of emotional regulation. Schore was one of the first researchers to grasp the fundamental importance of emotional regulation in human development. Schore not only knew the neurobiological intricacies of how brains develop, having received his Ph.D. from UCLA in this field. But he was also well-schooled in psychodynamic theory, which formed the basis of child psychology during the first three-quarters of the last century. Schore, like other psychologists who came before him, observed some obvious facts. During the first six months, infants have a very limited capacity to regulate their instinctual and emotional responses. During this time, the mother's capacity to respond and regulate the infant's affective state has a profound influence on the infant's subsequent development. But no one knew exactly how the mother's actions influenced the infant's nervous system, or how the nervous system developed in response to the mother's regulating behaviors. Schore's publication of *Affect Regulation and the Origin of the Self: The Neurobiology of Emotional Development* in 1994 detailed the neurobiological foundations of this process. This work revolutionized the study of developmental neuropsychology.

The Importance of Social Instincts

Through Schore's synthesizing work, developmental psychologists came to realize the importance of affective regulation. Its implications for the development of healthy instinctual functioning cannot be overstated. Many developmental researchers, working in different academic fields, have come to remarkably similar conclusions. In terms of social intelligence, how we respond to intimacy, friendship, and other forms of human connection is directly influenced by these early experiences. While the intricacies of emotional and instinctual regulation are complex, Schore identified the one region of the brain that was the center of the integration of instinctual impulses with social intelligence- the orbitofrontal cortex.

This cluster of neurons in the frontal lobes is a microcosm of instinctual intelligence unto itself. As children develop, they use the impressions stored in this region to guide all subsequent social interactions. The neurons of the orbitofrontal cortex- especially those in the earlier maturing right hemisphere- actually depend on affectionate and stimulating interactions with parents and caregivers to grow new connections. The release of opioids actually helps the neurons in the frontal lobes to form connections with other areas of the brain. The maturation of the frontal lobes is the basis for the development of cognitive processes like reasoning, linguistic communication, and planning. Schore was the first to understand how stimulation and growth of the frontal lobes- especially the orbitofrontal cortex- is essential for building interconnections between the frontal lobes and the areas of the brain that control the instinctual responses of the autonomic nervous system.

Fortunately, the majority of parents in the world have healthy bonding impulses with their children. From an evolutionary perspective, we can see why modern humans have a tendency to comfort cute and vulnerable babies. In the past, the offspring of parents that lacked this basic empathetic responsiveness had very little chance of surviving childhood, much less any chance of reproducing. They lacked the simple social grace of being able to connect with others. Each parent's capacity to empathetically bond with infants and the infant's capacity to respond to this affection form the basis of a lifelong instinctual intelligence.

Maternal Nurturance

One of our most basic visceral instincts is the need for nourishment. Every time we sit down at the dinner table with family or friends, we are implicitly reminded of a very basic fact: Our instinctual responses to food are deeply intertwined with the social matrix in which we live. Eating may often seem like a solitary act, something we do in response to our growling stomach or the mouthwatering lure of French fries. But if we look at our earliest experiences of feeding, we will see that this instinct has its roots in the earliest days of infancy.

The female nervous system is more neurophysiologically prepared to respond to infants than the nervous system of males. This is not to say that males do not engage in nurturing behaviors. Any father worth his salt will point to his willingness to work and gather resources for his children. Both males and females have a primary dopamine circuit that pushes up from the brainstem to the frontal cortex, stimulating the behaviors of foraging and nest building. These instinctual behaviors help provide the infant and the mother with food resources and environmental stability.

But there are a lot of things Dads just cannot do. The nurturing instincts of the mother provide for the immediate needs of the infant, such as maternal physical touching and nourishment through beastfeeding. Maternal behaviors are supported by a variety of subcortical brain regions that have specialized functions. All of these activities are closely associated with social connection and thus heavily influenced by opioid and oxytocin neuropeptides, just like the neurochemistry of social bonding described above.

Contact and Satisfaction

The infant's needs for nutritional sustenance are regulated by several areas of the nervous system. The brain has multiple sensory regions that monitor levels of glucose, lipids, amino acids, hydration, and various minerals. Any depletion of bodily energy is signaled via the lateral hypothalamatic gateway, a tiny group of cells deep in the center of the brain. These internal homeostatic monitoring systems enable the hypothalamus to activate a wide variety of systems that will stimulate emotional and behavioral programs needed to obtain nourishment. The hypothalamus might be small, but it is one of the most powerful instinctual centers of the brain. When it sends out the call that it is time to eat, our bodies respond in a big way. If we ignore that call, the hypothalamus can become very insistent. And I mean very insistent. Relentlessly insistent. Irritatingly insistent. *I have to eat right now* insistent.

But young infants can't just hop in a car and go to MacDonald's to get those fresh hot salty fries. They are totally and utterly dependent on Mom. And when Mom gives them what they want, life is good. As we saw above, early experiences of nourishing social interaction are stored in the frontal lobes, especially the orbitofrontal cortex. Early experiences of intense gustatory satiation and pleasure form deep impressions in this region. These experiences of satiation are associated with the presence of the mother, regardless if the mother is breastfeeding or bottle-feeding the infant. These early experiences will create lasting instinctual tendencies related to food and feeding. These tendencies directly influence the appraisal of the nutritive value of edible materials in the environment to areas of the brainstem. In other words, they influence what we will find pleasurable to eat. But they also form deep associations between social contact and the satisfaction of instinctual needs. This is a critical aspect of instinctual intelligence, so let's take a closer look at the social nature of instinctual gratification.

The mother's encouragement and affection during the feeding process will produce deep instinctual linkages between nutrition, pleasure, affection, and love. These pleasurable gustatory sensations are mediated within the brainstem and form a very basic core of our instinctual intelligence. The brainstem regulates the basic instinctual actions of chewing, swallowing, and gustatory acceptance. Consuming life-sustaining nutrients is one of the most primal behavioral instincts of the infant. The basic actions of chewing and swallowing later mature into more complex and mobile forms of proactive behaviors like seeking out and consuming food. They also promote the enhancement of social relations by the sharing of food resources. The active search for and acquisition of food (and feeding relationships) produces more energy which helps the child develop physically, leading to enhanced self-sufficiency and greater capacity to gather life-sustaining resources. This demonstrates that the pleasurable bonds between social connection, pleasure, and feeding are fundamental to our survival.

The Instinct for Nourishing Satisfaction

Under optimal conditions, the mother's emotional state would be essentially calm, nourishing, and responsive to the infant's instinctual need for nourishment. During this phase of development, the infant is beginning to experience the intensity of their instinctual embodied self-regulating needs. The mother's capacity to respond to those needs will have direct and lasting effects on the individual's responses to hunger, one of our most primal instinctual drives. Specifically, the capacity to tolerate internal states of agitation will be profoundly influenced by the responsiveness of the mother. In cases where the infant is fed in a timely and instinctually attuned manner, the infant will be better able to tolerate feelings of agitation and hunger when they arise. As instinctually intelligent adults, these individuals will be able to recognize, respond to, and gratify their needs for nourishment in a balanced and relaxed manner. Again, this is because they have a repository of embodied memories and impressions of satiating feeding experiences that were formed during infancy. The timely and loving responses to the infant's needs will help establish an innate sense of instinctually intelligent behaviors related to how much to eat and what to eat.

But it goes even deeper than that. The mother's responsiveness to the infant's nutritional needs has direct impact on the infant's subsequent capacity to express and gratify the full range of human instinctual needs. The basic template for this pattern comes from the mother's response to the infant's instinctual desire for nourishment from the breast. The innate reflex of infants to suckle and feed at the breast is a powerful instinct and a central part of the infant's emerging capacity to initiate self-regulating instinctual activity. Because this urge is so primal and so vital for survival, any restriction or limitation on this natural desire will be met with a powerful response. If the mother does not provide access to her breast (or to a bottle), the infant will experience a considerable amount of frustration and anxiety.

Under optimal conditions, the mother's response to the infant's instinctual needs will be timely, accurate, encouraging, and relaxed. This means that the mother will be quick to recognize that the infant is hungry and wants the breast. She will respond to the infant's needs with vocal encouragement, as well as making sure that there is easy access to her nipple or bottle. Under these conditions, the infant can exert their natural instinctual impulses. When the physical and needs are satiated, the infant then experiences a deep sense of relaxation and comfort. If the mother is also able to enjoy the infant's aliveness while sucking at the breast and share in the satiation of the natural cycle of feeding, then the mother and infant can relax into a state of deep contentment.

We can see a basic pattern within the infant's nervous system that takes place within this cycle:
 1) Feeling desire.
 2) Taking action.
 3) Being responded to, and;
 4) Experiencing mutual instinctual satiation.

This is an innate pattern of self-regulating instinctual behavior. As such, it forms a basic template for the infant's experience of *instinctual agency*. Instinctual agency is a basic intuitive knowledge that informs infants that they can feel their desire, initiate action, and obtain satisfaction. These experiences give them the ingrained confidence that *other humans will respond positively* to their instinctual desires. They will also experience satisfaction when they are able to satisfy the desires of others. This forms the basis of an instinctive social and moral intelligence that will be essential for success in the adult world.

However, there are many occasions when the mother is not so responsive. In these cases, she does not recognize the infant's desires in a timely fashion or she actively discourages the infant's basic needs. This leads to high levels of frustration in the infant. Their sense of instinctual agency will be influenced by the expectation that their efforts will not produce any satisfaction. As a result, these individuals will have trouble initiating and sustaining the full range of instinctually driven behaviors. The lack of maternal responsiveness affects how individuals will respond to all their other needs- warmth, physical touch and interaction, rest, and love- for the rest of their lives.

Integrating the Instincts with Social Reality

If we look at interconnections of the orbitofrontal cortex with the areas of the brain that control instinctual responses, we can see why Allan Schore and other researchers are so fascinated by this set of neurons in the frontal lobes. The orbitofrontal cortex (let's call it OFC for short) has direct connections to the amygdala. As we saw in the last chapter, the amygdala is at the very center of our self-protective instincts. The OFC can modify the activity of the amygdala in a variety of ways. If necessary, it can totally inhibit it. The OFC can generate images of the consequences of our actions. This capacity is how the OFC overrides the amygdala- and keeps us from hitting and injuring children when they do something that angers us.

It can also modulate the activity of the amygdala to help us function with more social grace. When you go for a job interview, imagine what you are thinking to yourself just before you walk in the door. *Be calm. Relax. I can do this.* You remember that in your last job people liked you and you did a good job. In your brain, the OFC is activating memories that signal the amygdala not to interpret the situation with fear, but with excitement and enthusiasm. This keeps us calm enough to walk through the door without tripping and to begin to connect with our new boss. And relax. He already likes your résumé. What he is assessing now is your instinctual intelligence. If your OFC is doing its job, your handshake will be warm and confident, and you will be able to connect with him on a visceral level. His gut instinct will tell him you are the right person for the job.

The OFC also has direct connections with the hypothalamus. Through these connections, it can modulate embodied instinctual impulses like hunger. This means that you can resist grabbing the ripe apple sitting on your potential boss' desk during the interview. Even though your stomach may be gurgling, the social intelligence embedded in the OFC will keep you focused on the social dynamics of the interview, suppressing thoughts of food and the comfort it will bring. The OFC, along with the neighboring prefrontal cortex, is the primary region of the brain responsible for impulse control and the delay of gratification. Without it, you might be stuffing your face with that apple- and never experience the delayed gratification of a big fat paycheck.

The Evolutionary Thread

Schore's contributions to the understanding of instinctual intelligence are not only useful for getting a great job. Knowledge of how the OFC works and how it regulates the autonomic nervous system is finding some rather unexpected applications. It is providing us with the knowledge to probe deeper into our consciousness, to the very heart of what it means to be human. The OFC, via its links to the amygdala and hypothalamus, can give us conscious access to the core of our instinctual regulating mechanisms: the autonomic nervous system. It is through the autonomic nervous system that we feel, express, and control our instinctual impulses. But there's something more. Schore and other researchers have also contributed to the deeper knowledge of instinctual intelligence in ways that are changing the evolution of human consciousness.

The OFC's capacity to regulate the autonomic nervous system has profound implications for the science of cultivating deeper levels of instinctual intelligence. In the chapters that follow, we will come to see how the basic forms of social intelligence that are established during infancy serve as a basis for the development of morality and compassion in later life. This is something that many people who have developed high levels of instinctual intelligence- including highly accomplished spiritual masters- have implicitly understood for several centuries. We will discover how they have used this knowledge to harness the biological energy of their instinctual impulses in order to transform the functioning of their nervous systems.

The social and moral intelligence of the orbitofrontal cortex is another essential thread in the evolution of human instinctual consciousness. As it weaves together with the protective intelligence of the amygdala, we can see the faint outlines a profound instinctual wisdom. It is a wisdom that functions with a self-organizing guidance- expanding the possibilities of human evolution- and bringing us closer to the deepest origins of the life-giving intelligence of the universe.

CHAPTER 3

Getting After It

You know you want it.
You can't stop thinking about it.
You're all about getting after it.

Have you ever wondered what drives us to get what we want? Most of the time, we don't stop to think about the impulses that compel us into action. We simply think how satisfied we'll be when we get our hands on what we want. We almost never think about why we feel hungry or why we want a new pair of shoes. We might be searching the internet for the set of high-tech golf clubs or the perfect end-table (you know the one that is not too big or too low, and not too dark, sort of modernish- but not sterile). But do we ever really notice the intelligence that is driving this search?

Why Mice Forage and Click

When you think about it, the ability to know what we want and the capacity to actually get it is no small miracle. And it is certainly not unique to humans. One of the most fundamental traits of living animal organisms is the organized capacity to seek out resources that will support environmental adaptation, reproduction, and survival. This *persevering drive* includes the behavioral, motivational, and cognitive processes necessary to secure both physical objects and social relationships from the external environment. It is a remarkable feat of adaptive biological engineering. When animals require some sort of protection from predators they will seek out protective enclosures or other means of physical safety. When animals need water and nutrients, they will seek out sources of food by looking for and following indirect environmental cues. When animals feel the mating urge, they will seek out the presence of attractive mating partners. When animals need social connection, they seek out the companionship of others of their own species. All of these seeking behaviors require perseverance- a steady, repetitive motivation that arises again and again to insure that a particular need or intermediate goal is met. With every click of your mouse in search of new toys or better information, you are tapping into this basic drive. In all its diverse manifestations, perseverance is a natural expression of the instinctual intelligence of all life.

The Seeking Circuits

Recent discoveries in evolutionary neurobiology have shed a great deal of light on the underlying neurobiological and evolutionary substrates of activities that require perseverance. Understanding the fundamental survival value of persevering and seeking behaviors then allows us to recognize how these basic motivational drives are constantly active in everything we do.

At many junctures of our evolutionary history, our ancestors were faced with environmental changes that reduced or eliminated their food supply. The most robust of our proto-human ancestors were not going to just give up and starve to death. Something within them pushed them over the next hill until they found the clues that led them to their next meal. In seeking out the food they needed to survive, these determined individuals lived on. And they reproduced. Their genetic tendencies of dogged persistence and goal-seeking determination were passed on to another generation. The humans alive today are the descendants of the most indefatigable and clever organisms to ever live on this planet. No wonder the pace of cultural evolution is growing at such a fast rate. As a result of natural selection, each generation of humans is more deeply driven to survive, explore, and thrive than the next.

The basic impulse toward persistent repetitive behaviors is controlled by the central motivational centers of the nervous system. The central motivational centers respond to both internal and external cues related to social, sexual, and survival needs. Internally, various types of persistent seeking behaviors are triggered by the activation of a region of the hypothalamus called the medial strata. In general, the hypothalamus is directly involved in most of our motivational instincts. This set of cells sits deep inside the brain, just behind the soft palate. It monitors the internal state of our bodies 24/7. It's quite tiny- but its influence is considerable. The internal monitoring functions of the medial strata are sensitive to several types neurochemical imbalances within our bodies. These imbalances can be nutritive, thus stimulating the search for water or certain types of food. French fries anyone?

This motivational center can also detect temperature imbalances. This is how we suddenly find ourselves turning up the heat in the house. Most of the time, we are not actually conscious that we are hungry or cold. We simply begin to make ourselves a sandwich or just put on a warm sweater. Deep in the core of our brains, the medial strata of the hypothalamus activates its connections to the motor regions of the brain that will lead to the alteration of body temperature. If we are outside and do not have a jacket, we rub our arms and move around a bit to feel warmer. Temperature regulation is one of our most basic forms of instinctual intelligence. The next time you adjust your thermostat, you might pause to consider its evolutionary brilliance. It is the pinnacle of adaptive ingenuity, the integration of our innate biological drives and modern technological innovation. Sure beats having to go look for wood and rub two sticks together every few hours.

How We Get After It

When an imbalance in our internal environment is detected, some very basic circuits and chemical pathways in the brain get busy. The technical explanation is that the hypothalamus will activate the *mesolimbic regions* of the *ascending dopamine circuits* which terminate in the amygdala and basal ganglia. These dopamine circuits are the biological source of the energy that fuels our most persistent survival behaviors. Their basic motivational impulses rise into the limbic regions and cortex where they encounter stored memories of previous experiences. The ascending dopamine's motivational force is tempered from above by the more cautious areas of the cortex. As we saw earlier, many of our instinctually driven social experiences are stored in the prefrontal and orbitofrontal regions of the cortex. In these two brain regions, various learned behavioral contingencies produce adaptive behavioral responses. In other words, we remember what worked in the past and we apply that knowledge to the current situation. We know certain stores have the food we like. Plus, we factor in the consequences of strategies that did not work in the past. Remember the time you offered to make a friend dinner if he helped you move a couch? After he criticized every dish you made and kept moaning about how much his back hurt, you realized it would have been easier to hire a moving company. Our brains keep a detailed inventory of these little incidents, using them to adjust our instinctual responses in any given situation.

Sometimes a Good Book is Your Best Option

The basic behavioral programs of foraging, nest building, seeking protection, mating behaviors, and social interaction are modified to respond to specific environmental conditions. A lot of times the things we want are not always immediately available. Under conditions of scarcity, our adaptive instinctual intelligence helps us make use of whatever is available. What happens when you wake up in the morning and have an insatiable craving for French fries? Everybody knows that MacDonald's does not serve French fries until 10:30AM (and 11AM on Sundays). Suddenly you have that flash of instinctual adaptation...Hash Browns! Problem solved. Sometimes our instinctual intelligence is quite ingenious at solving problems.

On the other hand, satisfying more complex desires is as a bit trickier and we need to resort to other strategies. I have a couple of friends who are foraging for mates in the internet jungle. That might not sound as romantic as "*E-Harmony*". But if people were to apply the insights of instinctual intelligence, their odds of finding a soulmate might drastically improve. Too often, my friends fall into the "making use of whatever is available" strategy. This works fine for satisfying your jones for a hot fried potato snack. But when it comes to finding a husband- or even a half way decent guy to date- a more sophisticated strategy will most likely be more effective.

When my friends first signed up with a matchmaking service, they poured over the thousands of pictures and descriptions. At first glance, it seemed like it would be hard to choose from all these great guys. However, as they began to investigate these potential mates more closely, they soon realized that many of these men were not exactly what they claimed to be. Once they began chatting with these fellows, they quickly learned that when he claimed he had a "comfortable living situation" it meant that he lived in his mother's basement. When he said he had "great career prospects" it meant that he was still waiting for a call regarding the interview he went on last month. You get the picture.

But here's the trap that my friends were falling into: as a response to apparent scarcity of good mates, they felt they needed to choose from *what was available*. They wound up dating all sorts of creeps, wasting valuable time and energy. Plus, they got quite discouraged in the process. They failed to consider another viable alternative- the *delayed gratification strategy*. When there are no decent options to choose from, my friends begin to feel desperate. Remember that our motivational urges for nest building, mating, and social contact are quite insistent. They scream out for some kind of gratification- even if it is just looking forward to a simple date on Friday night.

Here's what we need to remember: all of our basic motivational drives can be temporarily inhibited. We can wait until the golf clubs go on sale at the end of the season. We can drink a bottle of water after the meeting is over. The same principle applies to finding a suitable mate. Delaying a small short-term gratification can sometimes have big payoffs. If their search is yielding all duds and no studs, I encourage my friends to take a Friday night off, and stay at home and read a good book. Feeling a little lonely will never kill you. Thousands of new prospects are uploaded to the dating websites every day. While your competition is too depressed from yet another lousy, desperate date to even get out of bed, you can be scouting out the new prospects over a cup of coffee bright and early at your local Starbuck's. Plus, your social discernment skills are a lot sharper after a good night's sleep. Part of developing our instinctual intelligence is knowing when to conserve our resources of time and energy.

Pushing Our Buttons

The central motivational centers of the brain also respond to environmental cues that signal the presence of the rewards we are seeking. Every time we perceive something that is directly- or even indirectly- associated with a highly sought-after reward, our motivational centers are activated. Advertising executives know this quite well. All you need to do is suggest that your product will help people get the things they really want. What they are really offering you is the chance to increase likelihood of satisfying some very deep needs that go back deep into our evolutionary past. Ever wonder why there are so many TV commercials for "new and improved" cleaning products? Images of a big, clean house draw us back to the primal needs of having a safe shelter, free from rotting plants and animals, where we could rest and eat. The deeper the instinctual appeal, the more the likely our seeking circuits will be activated to obtain the product. It is no accident that MacDonald's always combines images of big juicy hamburgers and smiling people having a good time. The need for nourishment and social contact, as we saw in the last chapter, are as primal as it gets.

How do environmental cues trigger motivational responses? Or to put it in modern economic terms, how does advertising stimulate consumer demand? Much of what we know about this instinctual process has emerged from the study of addictive behaviors. Perceptual input flows through sensory and cortical networks, reaching various emotional salience detection regions like the amygdala, hypothalamus, the PAG, and brainstem. Specific stimuli in the environment will activate various dopaminergic circuits of the ventral tegmental area leading up to the *nucleus accumbens*. The nucleus accumbens is a small region of the brain that links the limbic system and the cortex via the thalamus. It's associated with a wide variety of motivational impulses. This system is acutely sensitive not only to direct perception of desired external rewards, but also to *environmental cues* that are directly or indirectly associated with sought-after goals. This system is what triggers the craving for a drink when the alcoholic walks by a bar. He hears the sounds of laughter and ice clinking in glasses- and before he knows what happened- he's in the bar having a drink.

If we look back to our evolutionary past, the triggering of our motivational instincts by indirect cues makes a lot of sense. Back in the day, our human ancestors did not have the luxury of refrigerators, supermarkets, or restaurants. Their next meal usually had to be hunted down or gathered up. The most effective hunters and gatherers were those individuals who could perceive and respond to the slightest environmental cues that indicated the presence of game, edible plants, or water. Sometimes the only clue might be a set of nearly imperceptible hoof prints trailing off into the distance. The humans that survived periods of scarcity were those who could sustain the motivation to follow the trail until the animal was spotted. While we often grumble about hard work, there is something innately pleasurable about seeking what we want. The most successful of these early hunters and gatherers were probably the ones who *enjoyed* the search for their next meal or a better spot to build a shelter. Their descendents are now happily traipsing all over the internet and shopping malls, seeking out their prey.

Setting Out Alone

The ability of human beings to explore their environments and search out what they need is a fairly extraordinary achievement of instinctual evolution. The capacities to recognize what we need, to negotiate environmental obstacles, and to respond to indirect incentives are all expressions of this intelligence. But these instinctual capacities require something more, something we take for granted. Foraging for resources often requires that we venture into the unknown. We have to leave what is familiar behind and explore new environments. Sometimes, as we all know, when we feel the drive to explore something new, we have to go it alone.

While many of our instinctual behaviors are often carried out in social contexts, our instinctual endowment has also equipped us to function independently. This capacity for autonomous functioning is an essential feature of our instinctual intelligence. In the previous chapter, I described how the regulation of our instinctual impulses is shaped by the early interactive experiences with our parents. You could say that parents are the primary civilizing force of humanity. But as children grow older, their parents cannot always be there to help them express their impulses in a socially intelligent manner. How do children learn to thrive in the world without their parents' direct supervision? In order to answer this question, we need to know how children become capable of regulating their own instinctual impulses.

Changing Our State

In the last 20 years, developmental psychologists have made enormous progress in understanding how children develop their own internalized sense of instinctual intelligence. Remember how the orbitofrontal cortex stores memories of all our interactions with our parents? Well, we not only use those memories to guide our instinctual behaviors- we also use those memories to modify our own subjective feelings, moods, and emotions. Around the age of 2 ½ to 3 years, young children are able to activate these stored impressions to alter the state of their nervous systems. This allows them to engage the world in a whole new way. Instead of needing Mom to be physically present to comfort every little distress, they now have a more efficient alternative.

Whenever they feel afraid, anxious, or lonely- they can think of Mom's smiling face. The activation of these memories calms the nervous system, and they can go back to what they are doing.

This is a remarkable developmental achievement that has altered the course of human evolution. Without this capacity for internal self-regulation, humans could not engage in the *autonomous* seeking behaviors that we need to survive. Our ancestors would have never ventured away from the comfort of the community and the warm fire. Individuals would have never wandered off and stumbled on a fresh stream or more fertile land. Think of a brave young man, thousands of years ago, that has journeyed out away from his clan. Food was scarce and the males had to spread out to cover more ground. Hopefully, one of them would find at least of sign that game was nearby. It's cold and the fall of evening chills his bones. He's tired. In his heart, he feels lonely. As he collapses on a soft pile of leaves, images of loved ones float through his head. He sees his younger brothers and sisters looking worried. They are hungry. Then he sees his mother's kind face. She tells him he must be strong and not give up. He does not know that the activation of his orbitofrontal cortex has sent signals to the rest of his nervous system- re-stimulating his dopaminergic motivational circuits. He only feels the surge of energy and the renewed will to hunt. He hears the sound of approaching hoofs. He raises his spear, his heart pounding. This is why the ability to alter the state of our nervous system without the *direct physical presence* of another human is so essential.

Each time we go to work, we carry the whole tribe with us in our hearts and minds- even as we drive off alone.

Keeping the Goal in Mind

The ability to use our minds to change the state of our nervous system is indispensable to the development of instinctual intelligence. Without this capacity, children would be afraid to adventure out into the world. Recalling Mom or Dad's smiling face helps reduce the natural fear and anxiety that arises when children are alone. But here is more to life than not being afraid. Sometimes there are some really cool things we want or a bunch of friends who are doing something really exciting. The desire for the exhilarating satisfaction of life can alter our nervous systems in a big way. Just like when children think of Mom to assuage their fears, our minds can alter our nervous system when we imagine the sweet rewards of satisfaction.

We experience this constantly throughout the day. What happens when you are thirsty? You being to notice images, perhaps faint at first, of a simple glass of water. You can almost feel the sensation of coolness on your lips. If you are unable to get that drink of water immediately, the flow of images will begin again, this time a little more clearly and intensely. The sound of the water filling your glass. The sparkle of its clarity. The soothing cool flow over your tongue. Perhaps you're on a phone call that you just cannot interrupt. The images of the water will arise in your instinctual consciousness even more vividly. Now water is pouring down your throat, an ocean of coolness and refreshment. The balm of its liquid cascade pouring into every cell in your parched body, the anticipation of pleasure and satisfaction reaching orgasmic proportions. As this urge builds, you finally say "Look, I gotta go", hanging up the phone and rushing off, your mouth already tasting the first drops of your own private oasis.

Without the capacity to imagine the reward of sweet satisfaction, we would never do anything. We would never check out the new playground, never want a new skateboard, or never go on our first date. We would probably just be happy living in our parents' basement forever. Images of desired rewards impact our nervous systems in the same way that direct sensory cues from the environment do. They stimulate the dopaminergic circuits of the ventral tegmental area leading up to the nucleus accumbens, amygdala, and basal ganglia. This surge propels us into action. The capacity to imagine future rewards is a fundamental feature of our instinctual intelligence. It gives us the ability to set goals, determine priorities, and sustain our motivation until we get what we are seeking. Without this fundamental persevering intelligence, we could never survive. And without the inspiration of imagination, human consciousness could never evolve.

Satisfaction and Imagination

The underlying neurobioligical networks that motivate the most basic survival behaviors also give rise to a uniquely human quality- the innate curiosity that energizes our search for meaning. The infinite array of ingenious human activity arises from the interaction of basic repetitive drives between the linguistic and conceptual centers of the neocortex. The innate drives of seeking and persistence are what propels us beyond the satisfaction of our immediate physical needs into the realms of exploration and imagination. The deep instinct to persevere and explore is what sustains the instinctual evolution of human beings. At the most basic level, it's a pure expression of the inherent dynamism of all creation.

Jaak Panksepp exemplifies the inexhaustible human impulse to explore and understand ourselves and the world around us. He has persevered through some of the most tragic and painful circumstance any father could ever face. In 1991, his daughter Tiina was tragically killed by a speeding drunk driver trying to evade arrest. Rather than give up under the weight of this loss, this brilliant neuroscientist gradually came to terms with his grief and continued to make prolific scholarly contributions. He has almost single-handedly established the field known as *affective neuroscience*. His scientific writings are etched with the depth of his loss, making his poetic insights into instinctual behavior at once scholarly and quintessentially human. He is now a professor emeritus at Bowling Green University. He also serves as a Director for the Memorial Foundation for Lost Children, which provides assistance to families with children who suffer from neuropsychiatric disorders.

Panksepp's discoveries allow us to peer deep into the core of our instinctual consciousness. In his many scientific articles, he has shed light on the specific circuits that underlie our instinctual behaviors. He has sketched out the paths along which our motivational drives emerge from the most primitive regions of the brainstem. One of the central areas of instinctual activity that Panksapp has studied is the periaqueductal gray (PAG) region of the midbrain. We have already seen how the PAG is instrumental in the production of protective and social behaviors. It is also directly tied to the motivational circuits of the dopamine networks. Through these neural and chemical networks, the PAG sends out the rudimentary impulses that will set us out in search of warmth, protection, and friends. Panksapp has also demonstrated that the PAG is also instrumental in our attachments to familiar environmental surroundings. Deep inside its neurons, the PAG wants us to be safe, warm, and comfortable.

But what is so essential about being safe, warm, and comfortable? When humans relax in the deep security of their social bonds and safe shelters, our instinctual consciousness begins to *evolve*. With our fears quieted, our bellies full, and our friends nearby- our minds might drift into a peaceful rest. In this twilight, our dreams and instinctual impulses blend with thoughts and images…until something new emerges- imagination. This imagination arises from the darkest churning of our instinctual swamp. It's the same primordial drive that first pushed fish to crawl on dry land- the first step in the morphagenic journey that would forever change life on this planet. In the human brain, the instinct for imagination dances more freely and flies higher than any animal. When our PAGs are satisfied, our instinctual consciousness transforms, and human awareness opens to the mysteries of existence. We begin to ask questions about our origins and dream about our future.

The Evolutionary Thread
What Jaak Panksepp discovered about the PAG is changing our understanding of human consciousness. His insights shed light on the mysterious origins of our instinctual heritage. Through the research of affective neuroscience, we are seeing how the primal tendencies of the PAG and other primitive instinctual areas of the brain can be systematically transformed to express a deeper level of human instinctual intelligence. As we weave the primitive impulses that emerge from the PAG with what we have learned about the amygdala and the orbitofrontal cortex, we are moving closer to a more complete understanding of the neurobiological basis of our instinctual nature. We are also beginning to recognize the extraordinary potentials of humanity to dream, to imagine, and to evolve.

CHAPTER 4

What Happens in Vegas

Las Vegas may be the most glitzy modern playground in the world. But the instinctual drives that fuel its 24/7 frenzy of lustful ambition are hardly anything new. Las Vegas is simply the latest and greatest incarnation of an evolutionary force that has been shaping this planet for billions of years. Here, the primal roots of our DNA are awakened and laid bare. The marketing geniuses who craft the veneer of Vegas know exactly how to trigger the impulses of sexual desire, competitiveness, envy, greed, and social dominance. They put the wildest fantasies of instinctual satisfaction right at your finger tips. And you can have it all- if you just hand over your credit card. The lure of this kind of paradise is just too much for some to resist. How else could you get people to come from all over the world to a God forsaken stretch of desert in the middle of nowhere?

Anything You Want

When you get off the plane at McCarran International Airport, you instantly know where you are. Within a few steps of your gate is a row of slot machines and their red and yellow blinking lights. As you walk to the terminal to get your bags, you pass the signs inviting you to for a free consultation for the cosmetic surgery of your choice. The ads are always the same, unabashedly straightforward as they are ubiquitous. Invariably, right smack in the middle of the picture is a blond woman with a low cut dress proudly displaying the tops of her enormous breasts. She is always smiling proudly, glowing with the perfect roundness and symmetry of her new found self-esteem. Her teeth are straight and devastatingly white, and she is draped with diamonds, suggesting both elegance and the primal radiance of sexual confidence. In the background, there is a picture of a respectable looking doctor, handsome but professionally attired in a suit and tie. He is the surgeon who can make this transformation happen, and he is just a phone call away. After a whole row of these ads, you see a bar (or a *lounge* as they like to call it), and it seems quite busy for an early afternoon in the middle of the week. Lo and behold, it is full of women who all seem to look exactly like the women in those ads for cosmetic surgery. The bartender beckons for you to join the party, but you move on, knowing that parties and alcohol, as well as around-the-clock cosmetic surgery, are always available, should you want them.

Weaving through the slot machines you wonder if it might not be a bad idea to pop a few bucks in the lucky slot machines. After all, all the signs say that they are *loose* and they have *progressive jackpots*. You're not quite sure what that means- but the image of winning a couple hundred thousand dollars has an appeal. Again, you are not quite sure what that appeal is, but there is a millisecond flash in your brain, an almost imperceptible cascade of images that have something to do with quitting your job and having a bigger house and no longer having to carry you own luggage and having people respect you and wearing clothes that proclaim in no uncertain terms that you are someone everyone wants to know. Of course, with your new fortune, you do not have to bother with all of these people, as then you do not have to answer to anyone. Your full-time job would be doing anything you want.

Yes, that's it! That's the appeal. *The ability to indulge your instincts*. Having whatever you want-when you want it. That's the lure of Vegas.

You pass by the slots, as there is no time now to pursue this dream right now. But deep inside your nervous system, a primordial agitation has been triggered. Without even really being invited, some very primitive desires have crept into your instinctual consciousness. The fun is just beginning.

Welcome to Vegas, baby!

More Than Meets the Eye

How do they do it? How do the various industries of Las Vegas manage to convince millions of people to spend billions of dollars in pursuit of an elusive dream? Sure, it is easy to see the primal appeal of sex, excitement, and money. But Las Vegas isn't the only place you can get these things. There is something more at work here, and our knowledge of instinctual intelligence can help us ferret it out. By studying the culture of Las Vegas, we can understand how some of our most basic instinctual programs operate. Our exploration will take us beyond the usual assumptions- it's easy to dismiss Las Vegas as superficial or even exploitive- to help us see that it actually offers something that is quite valuable.

Take, for example, gambling. The *gaming industry*, as it is called in Nevada, is enormously profitable, bringing in hundreds of billions of dollars every year. Everyone knows that the odds are slightly in favor of the casinos- and, that in the long run, almost everyone will eventually lose more than they win. Yet, in spite of these facts, people continue to lay their money down. From one perspective, this seemingly irrational behavior can be seen as an addiction or banal entertainment. But if we look a little closer, we can see a very basic form of instinctual intelligence at work.

The Rules of Instinctive Pleasure

Humans are social animals. Our social instincts have evolved to help us adapt to the challenges of survival. Over the course of evolution, individuals that experienced pleasure when engaging in survival-enhancing social behaviors were more likely to survive and reproduce. We could say that the basic intelligence of evolution makes sure we do what is necessary to keep us alive. In the last few chapters, we have seen how researchers have identified the neurobiological basis of many of our most basic survival programs. The motivational programs that are designed to ensure the basic needs of survival- like eating and staying warm for example- are directly tied to the pleasure centers of the brain. As humans evolved, the systems that linked pleasurable responses to eating behaviors grew in sophistication and complexity. These systems developed linkages with higher cortical areas, resulting in new behaviors that integrated increasingly complex social dynamics. The human nervous system evolved to ensure that the most instinctually useful behaviors were also *pleasurable*.

The results of this evolution are highly sophisticated neurobiological systems that mediate pleasurable experiences of social contact and sexual interaction. Unlike animals, humans don't just sit in trees eating food and sleeping all day, with a few days of mating frenzy each year mixed in. Our complex cultures and social networks have radically changed the basic adaptive functions of eating, social bonding, and reproduction. There are many intricate nuances that regulate the way that our basic instinctual impulses are expressed. The rules of engagement that determine how our instinctual urges are played out are all around us. Some rules are quite explicit, like the elaborate rules and regulations of professional sports. Other sets of rules are often taken for granted and we rarely notice how they shape our lives. Shopping at a grocery store is a fascinating place to see these rules in action. We have to suppress our immediate urge to eat whatever looks good. We don't touch other people's food. Unlike animals, we don't take little tastes of the various types of food that are available and then spit out what we don't like. We don't lie around, take a nap, and then defecate in the aisles. We gather our foods in a quick and orderly manner, then pay for them when we are done. We take it for granted that everyone knows these rules. But how did humans evolve to be so orderly? And what does that have to do with gambling?

The Adaptive Pleasures of Play

The answer is quite simple. Humans learn the rules of instinctual intelligence by *playing*. During childhood, physically energized play of different types is a behavior found in many animals- especially in mammals. There appear to be several evolutionarily adaptive consequences of this energetic play. This field of research was also pioneered by Jaak Panksepp, who has written extensively on the neurobiological basis of what he calls "rough and tumble" play. These forms of physical interaction activate intense emotional responses- allowing children to experience their instinctual energy in a safe and protective environment. The release of the excitatory neurotransmitters acetylcholine and glutamate cause the underlying neurobiological circuits to be exercised right up to the limits of a potentially dangerous or violent outburst. This gives children a direct embodied knowledge of the cycles of instinctual activation and just how far physiological arousal can be taken before an over-activated (and potentially socially damaging) response is triggered. In a very basic sense, play teaches children how to engage their instinctual drives but still remain within the rules of society. This form of instinctual intelligence is critical for the adaptive expression of more mature and adult-like instinctual energy. Professional competence and success are often built on the combination of persistent instinctual drive and social skills. Plus, the skills needed for dating and mating are highly dependent on the integration of instinctual energy and social grace developed by play. It also makes grocery shipping a hell of a lot easier.

Panksepp's research demonstrated that play is also innately pleasurable. Many of the games children play involve running and yelling, as well as all sorts of physical interaction. Whatever games children play- house, football, Laura Croft Tomb Raider, or Tag- play almost always takes place in a context of social connection. As we know, children experience a high level of brain opioid release during play. As the play of young children, especially boys, is often a bit rough-and-tumble, the physical touching also stimulates the release of brain opioids and the opioid-potentiating neruopeptide oxytocin. These neuropeptides create feelings of social confidence, allowing fuller expression of emotional and physical impulses within social contexts. Again, this helps children develop instinctual intelligence by letting them find the limits of acceptable behavior. Fairly often, impromptu games end when one child gets hurt or becomes upset. The injuries are usually minor- more emotional than physical- but they serve to indicate that a limit of instinctual intensity has been crossed. As children grow, the rules of the games they play become more formal, as in competitive sports or video games. Scores are kept and winners are rewarded. During adolescence, competition for even more pleasurable rewards is just heating up.

What Are Gamblers Paying For?

What can the games of children teach us about gambling? As it turns out, quite a lot. Let's look at your average Las Vegas casino, where some high-stakes gambling is going on. You can walk right by the 5 cent slots, where droves of people are staring blankly into at the screen, drearily pushing the same button over and over. These people are not really *playing* in the way I'm talking about, as they appear to be more interested in numbing themselves. The action we are looking for is at the craps table or over at the roulette wheel. It's also at the poker tables and the blackjack games. Here, the gamblers are engaged, their eyes intently focused on *the game*. They seem to be enjoying themselves, enthralled with the action whether they are winning or losing. This is the first key to understanding the instinctual intelligence at work here in the casino. These people know the odds are against them. But it's not just about the money. *They are paying for opportunity to play*. They like the feel of participating in the action. They like the social contact. They like the feeling of rubbing shoulders (and sometimes a bit more) with their new-found friends. The laughing and the nervous chatter all contribute to the release of opioids and oxytocin within the nervous systems of the players. The flow of alcohol further relaxes the inhibitions already loosened by the playful atmosphere. Some see this as a den of iniquity- or, at best- a sure fire way to lose money.

But look more closely.

By linking motor movements with affective expression, humans learn to express instinctual energy in a manner that reflects social competence. Here's how it happens: The release of opioids and oxytocin create sustained feelings of joy and relaxation, which allows the somatosensory cortex to integrate complex information from the midbrain, thalamus, and other regions of the neocortex. This neurocognitive integration of the motor subroutines of the somatosensory cortex with energetic emotional expressions is actually rewiring the brains of the gamblers. They are refining their instinctual intelligence. This integration of physical expression with innate emotional energy enhances the communicative skills of the individual, thus promoting social connection and the likelihood of survival. It also dramatically enhances their ability to express certain other instinctual impulses in a way that is socially smooth and sophisticated. Gambling can help people-men and women- become more charming and seductive.

Pathways in the male brain that allow the freer expression of emotions are reinforced. The opioids and oxytocin in their brains makes their touch a bit more playful and even provocative. They are more at ease and basically more fun to be around. Ladies, on the other hand, find themselves more apt to have conversations with a wide variety of men and women, depending on their orientation and mood. This allows them to survey the field- deftly moving from creep to catch- in the blink of a flirtatious eyelash. Feeling playful, a plain looking gal might even charm her way into rolling the dice for a high roller and suddenly Lady Luck is the center of attention. It's not about winning or losing- one moment of high-stakes confidence is enough to change the wiring of our brains. Just like when we climbed that tree when we were kids, there were no winners or losers. Deep in our instinctual consciousness, there is just a sensation of being excited, of taking a chance, and pushing the edges of what it feels like to be alive.

The Other Game

Let's face it- a lot of gamblers are not just interested in money. Like millions of others, they come to Las Vegas to play in another way. A stop at the gambling table is often the first phase of what many of them hope to be a long and passionate night. We're going to continue our exploration of the instinctual intelligence at work in Las Vegas upstairs from the casinos, in the fabulous lounges, where the rich and the beautiful play. But we are not so interested in the rich and beautiful. Rather, we will see how the poor and the plain are using their instinctual intelligence to get closer to that elusive dream that Las Vegas seems to evoke.

How Has Evolution Shaped Sexuality in Las Vegas?

The story of what happens in Vegas has been evolving for millions of years. In that sense, there is nothing new about sexual desire, playfulness, and seduction. What is amazing is the sophistication of the instinctual intelligence that underlies the infinite spectrum of human sexual activity. In the modern world, the basic drives of attraction need to navigate an astonishingly complex maze of social and cultural dynamics. The days of clubbing the woman over the head and dragging her back to the cave are long gone. In every Las Vegas lounge, every person in the room- male and female, lesbian and gay, transgender and fluid gender- makes thousands and thousands of intricate split-second decisions about how to assess potential sexual and reproductive partners. This goes on in every town and every city in every country of the world. While it rarely goes smoothly, humans continuously engage in this extraordinarily complex mating dance, somehow finding ways to make contact, connect, and sometimes reproduce. How did humans develop this intuitive knowledge?

This is the question that David Buss has spent his life trying to answer. Buss is currently the head of the Individual Differences and Evolutionary Psychology Area and a professor of Evolutionary Psychology at the University of Texas at Austin. Evolutionary psychology is a relatively new field of academic study that has only emerged in the last decade. The basic premise of evolutionary psychology is that the forces of natural selection shaped specific features of human cognitive, emotional, and behavioral physiology. Thus, the functioning of our basic instincts can best be explained by taking into consideration the various circumstances that allowed some of our ancestors to survive and reproduce more effectively than others. It is a powerful explanatory tool that has great significance for understanding the roots of instinctual intelligence. From the perspective of evolutionary psychology, many of the intuitive behaviors that surround mate selection are influenced by instinctual appraisal systems that have evolved over millions of years.

Buss has written several books that have created controversy in the worlds of psychology and anthropology. His provocative 1994 work, *The Evolution of Desire: Strategies of Human Mating*, was one of the first attempts to systematically study the dynamics of sexual attraction on a cross-cultural basis. Many of Buss' conclusions angered supporters of mainstream psychological theories and feminist thinkers. Many psychologists saw Buss' analysis as speculative and superficial. Feminist scholars were insulted by Buss' observations that what females found attractive in men was wealth and status. Judging by the intensity of these reactions, it was clear that Buss had struck a deep nerve in the collective psyche. Clearly he was on to something. Let's take a closer look at the dynamics of sexual attraction in the microcosm of a Vegas lounge. Here, we can clearly see how natural selection has shaped the modern sexual intelligence of both men and women. Of course, human relationships, especially sexual ones, are infinitely complex. Some of this analysis may seem superficial or simplistic. But the more we understand the underlying instinctual dynamics, the more we can begin to appreciate the sophisticated intelligence behind the magical pulse of human life.

Flirting Your Way In

The first thing we notice in the chic lounges is that there are no kids around, and no old folks either. This is strictly a playground for young adults. It's a basic fact of life that the maturation of the pituitary gonadal axis during puberty stimulates the production of hormones that awaken the specific brain regions that mediate sexual motivation. All the people we see are at the height of their sexual and reproductive capacities, surging with hormones. Throughout the world, each culture has its own particular dynamics of sexual playfulness and attraction that determine the age, behaviors, rituals, and selection criteria. In Vegas, the mating game is all about competition. You can smell the attitude. One needs high levels of hormones to even get in the door. The bouncers are very selective about who enters the club, seeking to let in the most instinctually intelligent looking people into their exclusive lounges. Here, the playful openness that was stimulated by the social interaction of the casino can be advantageous. The same circuits that are active during energized physical play are also activated in flirtatious behaviors, especially the initial dance of social interaction and physical touching. This knowledge can be helpful in the competition for sexually attractive mates.

The exclusive clubs in Vegas count on good-looking, socially sophisticated people to set trends and influence people to spend big money. In this situation, an average looking guy standing around with his hands in his pockets has very little chance of being admitted. However, if Mr. Average has ignited his social circuits at the casino, he can improve his chances dramatically. He might just walk up to one of the endless stream of seductively clad young ladies strolling through the doors (they are always welcome by the bouncers) and put his arm around her, ever so playfully. With a charming grin he says "I just got incredibly lucky at the blackjack table." The woman smiles with surprise and he flashes the bouncer a confident nod as he strolls by. The bouncer figures this guy is good for business, and lets him roll in without a second thought.

Meanwhile the rather plain looking girl from the casino strolls up to the bouncer, and seductively whispers in his ear "I'd do *anything* to get in here and party with you." She touches his arm, still feeling the juice from her lucky roll of the dice downstairs. He waves her in with a dazed smile.

What the bouncer might not know is that opioids play a large role in the subjective experience of pleasure. When she touched his arm, he experienced the release of these neruopeptides in several regions of his brain. He could feel the suggestion of sexual pleasure in his higher cortical and limbic regions at the same time. He was thinking about and feeling the anticipation of sexual pleasure. Visually, he might not have even thought that our plain friend was very attractive. However, deep in his septal area, cingulate cortex, and somatosensory cortex, neurons were firing away, signaling the pleasure laden promise of desire. She was feeling the same sensations, and transmitted this to him by her sensual whisper and the touching of his skin. This is limbic resonance of the adult variety.

The neural circuits that coordinate the motivation and behavioral expression of sexual activity are also part of the underlying neurophysiology of persistent seeking behaviors described in the last chapter. The medial hypothalamus and the ventral tegmental area both contain steroid receptors that are sensitive to testosterone, diydrotestosterone, estrogen, and progesterone- the main hormones that promote sexual behaviors. Activation of these areas will stimulate various types of sexual behavior patterns. While many clubs in Vegas revolve primarily around the gender–typical patterns of heterosexual activity, there is a growing variety of sexual orientations that are catered to in Vegas. This is true in most major cities of the world. The primary reason men, women, and transgendered folks are in the lounge tonight is that are feeling the instinctual drive to seek out sexual partners. But they'll go about it in radically different ways.

Standing Around Won't Cut It

For men to be sought after sexual partners, they have to have *game*. Having game is the latest slang for instinctual intelligence of a sexual nature. Men possess a unique set of factors that shape the expression of their sexual intelligence. One of the most important differences in the sexual neurochemistry between genders is the role of arginine vassopressin (AVP) in male sexual motivation and behavior. AVP is a hormone released by the pituitary into several areas of the brain during the initial stages of male sexual arousal. The actions of AVP account for many of the male-typical attributes of sexual behavior, including persistence and inter-male aggression. AVP can be seen as the overall arousal inducing hormone that accounts for the eagerness of male sexual motivation. At a basic level, it explains why guys have to make the first move with women. For gay men, it explains way it is never hard to find a first date.

One of the first screening criteria for hetero women is assessment of the levels of AVP in a prospective mate's system. Being the product of countless generations of successful reproducers, she cannot help but draw an instinctive conclusion that a guy who is sexually persistent would be good at gathering resources. She also intuitively knows that a man who can keep other males from stealing his resources will increase the likelihood of her children's survival. All of this is subliminal, derived from subtle cues and intuition. All she really notices is the feel of his confidence as he locked eyes on her from across the room and made his way through sea of people directly to her. His cute smile didn't hurt either.

Because he is not a rock star or otherwise wildly rich, famous, and handsome, Mr. Average will have to compete fairly aggressively for attractive women- or attractive men, if he is drawn in that direction. Either way, securing contact with the most sought after partners will call for a great deal of sexual persistence. Fortunately, AVP activates the seeking systems of the ascending dopamine circuits of the ventral tegmental region. This is how a lot of men get to Vegas in the first place. The combination of AVP and testosterone receptors released into the amygdalar tissue of the temporal lobes appears to be the primary contributors to inter-male competition and territorial protection. While playing has its roots in childhood, adult male competition is a high-stakes game. It's all about status and hierarchy. Star athletes are some of the most sexually sought-after males on the planet, as well as the highest paid. They can defend their turf. As dominant males, they have their pick of sexual partners. Women automatically factor in that their ability to control resources and physically intimidate other males will enhance the ability of their offspring to thrive- both socially and physically. This is why the hetero men in the lounge are all trying to look confident and successful. Displays of wealth signal to women that they control resources and that they have social status. For gay men, economic and social status may not be quite that important- but it never hurts. Often, it is physical prowess and attractiveness that will ignite the initial flames of deeper attraction. Most men, regardless of their orientation, will try to dance in a way that suggests they have physical prowess, or at least artfully hide the fact that it is lacking.

As all women know, men make great efforts to create displays wealth they do not really have and are apt to lie about their jobs and income. Discerning as they may be, it is not easy for women to evaluate the economic and physical prowess of men in this setting. That is why when a movie star rolls into the club, all heads will turn his way. Women can be sure of his social status and his resources. The only chance the males lower in the social hierarchy have is to persist. And persist they will. There are a lot more available women than there are movie stars in the club tonight. Still, Mr. Average will need to use every ounce of instinctual intelligence he can muster to increase his odds.

Remember Those Ads at the Airport?

But which women are the targets of men's sexual persistence? That's pretty obvious. Men initially evaluate potential partners primarily on physical appearance. Now this may sound crude or superficial, but we are talking about primal, gut-level responses. Males, on average, have far more neurons in the preoptic area of the hypothalamus compared to females. These cells are sensitive to the effects of testosterone, thus heightening the stimulating pleasure experienced by males in the presence of visual stimuli that signal sexual attractiveness. It is now widely recognized that male sexual responses are highly correlated with specific physical attributes. For gay men, trim and muscular physiques signal sexual vitality. Youthfulness signals to heterosexual men that women are at the height of their reproductive capacities. Wide hips indicate the ability to bear children with ease. Smooth clear skin indicates healthy and robust genes. In Las Vegas, it is seems that men respond to one thing above all else. Well, make that *two* things. Large round breasts indicate that the woman is capable of producing copious amounts of milk, thus insuring the nourishment of several children. The evolutionary basis of female sexual attractiveness to men is clear. This is the basic instinctual package men are born with. It also explains why a lot of the young women at the club have surgically enhanced breasts. But these are only the most primitive of instinctual impulses and strategies. How can Mr. Average use a more refined understanding of instinctual intelligence to his advantage?

First of all, he will realize that his goal for the night is not reproduction; it is indulging his sexual pleasure. Whether this amounts to flirting, getting a telephone number, or something more will depend on a lot of things that are often beyond his control. Knowing this, he relaxes. Women go for guys that are persistent and relaxed, not rude or pushy. Repeating his mantra that reproduction is not the name of the game tonight, he ignores the initial appeal of the women with the huge and obviously fake breasts. His frontal lobes can override his testosterone driven amygdala- and he will realize that those breasts are full of silicone- not life-giving milk. His perception altered through this insight, he recognizes the room of full of attractive smiling women. The majority of men in the room have staked out their turf around a few of the cosmetically enhanced models. Our instinctually intelligent friend is poised to take advantage of this situation. He knows that oxytocin is involved in pleasurable sexual sensations in both sexes. In males, oxytocin usually has a more limited role, with peak release during orgasm. The effects of oxytocin are easily recognized as the afterglow of sexual satisfaction. However, he knows that if he just relaxes and makes genuine contact with one of the overlooked but very attractive women, they will both be in the flow of an oxytocin rush in no time at all. Before long, he finds a smile that draws him in. Staring in the eyes of his new friend, he realizes that the sensation of relaxed sexually charged contact is not only arousing but pleasurable and playful. It is also mutually reinforcing. The more she relaxes and opens to her sexual desire, the more compelling the adventure becomes. He has not lost any of his predatory glow, but he also feels a sweetness. He can sense her pleasure and wants to give her more. With a little luck, he his on his way to a weekend of sensual delight that his less instinctually intelligent friends cannot even imagine.

Sexy Smart

Even cavemen knew that the innate sexual intelligence of women operates differently than men. It's simply taken several hundreds of thousands of years to even begin to figure out what that difference was. This is also true in the world of science. Researchers have a far more detailed understanding of the neurophysiology of male sexuality. With a little blue pill men can be well on their way to orgasm. With women, the psychoneuroendocrinology of sexuality is a lot more complex. I don't think that anyone has it all figured out yet, even women. Maybe it's the mystery that makes it so exciting.

Neurobiologically, one thing we know for sure is that oxytocin appears to play a far greater role in female sexuality than in males. While females also experience an increase in oxytocin levels during orgasm, their levels of oxytocin are already quite high during the initial courtship and arousal phases that lead up to copulation. Chances are many of the young women at the club spent the day getting their hair done, their nails polished, and their skin smoothed and tanned. They likely shopped for a new dress and- it goes without saying- a new pair of shoes. They probably did this together, in a modern social ritual that young women perform with utmost relish. Spending the day grooming and gossiping is probably nothing new. We see rudiments of this behavior among our primate cousins and most likely it was a favorite pastime of our ancestral mothers. By now we should be quick to realize the adaptive intelligence of social bonding. These women are not just being indulgent. They are actually refining their instinctual intelligence by enhancing their social network and learning to evaluate the suitability of potential mates. Remember that females have to carry the baby for nine months and then care for it of several years. Taking some time to get your friend's analysis of why your boyfriend acts the way he does is quite wise. The instinctual intelligence of females is often a collective wisdom.

Females are more engaged in the social dimensions of sexual activity than males. Women can be quite competitive with each other socially. Friends will often compete for status in the various types of social groups to which they belong. For instance, women who work at the same club might be fiercely competitive for social position. In order to destabilize the confidence and social standing of a competitor, a social climbing female might employ social gossip, deception, and sabotage. Males are not so embedded in the social dimensions of sexual competition. The men at the club are lone wolves. They may show up with friends, but for the most part they need to pursue sexual mates alone. Heterosexual men do not dance together. In the other hand, women usually hang out together, often dancing in groups. Women don't have to be lesbians to enjoy close physical contact with each other. Again, oxytocin is involved in all levels of social interaction, especially bonding and playful physical contact that signals receptivity. For females, physical playfulness activates the release of opioids and oxytocin- it makes them feel sexy. The innate instinctual intelligence in sensual touching is quite potent. It's what helped our plain friend become a lighting bolt of female sexual energy and charm her way into the club.

In most modern cultures, an increasing number of young women are bisexual in their sexual orientation. The rigid gender roles of the past are largely a thing of the past in most urban areas. These women enjoy a very fluid sense of sexuality, intricately woven into the social dimensions of their lives. Biologically, the social dimensions of sexuality are more developed in women because, on average, they have far more connections between the left and right sides of their brains. This greater cross-hemispheric interaction allows women to link language and sensation more intuitively than men. They have larger numbers of circuits within the corpus collosum, a set of neurons that connects the two sides of the brain. This makes a lot of sense in terms of instinctual intelligence. Men compete with each other physically, usually through intimidation but also directly, through aggression and violence. Women, often covertly compete with each other using social intelligence. They need both sides of their brains to be socially and sexually successful with their own gender. They also need social intelligence to evaluate prospective reproductive partners. Heterosexual women are not only feeling the way men are responding to them physically, they are also listening to what the man says.

But years before they ever get to the sight of babies and diapers, each man must pass a critical test if they hope to get a real phone number, much less hook up with a woman at the club tonight. They not only have to be confident and appear reasonably good-looking. They also have to sound somewhat intelligent and even manage to be witty and clever. A beautiful woman can say almost anything and a guy will rarely even notice a slip of logic or an inconsistency in her story. Well, he might notice- but he doesn't care. On the other hand, even a good looking guy can be rejected on the spot with one stupid comment or even if he gets caught in a little lie that makes him look untrustworthy. Once a woman's radar is tipped off that a guy is somehow bogus, her defenses will go up and her sexual openness will shut down. This kind of relational integrity is also central to the formation of lesbian relationships. Again, it is an evolutionarily honed blend of sexual and social intelligence that shapes female intimate relationships.

Getting Closer

Complex as it may seem, an instinctually intelligent woman can get through the basic screening and appraisal process in less than two or three minutes. If a potential partner passes these tests, then the woman begins to relax into another layer of sexual arousal. Women show high levels of activation in the ventromedial hypothalamus during sexual arousal. This is due to the high concentrations of oxytocin, estrogen and progesterone in this area, all of which appear to by linked to social connectivity. Totally unaware of the role of her hypothalamus, she will nonetheless start to signal sexual receptivity more directly through flirtatious behaviors. The instinctually intelligent male knows that this phase of courtship is quite enjoyable for women and he had best relax and enjoy it also. Any attempt to rush this process- and get back to the hotel room too quickly- will spoil the romance. The woman will respond to gentle physical touches that signal to her that the male has physical grace and patience.

Every moment, everywhere in the world, the mating dance continues. Every possible combination of men, women, bisexual, transgender, every possible way- every molecule of the human race finds its own sexual frequency. Between a man and a woman, there is the possibility of creating new life. In this timeless magnetic dance, the flirting and the talking and the romance may go on for some time. The couple might exchange phone numbers or they might continue the evening in a more private setting. For the man, this is a delicate phase. He feels the deep urges of millions of generations of males of every species. He wants to get close to her, to get her naked, to feel her skin, and to get his genitals next to hers. This is the drive, the delicious instinct of life. As the opportunity for this consummation draws near, every system in his sexual repertoire is firing. If he has some refinement of his instinctual intelligence, he will find the balance between raw persistence and a reassuring sweetness. As they kiss, his hands touch her body. He is looking for a signal of her readiness, a sign that he can proceed with his immediate goal, the primary goal of every male of every species that has ever lived. He kisses her and he senses the electric arch of her back. This is the deep instinctual response of lordosis, signaling the female's readiness to copulate. Lordosis is the arching of the back that allows easy access to the genital area. This reflex is mediated by the spinal cord, as well as the ventromedial hypothalamus, especially when it is primed with steady levels of estrogen and the sudden surge of progesterone that prepares the egg for fertilization. Because this couple has no interest in reproduction tonight, they use a condom, using their modern instinctual intelligence to outsmart the biochemical systems that have helped to fertilize countless eggs. In the peak of passion, their mutual orgasms release a flood of oxytocin, and they drift off into a contented sleep.

The Darker Side of Human Nature

David Buss has not limited himself to the exploration of sexuality. He has recently authored several more books on primal human impulses. One of these, *The Dangerous Passion: Why*

Jealousy is as Necessary as Love and Sex, explores the role of jealousy in human mating. Buss argues that sexual jealousy is a natural part of our instinctual endowment. It helps to insure the sexual fidelity of our partners and increases the odds that our genes will reproduce and our offspring will thrive. Another has the alarming title *The Murderer Next Door: Why the Mind is Designed to Kill*. Buss again uses his knowledge of evolutionary psychology to highlight the adaptive advantages to murder. In the past, there were no CSI teams to catch the culprits. Getting away with murder was relatively easy. Problems could vanish, resources could be acquired, and social hierarchies could change just by pushing a competitor off a cliff or pounding a rock into someone's skull. Chances are many of our distant ancestors advanced within their social hierarchies through acts of violence and treachery. Some of those adaptive and potentially violent circuits are still at work today, shaping our thoughts in clandestine ways.

Buss has been courageous in his willingness to explore the darker side of human instincts. This makes a lot of people uncomfortable. Some have even gone on to suggest that Buss is somehow advocating violence, murder, and other instinctually irresponsible acts. Nothing could be further from the truth. Buss has been a rational voice in helping modern humans to come to grips with the reality of their instinctual heritage. His writings are an important first step to a deeper understanding of true nature of the primal forces that have shaped our evolution. Ignoring the reality of these impulses can have disastrous consequences. Throughout history, many moral, legal, and spiritual traditions have focused on the more enlightened qualities of human nature. They sought to promote the good while throwing out the bad. From the days of Moses, humans have sought to repress, deny, purge, outlaw- or just plain ignore- certain aspects of human instinctual energy.

The Evolutionary Thread

One of the indispensable elements of our instinctual intelligence is its raw passion and power. If we deny this or regard it as somehow wrong or immoral, then we are cutting off a part of ourselves. Competition, violence, and sexual aggression are the raw materials of our evolving instinctual consciousness. In order to uncover the deeper intelligence that lies behind them, we have to understand how they work. This dark underbelly of the human soul needs to be brought out into the full light of day, to see both its ugly distortions and its potential for transformation. As we will see, the so-called dark underbelly of the human soul has in it the seeds of a wisdom we are just beginning to recognize.

CHAPTER 5

At the Edge of Life and Death

There's a reason they call it Hell Week.

In the deadly realities of warfare, superior training is the difference between life and death. On this edge, the slightest nervous system imbalance can lead to instant death. The warriors who lay their lives on the line need to master that edge. They need to know every intimate detail of what separates life from death.

Hell Week is the how Navy SEALs are introduced to that edge. SEAL training is widely regarded as the most challenging form of military training ever devised in the history of warfare. Completing the full 32 months of training earns the individual the privilege of being awarded the Navy SEAL Trident. SEAL stands for Sea, Air, and Land- the elements in which these warriors operate. SEALs are the heart and soul of the US Special Forces. Completing the training and becoming a Navy SEAL allows you to join the most secret and elite military group on the planet. They are called in when a mission is judged to be too difficult and too dangerous for any other military personnel. During the 32 months of training, each candidate is pushed to the limit of his instinctual capacity. Very few of those who begin the program have the physical stamina, strength, and nervous system constitution to successfully complete the entire training. It requires a very particular type of instinctual intelligence to become a SEAL. To thrive under the constant threat of death, the human body must learn to draw on the deepest reserves of instinctual energy. To do this, it is necessary to overcome the tendency of the nervous system to go into a state of shock- an incapacitating freezing response- under conditions of extreme and overwhelming terror. In warfare, if your nervous system seizes up, chances are you will die and the mission will fail. SEALs training is not about improving the weakest candidates. It is about identifying the individuals with the strongest survival instincts and transforming them into superior warriors. They need to weed out any individuals who cannot endure mind-bending levels of pain, cold, exhaustion, and fear. This is exactly why they created Hell Week.

Survival Instincts

We can learn a lot about how our basic survival instincts function by studying the training procedures of Navy SEALs. Their training programs are systematically designed to push these survival instincts to the absolute limits that the human body can endure. Every hour of the training brings candidates closer to the fine edge between life and death. At this edge, we can begin to see how the human nervous system responds to the most stressful and life-threatening conditions imaginable. Under these conditions, our basic programs hover between a fully energized survival response and a complete neurobiological collapse. As we explore this edge, we will be confronting a profound mystery. It is the same mystery that the officer in charge of the training- the Master Chief- ponders every hour of Hell Week:

What is the deep intelligence of our survival instincts that arises in response to the most terrifying conditions?

In the days leading up to Hell Week, every SEAL candidate quickly learns that humans have several instinctual programs that are designed to respond to a variety of life-threatening conditions. As we will see, there are distinct neurobiological systems designed to respond to pain, cold, suffocation, and the threat of physical violence. SEAL training deliberately stresses each one of those systems in a systematic and precise way. As each test grows more intense, it becomes readily apparent which candidates cannot handle the extreme stress placed on each of the neurobiological survival systems. When the stress grows too great, candidates that feel they can no longer go on can quit the training at any time. All they have to do is ring the bell that hangs in the middle of the training compound three times. Why do some of the candidates quit and others go on to earn their Tridents? The answer lies deep in the nervous system of each individual. Each one of them will respond to the specific challenges posed by the training in their own unique way. Only those who can respond with instinctual intelligence to the stress applied to all of the individual systems will continue. Just like in the days of the dinosaurs, only the fittest will survive.

Insights from Our Reptilian Past

The basic programs for human survival responses are the result of an evolutionary journey that began long ago. Most researchers believe that we can trace the origins of our survival instincts by examining the nervous systems of contemporary humans- if we just look hard enough. It's difficult and painstaking work. Even then, there's no guarantee that other scientists will notice your work. Sometimes the most profound insights into human evolution take a small step ahead in the most obscure conditions. At first, almost no one notices it. But slowly- if the insight has great explanatory power- it begins to take hold. What starts out as a footnote becomes a fundamental theoretical paradigm. This is what happened with the writings of Stephen Porges, a professor of psychiatry, and co-director of the Brain Body Center at the University of Illinois at Chicago. In 1995, he published a short article in the academic journal *Psychophysiology*. The article was called "Orienting in a Defensive World: Mammalian Modification of Our Evolutionary Heritage. A Polyvagal Theory." For several years, very few scholars or psychologists appreciated the significance of what Porges had written.

In this article, Porges outlined the evolutionary development of nervous system regulating mechanisms of the humans. He observed that humans have three discrete systems that help them adapt to social and environmental conditions. Under normal, non-stressful conditions, our nervous system regulates metabolic and neural systems by means of transitory arousal or relaxation of discrete regions of the *ventral vagal complex* without the activation of the sympathetic system. The vagal complex is a network of nerves that emanate from the midbrain. Certain nerves act as a "vagal brake" that allows quick adjustments in heart rate, blood pressure, and metabolic level without the severe biological costs of a system-wide activation of the sympathetic system. It also provides a burst of energy that enhances neural outflow to the communication systems of the face and throat that supports the expression of richly nuanced facial communication gestures. This is the most efficient mode of nervous system regulation.

The next level of nervous system regulation is the sympathetic response. This is activated when the external social or physical environment is perceived as threatening and vagal complex activation is not enhancing the chances for adaptation or survival. In other words, when talking or yelling is not helping, it is time for the fight-or-flight sympathetic response- characterized by an increase in heart rate, activation of sweat glands, dramatic increases in circulating catecholamines (dopamine, adrenaline, and norepinephrine) throughout the nervous system, and a general increase in mobilizing metabolic activity. This response is extremely metabolically costly.

The final and most phylogenetically primitive response of the polyvagal regulating system is the activation of the *dorsal vagal system* located in the midbrain. As we will see in our exploration of Navy SEAL training, the dorsal vagal region responds to pain, social anxiety, and temperature dysregulation through depressing metabolic activity. It has its origins in our reptilian past, where remaining motionless often averted detection by larger predators. Smaller lizards did not have the physical capacity to fight hungry dinosaurs. Nor did they have the luxury of ironing out their differences through diplomatic negotiations. In humans, the dorsal vagal system will only be activated in the most extreme conditions of stress not alleviated by the activation of the sympathetic or vagal complex systems. However, when the dorsal vagal system is activated, the sympathetic excitatory systems of the brainstem remain active, albeit at a slightly reduced level. The net effect is a state of prolonged semi-conscious distress, in which the dorsal vagal activation immobilizes motor responses but does not shut off the stress response.

Porges' insights into the evolutionary roots of human survival responses are now emerging as a central paradigm for the modern understanding of instinctual intelligence. So much so that we studying its applications throughout the remainder of this book. But before we see how polyvagal theory can help us understand the skills of master nervous system regulators like Tiger Woods and the Dalai Lama, let's see how it functions in the grueling Navy SEALs training. This will give a clear picture of how the polyvagal system responds to a variety of threatening conditions.

Making Friends with Pain

Within the very first hour of the first day of SEALs training, candidates will have done 500 push-ups and 60 pull-ups. The pain experienced in that first hour shocks the nervous system into survival mode. The training continues with endless physical conditioning drills where the candidates are forced to roll heavy containers up and down the dunes on the beach training areas. Extreme levels of pain are experienced as muscles begin to fatigue in the intense heat. Fingers are crushed. Knees and ankles are stressed to the point of injury. The sting of sand in their eyes, combined with the constant strain on every muscle in their backs, pushes pain intensity levels through the roof. For most of us, the urge to cry out would simply take over. It's a natural impulse to cry out when we are in pain or injured. These cries are the adult versions of *distress vocalizations* made by infants. This is one of the basic survival responses with which we are born. As we saw in chapter two, infants under the age of 9 months do not have a full repertoire of mature sympathetic nervous system responses and motor development that allow them to fight or flee. They do, however, have specific neural systems that serve to activate instinctual responses that help their bodies to tolerate potentially life-threatening conditions. Distress vocalizations help dissipate stress from the infant's nervous system. More importantly, these cries of distress signal caregivers to attend to the survival needs of the infant.

For Navy SEALs, infantile responses to pain are not an option. Whining to the Master Chief that you are tired and sore will get you nothing but ridicule and humiliation. Getting angry with him and yelling at him to let him know that he is being *too mean* will only increase your pain. To continue with the training, the instinctually intelligent SEAL candidate must use his (or occasionally her) instinctual intelligence to modify the crying response. He knows that the urge to cry or to yell in anger is an attempt by his nervous system to respond in an adaptive manner to pain. But he also realizes he cannot complain to or bitch at the Master Chief. If he submits to this urge, he is finished. In our earlier exploration of basic programs of social bonding, we saw that the crying response is regulated by the periaqueductal gray (PAG) region of the midbrain. Even if he does not know the precise neuroanatomical details, the instinctually intelligent SEAL candidate can use his knowledge of distress vocalization responses to his advantage.

Intuitively, a true warrior respects pain. It informs him with a wisdom that helps him survive. If we look closely at this intuitive knowledge of pain, we will see that the crying response is a parasympathetic modulation of the basic fight-or-flight response of the sympathetic system. In general, parasympathetic responses often balance sympathetic activation of our survival systems. Think of what happens when you accidentally hit your finger with a hammer. For most people, the pain is accompanied by an intense feeling of anger, verging on violence. You're *really* pissed. You want to yell at or hit somebody. This is the initial sympathetic reaction, evolved over millions of years to protect us from further injury. However, the parasympathetic modulation of the distress vocalization can dampen the expression of the sympathetic system just enough to inhibit its most impulsive and physically violent responses. Instead of hitting somebody, we yell and curse. The instinctually intelligent warrior intuitively takes the parasympathetic modulation one step further. He knows how to transform the boiling rage he is feeling into a source of extraordinary power.

Predatory Aggression

The primary brain region that mediates feelings of extreme aggression is the amygdala. With its direct inputs to the deepest centers of arousal within the limbic system and brainstem, the amygdala can trigger two different types of aggressive responses- the *fight/ flight response* or *predatory aggression*. We saw how the amygdala activates the basic fight/flight instinctual programs in the first chapter. Predatory aggression is activated via a neurobiological pathway that is distinct from the fight/flight response. Activation of the predatory aggression system is controlled by the parasympathetic lateral hypothalamus, which directly adjusts the responses of the amygdala and the PAG region. Subjectively, the involvement of the parasympathetic system makes this form of rage less impulsive and immediate, imbuing it with the qualities of cool, deliberate vengeance.

SEALs are trained to consciously use pain to maintain the activation of the predatory aggression system. This helps them operate with instinctual intelligence on the battlefield. Because their nervous systems are not boiling over with rage, they do not impulsively discharge their aggressive energy with unnecessary outbursts. At the same time, they can dial up their aggression instantly because they use their conscious awareness of pain to keep their nervous systems fully alert and primed for attack. In any given situation, they may be experiencing a great deal of pain. The urge to cry out with distress vocalizations is always there. But instead of crying out, the pain becomes the silent battle cry of the warrior. Pain becomes an inner strength, galvanizing the nervous system with the fortitude of unflinching resolve.

From an evolutionary perspective, the predatory aggression system has unique adaptive advantages. In hunting and gathering societies, the ability of early humans to activate this basic instinctual program often meant the difference between life and death. Those individuals who were best able direct their aggression towards prey- while simultaneously inhibiting aggressive responses to family and friends- were regarded as great warriors and effective leaders. A capacity to activate the predatory aggression system allowed them to defend their territory and protect their families. This helped them to amass resources that would ensure their survival and reproductive success. Predatory aggression is a form of instinctual intelligence that is not exclusive to males. Throughout history, females emerged as excellent hunters and leaders in a variety of cultures. However, the finest examples of predatory aggression in females can be found in the protective instincts they have for their children. Mothers can become cold-blooded killers at the first sign of a threat to their offspring. Anyone who has the misfortune of stumbling between a mamma and her cubs will encounter a fury that would make even a Navy SEAL piss in his pants. It's interesting to note that arginine vassopressin (one of the primary sources of male sexual aggressiveness) peaks in females after childbirth. This appears to account for some of the features of maternal aggression.

SEALs Do Not Submit

During the first three or four weeks of training, SEAL candidates are in a constant state of misery. Wet clothes drain the last vestige of warmth and comfort from their bodies. Unrelenting pain in their bones. No Sleep. If that weren't enough, they are subject to the devastating harassment of the Master Chief around the clock. His tone and demeanor are deliberately designed to trigger feelings of shame and humiliation. His abuse is relentless. Any candidate who shows the slightest sign of weakness will instantly become the target of the most ferocious attacks. The only way to get him to stop is to ring the bell three times- and forever surrender the chance to become a Navy SEAL.

SEAL training systematically probes the instinctual systems of every candidate to bring out the primal response of predatory aggression. For most of the candidates, the slightest weakness is exploited until they are forced to quit. For the most adaptive, this instinct is honed to a razor's edge of power and resiliency. Take, for example, the suffocation reflex. Throughout the training, candidates will be forced to submit to drown-proofing tests. Their arms and legs are bound and water is poured into their mouths and noses. This triggers involuntary panic and suffocation responses. A Navy SEAL needs to become familiar with these primal instinctual responses if they are to succeed as warriors. Temporarily inhibiting the choking and coughing of the suffocation reflex might allow the SEAL to survive a few more seconds in combat conditions. This training is designed to help the candidate find the perfect balance between the hyper-aroused state of panic and the submissive response of distress vocalizations. At the edge of life and death, every second is an eternity. Being able to maintain the nervous system in a state of balanced predatory aggression allows a warrior to maintain an awareness of the external surroundings and recognize opportunities for escape- or an opening for a last-second attack.

The Inner Fire of a Cold Warrior

If you cannot tolerate being cold and wet for long periods of time, forget about becoming a Navy SEAL. During the first few weeks of SEALs training, candidates are forced to endure endless hours in the surf. Sometimes they are forced to do push-ups and other exercises in knee-deep water. Other times, they are force to stand in chest high water for hours, while the Master Chief goads the coldest and most miserable candidates to ring the bell and end their suffering. The SEALs training program subjects candidates to extremes of temperature conditions for a very particular set of reasons. First, it will efficiently weed out any individuals whose nervous systems cannot adaptively respond to extremes of environmental temperature dysregulation. During the afternoon, many of their exercises are performed on sweltering beaches under humid conditions. High temperatures and fatigue quickly begin to wear down the candidates' nervous systems, and stress responses escalate. Candidates who cannot regulate their body temperatures through the sympathetic response of sweating are doomed to failure. However, it is in the evening and early dawn where the capacity of candidates to endure thermal extremes is put to the test. Hour after hour they are marched in and out of the water, never drying off, always wet and cold. Endless drills are carried out in the water, their body temperatures dropping. Medical personnel are always monitoring the situation, making sure no one slips into hypothermia. To some, this may seem like a cruel and pointless exercise. However, if we look more closely, we can observe the underlying instinctual intelligence that makes Navy SEAL training so effective.

Deep inside the nervous system of each candidate, their over-stressed survival systems are hovering at the edge of failure. The instinctual centers that respond to *cold* share nearly the exact same neural networks as those that respond to *pain*. Again, the PAG is at the center of all the action. In an attempt to keep the body from freezing, it will initiate various behaviors to help the body restore its optimal temperature. The first response is always the most obvious- move away from the cold to where it is warmer. But for a SEAL candidate required to stand in chest-high water in the middle of the night as a training exercise, getting out of the water is not an option. This is when some of the most primitive survival responses will kick in. Candidates will begin to shake and tremble as their muscles involuntarily tremor in an attempt to generate heat. Just like the reflexive responses to pain, candidates will feel the urge to complain or get angry. However, those with superior instinctual intelligence will guide their nervous systems to a more adaptive response. By consciously focusing on the pain of coldness, they welcome it as an ally. The impulse to whine or cry is recognized as a way to activate the predatory aggression system. As we saw earlier, this system utilizes a delicate balance between the sympathetic and parasympathetic systems to allow the nervous system to thrive in life-threatening conditions.

The Source of Strength: Inner Balance

At a certain point in the training, some of the candidates' nervous systems will learn to settle in on the razor's edge balance that characterizes predatory aggression. To do accomplish this, they will recruit specific regions of the prefrontal cortex to produce mental images that will continuously reactivate the amygdala over and over again. These mental images often consist of strategic initiatives, powerful actions, and certainty of effective and focused violence. These images are all focused in the success of the mission. This generates feelings of cold aggressive hatred that have the incessant, driving quality of persistent vengeance. In this way, they keep their amygdalas on the edge of hyperarousal, carefully amplifying the classic fight-or flight sympathetic and stress responses. The increase in the circulating catecholamines dopamine, adrenaline, and norepinephrine in the nervous system will continuously re-stimulate the prefrontal cortex and the amygdala. This feedback loop makes the predatory aggression response way more intense and persistent than the activation of the neural circuits that underlie anger.

Meanwhile, the parasympathetic responses of the lateral hypothalamus open an important neurobiological pathway. This pathway allows neural input from the viscera to enter the amygdala via the vagal afferent nerves that terminate in the nucleus of the solitary tract. This internal pathway is the result of millions of years of nervous system evolution. Any injury or malfunction of internal organs is an obvious threat to survival. This *internal warning system*- based in the amygdala and its cortical interconnections- pulls attention away from the external environment and directs it to inner sensations and self-protective behavioral responses. This inner awareness not only tempers the outward aggressive responses of the amygdala, it is also the source of the inner instinctual fortitude of a SEAL. They are not driven by a hatred of the cold. The source of their balanced power is a warmth generated by the gut level intimacy with their instinctual intelligence. This inner intimacy transforms the cold into a slow burning fire in the belly of a warrior, fueled by the fierce desire to survive. For those who cannot find this inner balance in the face of extreme cold, a warm shower is only three rings of the bell away.

Hell Week

Being abandoned in a cold place and left to die is the ultimate fear that lurks in the deepest recesses of our instinctual consciousness. Just as with pain and cold, the awareness of death is the ultimate source of wisdom for every true warrior. Warriors must learn to thrive in the face of death. They must learn to value the lives of others as dearly as their own. That is why SEALs never to leave their wounded or dead behind. It's more than just a code of honor. By never turning their backs on death, SEALs are able to access deeper and deeper levels of instinctual intelligence. This is how they thrive under the most hellish of conditions.

During Hell Week, SEAL candidates are brought face to face with death. They are already exhausted by the first three or four weeks of training and as many as half the original training group has already quit. Hell Week is designed to break the spirit of those who remain. The drills are endless. The abuse of the Master Chief is incessant. Sleep is out of the question. They are marched in and out of the water until they are so cold and so wet and so miserable that nearly half of the remaining class of trainees will ring the bell just to end their suffering. To top it off, each team is required to carry 185-pound boats above their heads everywhere they go. They carry the boats up and down the beach, from exercise to exercise. They carry the boats to the mess hall. Sometimes they just stand still and hold the boats over their heads. The pain, the cold, the abusive threats, and the fatigue take their toll on the nervous system. In the crucible of Hell Week, the primal survival instincts of the human nervous system are exposed.

By now, it should be obvious that there is a method to this madness. The Master Chief knows that his abuse has the potential to activate the most primitive survival system in the human body. He also knows that, in some candidates, this system will become overloaded. When it is overloaded, an individual's nervous system goes into a state of shock, and the dream of becoming a SEAL fades into blackness. The last thing that the overwhelmed candidate may remember is feeling vague sensations of panic and nausea. Dissociation and nausea are signals that the most evolutionary primitive instinctual mechanisms have been activated. This inhibitory system is only triggered when all other survival instincts have failed. This system is located in the dorsal vagal complex in the medulla. Its activation will immediately reduce the individual's heart rate, blood pressure, and overall metabolic level. The perceptual awareness of all external sensory stimuli will be blocked from conscious awareness. They simply go blank, staring into space, cut off from everything, including themselves. The activation of dorsal vagal complex will suppress distress vocalizations and motor movements. In essence, they are frozen.

This primitive inhibitory response strategy is a last-ditch effort of the nervous system to help individuals adapt to overwhelming threats. According to Stephen Porges, it has its roots in our reptilian past, where motor inhibition and other freezing responses helped our distant ancestors avoid attention of predators. In one sense, it is the most primitive form of our instinctual intelligence. In the face of an overwhelming threat and certain death, freezing can sometimes be an adaptive response. As we will see in later chapters, this freezing response can help individuals survive life-threatening conditions of abuse or traumatic injury. However, when the human body is forced to resort to this primitive level of defense, the metabolic costs are extreme. The primary outflow of the dorsal vagal complex in the medulla provides parasympathetic input to the stomach and intestinal tracts. This increases the production of digestive acids and increases intestinal motility. This is why some SEALs candidates actually end up shitting in their pants. At the same time, the extreme activation of the stress response causes areas of the midbrain and brainstem to send sympathetic outflow to the gastrointestinal system, which inhibits digestive processes and intestinal motility. The net result of this is a state of extreme physiological distress involving inescapable nausea and severe visceral and somatic dysregualtion. This paralyzing state of misery will totally inhibit all motor movement. This is the most primitive survival response of the human instinctual system. It is a total and complete submission to the overwhelming forces in the external environment. If this happens to a SEAL in a combat situation, the results will be disastrous. It is the job of the Master Chief to provoke this response in any candidates whose nervous system is predisposed to this freezing response. He will verbally and emotionally abuse them until they ring the bell. It's not pretty, but there is an instinctual wisdom behind it.

The Evolutionary Thread

Over the last few years, researchers in several fields began picking up on Porges' work. Allan Schore, who we first met in Chapter Two, was one of the first developmental neuropsychologists to recognize the significance of Porges' polyvagal theory. Schore realized that the nervous system immobilization caused by the activation of the dorsal vagal complex was an exact description of what happens to children when they are abused or suffer from physical trauma. Following this insight, Schore and other researchers were able to integrate seemingly diverse observations regarding the effects of abuse and trauma on the nervous systems of infants. Polyvagal theory has helped developmental scientists understand the neurobiological basis of the *dissociative response* that was first described clinically by Bruce Perry and his colleagues at the Baylor College of Medicine in Houston, Texas. The dissociative response is characterized by a sensory and perceptual numbing and behavioral flatness that occurs in response to extreme levels of hypermetabolic arousal in the infant's nervous system. Thanks to Porges, psychologists have a solid evolutionary and neurobiological basis to understand the impacts of trauma on the developing human nervous system.

Porges' work has profound implications for our modern understanding of instinctual intelligence. Polyvagal theory has helped researchers and therapists develop sophisticated techniques to treat the life-threatening dissociative responses caused by trauma. These dissociative responses dampen or even totally inhibit the functioning of many of the basic instinctual programs we need to survive. This clinical research and practice has examined the long-term cognitive, behavioural, emotional, social, and somatic effects of abuse and trauma in children, adolescents and adults. The efforts of Porges, Schore, and Perry- along with numerous other researchers and clinical psychologists- have revolutionized our understanding of how childhood experiences alter the neural networks of the brain and nervous system. The new therapeutic techniques derived from this research have improved the lives of countless people by helping them restore the natural adaptive responsiveness of their instinctual intelligence.

As researchers continue investigating the neurobiological basis of our survival instincts more closely, they are discovering something quite remarkable. Through the excavation of our evolutionary past, we are now able to link the deepest survival instincts of the polyvagal systems and PAG with the amygdala and the more evolutionarily advanced orbitofrontal cortex. This gives us a complete picture of the neurobiological basis of our instinctual intelligence, from its most lizard-like impulses to its most refined human expressions. We have identified, for the first time, the biological substrates that support the vital link necessary for the evolution of human consciousness.

Unless we learn to unlock their hidden secrets, the primitive survival instincts buried in the polyvagal systems act as a formidable barrier to the development of higher levels of instinctual intelligence.

However, does this mean we have to become Navy SEALs to utilize this source of power?

No. In the chapters that follow, we will explore how individuals working on the cutting edge of human development are using the ever-expanding knowledge of these survival instincts to transform this barrier. We will discover how the primitive impulses of hatred and predatory aggression are actually doorways to the extraordinarily wise power and peacefulness that usually lie dormant within our consciousness. And you don't have to be a SEAL to join in this exploration- all you need is a willingness to embrace the unlimited possibilities of human nature.

CHAPTER 6

The Seeds of Stress

One of the hardest things to do in life is acknowledge that our bodies have a wisdom of their own. They move through natural cycles of activity and rest, without any conscious direction from our minds. The human body ebbs and flows with its own rhythm, a rhythm that is not always in synch with the demands of modern life.

How many times have you gone to bed on Friday night- determined to start a project Saturday morning- only to awake in a pool of lethargy? Your ambitions seem to be drowned by a wave of fatigue. Your body feels heavier that usual. Getting out of bed seems impossible. Even walking a few steps will result in bone crushing misery. We try to raise the covers, but before our arms can even move, the sweet call of our pillow swallows us back into a deep sleep.

Suddenly, your eyes open and you find yourself hopping out of bed. You feel energized and awake- already planning your first, second, and third moves of the day- before you have turned on the coffee maker. You feel quick. Alive. Alert. That extra hour of sleep seemed to have made a world of difference. You might begin to wonder if your body has a subconscious way of knowing when it is time to rest and time to get going.

Well, in fact, it does.

The Ebb and Flow of Energy

How does the human body regulate itself, innately knowing when to charge up and when to relax? This is one of the most fundamental aspects of our instinctual intelligence, and yet, very few people understand how it functions. Many of us live in a state of constant struggle with the natural activation and relaxation cycles of our bodies. Physicians and psychologists all over the globe are increasingly encountering an unprecedented degree of nervous system exhaustion experienced by overworked and stressed workers. The incessant demands placed on the human body can lead to stress-induced physical illness, as well as psychological conflicts- not to mention the endless mental agitation with which we are all familiar. We constantly push ourselves beyond our healthy limits. Clearly, it is not very easy for most people to recognize- much less honor- the natural instinctual intelligence that regulates the body's arousal level. Why are we doing this? Why are so many of us increasingly willing to ignore the obvious signs of physical, emotional, and mental exhaustion?

The answer to this question is that the patterns of excitation and relaxation are deeply engrained in our nervous systems. They are established at an early age. These engrained patterns seem so much part of our bodies that we are rarely aware of their functioning. The demands of work, family- and the thousand other pursuits of modern life- all obscure the subtle rhythms of our bodies. Advances in technology and biochemistry have enabled us to alter the arousal patterns of our nervous system with ease. Caffeine gets us going. Children need to get to school. Cell phones call out to us. Televisions blare. Pornography titillates us. Email awaits a response. But these seemingly helpful interventions have an unsuspected toll. Chronic stress accumulates in our bodies. Eventually, the cracks begin to show. High blood pressure. Lower back pain. Immune system deficiencies. Unexplained fatigue. Even heart disease. It starts slowly at first. We skip the extra hour of sleep to get a head start on a project. We burn the midnight oil to beat a deadline. We allow ourselves to be driven by an schedules and responsibilities and an avalanche of things that just *have* to get done and a compulsion to prove that we are competent and successful and we stretch ourselves and run to Starbuck's and push and rush on to the next pressing issue before we even finished the last thing that still isn't quite done. Sound familiar?

Before we know it, we have nothing left. We have fallen victim to the modern phenomena of *burnout*.

In the last decade, neuropsychologists have made great strides in understanding how the basic patterns of excitation and relaxation operate in the human body. This knowledge is being applied in clinical settings across the world. Psychologists are formulating new treatments for anxiety and depression that incorporate the understanding of the innate arousal patterns of the nervous system. This research is dramatically enhancing our knowledge of instinctual intelligence and opening up new possibilities for thriving in the modern world. It is helping countless people move away from the outdated paradigms of anti-anxiety medication and triple bypass surgery. One of the most important findings has been that the functioning of the sympathetic and para-sympathetic systems- which are referred to collectively as the *autonomic nervous system*- develops based on parental interaction during the first three years of life. This cutting-edge knowledge is not only being used by clinical psychologists treating depression and anxiety disorders. It's being applied by people working on the frontiers of human development. These pioneers of human evolution are using this state-of-the-art instinctual intelligence to help people pursue extraordinary levels of effectiveness in their professional, personal, athletic, artistic, and spiritual endeavors. The goal of the next three chapters is to demonstrate how our basic instinctual responses are shaped by early childhood experiences. Equipped with this knowledge, we can then understand how- as adults- the specific instinctual programs described in earlier chapters are influenced by the autonomic nervous system.

The Drive to Separate

Sometime during the fifth or sixth month of life, an innate instinctual drive of human nature awakens. The impulse of infants to break free from the all-encompassing presence of the mother begins to emerge. It starts with a kick here, or a sudden squirm there. Before you know it, they are off crawling as fast as they can. Without this primal instinct to *separate* from our mothers, we would never be able to leave the house, go to school, drive a car, or any of other things that we take for granted as independent adults. However, developmental scientists have discovered a very important fact: the interactions that occur between the mother and the infant during this phase will have a lasting impact on the infant's instinctual intelligence. Understanding what happens at this early stage of life gives us direct insight into how our instincts function as adults-especially how we respond to stress.

The Physiological Basis of Separation

Nature equips infants with everything they need to begin their journey into the world as distinct individuals. During the first few months of life, infants experience a rapid development of the nervous and motor systems. Somewhere between 6-9 months the neurobiological structures of the sympathetic nervous system are established. This neural maturation process will take several more years to complete, but this system is more or less fully functional by the age of nine months. The development of the sympathetic nervous system allows the infant to tolerate higher levels of stimulation and excitation. As we saw in the first chapter, the sympathetic nervous system prepares the body for action by increasing heart rate, activating sweat glands, and increasing the levels of excitatory neurochemicals throughout the body. All of these factors will rapidly mobilize metabolic activity. This means that more energy will be made available to the motor systems. This energy will fuel the natural development of crawling- and, in a few months time-walking. It also provides the bursts of physical energy necessary to push away from the mother. The dynamic activity of pushing and squirming is an innate instinctual capacity of the infant. It is essential for physically separating from the embrace and protection of the mother.

The burst of energy provided by the sympathetic nervous system also brings new capacities for delight and pleasure. Infants are quite thrilled to explore new toys and new surroundings. At this age, there is also far more interest in sustained physical, visual, and vocal contact with adult caregivers. As we have seen in previous chapters, this social contact stimulates the production of opioids and oxytocin. This makes the sympathetically-fueled desire of infants to expand the borders of their experiences even more naturally and innately pleasurable. Cognitively, the rapid neural growth that is stimulated by the expansion of the sympathetic nervous system into the neo-cortex supports new perceptual and sensory capacities. Kids get smarter right in front of our eyes. The continuing development of the neo-cortex- especially the prefrontal and orbitofrontal corticies- allows sensory input and the memories of previous experiences to modify instinctual impulses. Infants are able to match their motor movements to the outside environment with increasing accuracy. The increase in opioids facilitated by social contact allows infants to tolerate a more intense and varied range of stimuli. It also stimulates their sense of curiosity and discovery of the world around them. As we can see, there is an organic biochemical intelligence at work during the first year of human life. It propels the lifelong journey that results in an independent, autonomous human being that is capable of surviving on its own.

Sympathetic Adaptation and Survival

At the beginning of this journey, however, young infants are still completely dependent on the mother and other parental caregivers for survival. They cannot simply just get up and start taking care of themselves. The emergence of their instinct to separate comes on gradually. But it does not just emerge on its own. It develops in conjunction with the social environment in which infants live. Developmental scientists now recognize that each mother's unique reactions to her infant's desire to separate will have a direct impact on the infant's developing sympathetic nervous system. Infants will intuitively adapt the functioning of their sympathetic nervous systems based on the reaction of the mother or other primary caregivers. The ability of infants to modify the responsiveness of their nervous systems is a true miracle of instinctual intelligence. It's an ingenious adaptive response that dramatically increases the odds of survival for infants. Let's take a closer look at why this is.

The Advantages of Inhibition

Think back to what happened in earlier times. Nomadic families were frequently wandering though strange or hostile environments. If infants simply began crying out or crawling off totally outside their mother's control, the survival of the entire tribe might be jeopardized. The ability to temporarily inhibit the nervous system of an infant might have been a matter or life or death. In other cases, the mother may have been absent or deceased. The child is then left with the father or other relatives. In the absence of the maternal caregiver, the ability to restrict the child's sympathetic nervous system discharge increased the odds of survival for the remaining members of the family. By restricting the infant's arousal levels, adults did not have to spend as much time attending to the infant. At the same time, the innate instinctual responsiveness of the infant's nervous system somehow recognizes that his or her chances of survival would be increased by reducing the frequency and intensity of sympathetic activation. Back in the days of survival of the fittest, any infant that was too cranky, too loud- or required too many resources- was simply abandoned, especially if the mother was dead or missing. Infants that could adapt their nervous systems to the needs of the rest of the tribe had the best chance of survival.

In the modern world, recent research has demonstrated that the mother's own childhood experiences of inhibition of her sympathetic nervous system also have a direct impact on the infant. If the mother lacks her own sense of instinctual independence, then it is likely that she will grow dependent on the infant for companionship and contact. The infant's desire to separate will be experienced by the mother as a threat to her emotional, psychological, and even physical well-being. Most mothers aren't directly conscious of this tendency, but will communicate this to the infant's nervous system through her instinctual reactions. It may be that *her* mother may have also thwarted her initial impulses to separate. Now, she responds in a similar way (albeit unconsciously and automatically) to her child. In cases where the mother is a single parent or has a poor relationship with the infant's father, the mother will have a natural tendency to use the infant as a substitute for the intimacy that is missing in her adult relationships. When it comes time for the infant to separate, the mother will be unprepared to let the infant have the freedom necessary for healthy individuation. The mother might hold the infant close to her and physically restrict the infant's exploration. Emotionally, she might verbally or non-verbally discourage the infant when he or she is becoming physically energized and wanting to get away. Because at this age the infant's nervous system is not yet fully developed, the primal impulse to fight or flee is easily restricted by the mother. Utterly dependant, the infant has no choice but to acquiesce.

Overcharge

The capacity of human infants to modulate their nervous system functioning in response to their social environments is quite flexible. Not only can they *inhibit* their sympathetic system responses, they can also *increase* its level of activation. This can be quite an adaptive response in certain circumstances. Consider the situation for infants if the mother is largely unresponsive to their initial first attempts at crawling. Once infants learn to crawl, they will often start exploring the surrounding environment and this can lead to all sorts of trouble. As every parent knows, unless you watch them closely, disaster is just around the corner. If infants are left unattended in this situation for extended periods of time, they have to fend for themselves. Inevitably, they will find something to put in their mouths or something to pull off a shelf. As they begin to walk, the potential of mishaps multiplies exponentially. If infants are left unattended during these initial exploratory adventures, their nervous systems will adapt in a very specific manner. Every time they are shocked or hurt or stunned, they will experience a heart-pounding sympathetic reaction. Without the reassuring presence of a mother or adult caregiver, they will not be able to calm themselves down. Infants of this age have very few capacities for self-soothing.

For most kids that have attentive parents, this might only happen a few times and there will be no life-threatening incidents. This happens to every child occasionally, because even the most vigilant mother can be momentarily distracted or absent. It's no big deal and there will be no major impact on the infant's nervous system. However, if infants are left alone or poorly supervised on a *regular basis*, then their nervous system must adapt to this situation. As we saw above, every time they run into trouble, they will experience a sympathetic response. This is nature's way of protecting them. The sympathetic response will help them get out of dangerous situations. Again, think of the situation tens of thousands of years ago. A child left alone might run into a small animal. The natural fear response would have made them run away or produced a scream of surprise. This would have most likely scared the animal away. Or a child might fall into a small hole in the ground. A healthy jolt of sympathetic arousal would have provided the energy needed to crawl out to safety. If this happens over and over, in both minor and major ways, the overall level of arousal of the infant's sympathetic nervous system increases. Because there is no parent or caregiver to calm the child down, this can result in the excessive release of corticotrophin releasing factor (CRF) and the secretion of noradrenaline from the locus coeruleus, a small cluster of neurons located in the top portion of the brainstem. The cumulative effects of excessive levels of CRF and noradrenaline - as well as other excitatory neurochemicals like adrenaline and glutamate- predispose the infant's nervous system to be easily triggered into high levels of sympathetic arousal. When a young child is abandoned or neglected in this way, this hyperarousal of the sympathetic system optimizes the odds of survival.

Developmental scientists have also gained a deeper understanding of the consequence of chronic abusive experiences during infancy. The first and most obvious neuropsychological effect of abuse is that infants live in a state of sympathetic hyperarousal. The cumulative effects of violence and the absence of soothing parental interaction leave them more susceptible to the triggering of the sympathetic hyperarousal responses. This means they will develop a life-long predisposition toward anxiety, because their baseline level of sympathetic nervous system arousal is higher than average. As they get older, many these individuals who experienced neglect and/or abuse will often develop an emotional and behavioral disposition towards anger. Their nervous systems have adapted to respond to even mild frustrations with a very intense sympathetic activation. They will respond to the demands of the social environment in a similar way. Whenever they experience the slightest social irritation- a complaint, a rejection, a snide remark- they fly off the handle with an angry outburst or even a violent response. The memories of neglect or abuse are deeply etched into the nervous system.

The Costs of Inhibition

The ability of infants to adapt their nervous systems to the surrounding social environment carries with it some serious costs. Modern developmental researchers now understand the complex consequences of the chronic under or overarousal of the infant's sympathetic system during this phase of development. These effects can last an entire lifetime and can impair the somatic, emotional, and cognitive aspects of instinctual intelligence. The absence of early relationship-based encouragement of sympathetic nervous system responses impacts the entire nervous system. Most significantly, it restricts the development of the frontal lobes, the region of the brain that gives us *conscious control* of our instinctual responses. The failure to develop the full capacities of the sympathetic system- including the control centers in the orbitofrontal and prefrontal corticies- leads to a wide variety of sub-optimal coping strategies. These clinical findings are revealing the consequences of the habitual automatic tendency toward modifying the arousal levels of the sympathetic nervous system to adapt to the demands of the social environment. A poorly developed fight or flight response will leave the individual insufficiently equipped to respond to the stressors of life. Chronic sympathetic overcharge is now recognized as an underlying cause of burnout and other stress-related syndromes. It's hard to let go of what our nervous systems learn at an early age.

The Sympathetic Signature

Fortunately, the majority of children growing up in today's world have parents that fall in between the two extremes of neglect and smothering. Some parents might learn to the over-protective side and others might have a bit of a hands-off policy. Either way, we now have a pretty clear picture of how each individual's characteristic *sympathetic signature* is formed during the first year or two of life. This sympathetic signature becomes a central feature of our adult instinctual intelligence, influencing almost everything we do. It determines how we respond and adapt to stressful social situations. It also influences the degree of arousal we experience when we activate our basic instinctual programs. Most of the time, our sympathetic responses occur automatically and unconsciously. And because these responses helped us get through difficult situations when we were growing up, we have very little reason to question them. However, certain life events may force us to question this basic instinctual response. We may find ourselves working 70 or 80 hours a week to please our demanding boss. We might feel the impulse of reacting violently to our children. We may notice that our daughter is inhibiting her natural intelligence to conform to the pressures of her social environment. Or we may simply grow frustrated for allowing a friend walk all over us.

What can we do about it? Is it possible to change such deeply ingrained habits?

The short answer is yes. However, the sympathetic system is not the only force that shapes the expression of our instinctual behaviors. It's only one half of the equation. To understand how our knowledge of instinctual intelligence can be used to recalibrate the habitual functioning of the entire autonomic nervous system, we have to consider the counterpart the sympathetic system- the parasympathetic system. As adults, our sympathetic nervous system does not become over- or undercharged by itself. The relaxing and inhibiting actions of the parasympathetic system work in conjunction with the sympathetic system. They function together, in concert, to shape the expression of instinctual energy within our bodies. Knowledge of these two systems paves the way for us to find a more realistic and workable equilibrium between arousal and relaxation. In this equilibrium, the conditions for developing instinctual intelligence are optimized.

Instinctual Intelligence

CHAPTER 7

What Holds Us Back?

Have you ever wanted to dance with total abandon? Or sing triumphantly at the top of your lungs? To be a rock star? A famous actress? Have you ever wanted to walk into a room and express your sexual attraction to someone without fear or shame? Have you ever simply wanted to speak your mind, unafraid of what others will think?

Well, you're not alone. If you're like every other human being, you probably secretly and passionately crave the thrill of unbridled instinctual freedom. Yet, so many of us live with a less than passionate intensity. It is as if some mysterious force shrivels up our instinctual energy- leaving us frustrated and unsatisfied. This inhibiting force dampens and restricts our natural instinctive exuberance. At the same time, it leaves us feeling tense and unable to relax fully and completely. For others, a feeling of shame permeates their bodily impulses and cuts off their instinctual potency. When this happens, a nagging sense of depression can dampen each day, as passionate dreams fade into quiet resignation. As adults, we have two choices: we can accept this as an inevitable fact of life. Or we can begin to question this mysterious inhibiting force that robs us of our life energy and blocks our most passionate desires.

If we choose the latter option, we will discover that this inhibiting force is not so mysterious after all. Armed with our modern knowledge of instinctual intelligence, we will come to recognize how we first learned to feel shame as children. By understanding its origins, we can then see how we slowly lost touch with our instinctual aliveness in the process of becoming adults. Our investigation will also help explain why it is so difficult to relax as adults. This inability to enjoy the restorative benefits of a healthy parasympathetic response is another underlying cause of the modern phenomena of burnout. If we want to understand how modern science is helping individuals regain the most vital and dynamic parts of their instinctual intelligence, we need to look a bit more closely at the development of the other half of the autonomic nervous system- the parasympathetic system. This exploration can help us understand the deeper origins of the nagging sense of shame and restless discontent many of us feel. This knowledge holds the key to unlocking the full passionate and restorative potentials of our adult instinctual intelligence.

The Inhibiting Force

The development of the human nervous system is a true miracle of nature. You could say that it is a brilliant piece of engineering, an exquisite product of millions of years of research and design. It has a built-in system of checks and balances that maximize the chances of each human to survive and reach adulthood. At each stage of development, new instinctual programs are activated. As children reach the age of 16-18 months, their ability to explore their environment increases dramatically. They become capable of walking (and running!) and thus now have the means to physically separate from the mother. Continuing maturation of the sympathetic nervous system provides a spark to propel energetic exploration of the external world. The sense of willfulness and independence begins to emerge as children complete their second full year. The desire to oppose the wishes and commands of the mother by saying "NO!" also emerges around this time. In general, children at this age are quite enthralled with the notion that they can do what they want-whenever they want. All parents know that this is a precarious time for the young toddler. They can run off and get into unimaginable difficulties in the blink of an eye. The natural intelligence that guides instinctual development provides parents with two distinct pathways that enable them to regulate the nervous systems of their children- *energetic refueling* and the *shame response*.

Energetic Refueling

As children explore the world away from the mother, they are likely to run into situations that will frighten or upset them in some way. This results in a radical diminishment of their excitatory physical and emotional states. Discouraged by some mishap or frightening experience, the crestfallen youngster looks to the mother (or other adult caregiver) for comfort and support. During the period of 16-30 months, the mother plays a key role in re-stimulating the child's nervous system. Her responsiveness, particularly her direct face-to-face smiling positive expressions, acts to soothe the child and re-energize his or her emotional state. Recent neuro-imaging studies indicate that a number of brain regions- especially the affective modulation centers of the prefrontal cortex- are activated in both mothers and their children during intense gaze transactions. This re-stimulating interaction jump-starts the child's excitatory and exploratory behaviors. With the sense of confidence and well-being regained, the child heads back out into the world, feeling bolder. This interactive dynamic forms a deep and lasting imprint on the child's instinctual intelligence: the reassuring support of another human being is essential for being able to cope with the challenges of the world. In short, the child develops a visceral sense of depending on the mother for survival.

The Disapproving Gaze and the Shame Response

Deep in the core of their instinctual consciousness, children know that without their life-sustaining caregivers they cannot survive. However, they are often swept up in the powerful rush of the basic instinctual programs that are pushing them to explore the world away from their parents. Because the influence of the excitatory systems is so powerful during this developmental phase, children are at considerable risk. Their energetic exploration of the environment, combined with the new capacity to walk and willfully distance themselves from their mothers, results in a high likelihood of encountering dangerous situations. The young innocent child has no previous knowledge to guide them away from potential danger, so vigilant caregivers are required to keep them from potential harm. Nature, in its infinite wisdom, provides both the child and the mother with a potent neurobiological mechanism that regulates the child's behavior.

Sometime between 18 and 24 months, the child's parasympathetic nervous system begins to establish powerful *inhibitory* neural pathways that balance the already-established *excitatory* sympathetic system. The inhibitory parasympathetic system has deep evolutionary and survival value. When it is activated a moderate amount, the parasympathetic system produces a cascade of relaxing effects that are vital for the restoration and growth of the body. This moderate activation promotes growth of body tissues, facilitates digestion, and restores synaptic balance after a cycle of excitation. However, in young children that have incurred the wrath of their mothers, the parasympathetic activation is off the scale. The intense activation of the neural circuits of the parasympathetic nervous system in a social context is referred to as the *shame response*. Shame has the immediate effect of shutting down the excitatory systems that usually dominate the young child's nervous system. Working in direct opposition to the sympathetic system, the parasympathetic shame response reduces blood flow to the motor muscle systems, dampens the child's affective state, and greatly restricts external perceptual awareness.

This inhibition of the child's nervous system arousal is achieved through specific neurobiological pathways. Infants are born with a pre-wired perceptual attunement to the voices and facial gestures of other humans- especially the mother. This perceptual predisposition continues to develop as the infant matures. At about 16-18 months, the facial perception and response systems acquires a stunning sensitivity to the mother's disapproving facial gestures. The perception of the mother's angry face, combined with the angry tone of her voice, will instantly activate the parasympathetic nervous system. One glance and the child shuts down. Viewed from an evolutionary perspective, this innate neuro-behavioral mechanism is a very efficient method of regulating the child's behavior at a time when they are subject to considerable risk.

Parasympathetic Adaptation

For the child, the feeling of shame that results from the mother's disapproving gestures carries with it some very frightening implications. These fears were burned into the human nervous system deep in our evolutionary past. The mother's disapproval will often imply the possibility of rejection and abandonment. This fear is rarely a conscious, rational thought- it is more of an instinctual fear of social isolation- hardwired into the periaquaductal grey (PAG) region in the midbrain, as we have seen in previous chapters. The child intuitively fears that his or her actions were so contemptible that they will be severely punished or abandoned. The activation of the parasympathetic nervous system is often accompanied by physiological sensations of coldness and isolation. Inwardly, the fear of abandonment can be experienced as a feeling of worthlessness and aloneness. In addition, the threat of the mother's rejecting disapproval can then become a nagging sense of doubt or fear for the child. The phase-appropriate exploratory behavior can become severely restricted by the looming threat of an unfavorable maternal response. On top of it all, shame affects the child's innermost sense of self. During this developmental phase, the proud feeling of being unconditionally adored by the mother is gradually being eroded. The child loses the sense of grandiosity due to their dependence on the mother for the simplest of needs.

The threat of the mother's rejection further compounds this loss of self-confidence. In all, it is a pretty rough time for the young child.

Just as we saw with the adaptive responses of the sympathetic nervous system, children will adapt the responses of their parasympathetic systems to maximize their chances of survival. The child's parasympathetic system will adjust its activity in response to the type of parental interaction that is present. Consider, for example, the case of the *smothering mother*. The overprotective mother will not allow the child have any degree physical independence. She will follow the child around, eliminating the opportunity for healthy struggle with the challenges presented by the external environment. The child has little or no opportunity to explore novel situations and difficulties. Because the mother artificially limits the child's sense of frustration, there are little or no opportunities for the natural cycle of sympathetic arousal and parasympathetic relaxation. This cycle is foundational to the development of the healthy balance that characterizes autonomous instinctual functioning.

Just as we saw with the sympathetic system, the toddler's parasympathetic system will modulate its functioning to adjust to this overprotective social environment. Because the mother is not communicating disapproval or anger, the child's parasympathetic nervous system is rarely activated. The child will feel very little shame or guilt. As a result, they will fully expect that their mothers (or someone else) will be there to help them with any difficulty they encounter. The under-activation of their parasympathetic systems will result in a compensating over-activation of the sympathetic system. Angry outbursts will solicit the help of the mother or other adult caregivers. Under these conditions, individuals will lack realistic self-awareness and will likely grow up to be self-indulgent, spoiled, and even pathologically narcissistic.

Plagued by Shame

In other cases, the emerging independence of the child is met with disapproval and aggressive inhibition. The mother will actively restrict the child's exploration with threatening verbal, emotional, and physical expressions. As the parasympathetic nervous system becomes more functionally established, the effects of the mother's admonitions have a powerful dampening effect on the child's energy and self-confidence. When the mother *constantly* inhibits the child with a severe tone and even physical abuse, the child's parasympathetic system will become over-activated. Feelings of low self-worth, physical inadequacy, and humiliation will arise whenever they initiate independent activity, even if the mother is not actually present. The pervasive sense of maternal punishment will likely result in the individual experiencing a pervasive fear of taking action in all areas of life. Guilt, shame, and self-doubt are all signs of an over-activated parasympathetic system. As adults, the tendency towards over-activation will prevent the individual from enjoying the relaxing and restorative benefits that flow from more moderate levels of parasympathetic activation. Even more importantly, this nagging sense of shame will prevent them from fully activating many of their basic instinctual programs. The result is that many of the most fulfilling activities of life- self-assertion, sexuality, creativity, exploration- will be unconsciously restricted by severe behavioral and emotional inhibition. However, it is important to recognize the fundamental adaptiveness of the child's original response. Harsh parental disapproval and shaming admonitions always carry with them the *implicit* threat of abandonment. By activating the parasympathetic nervous system- and thus inhibiting the offending behaviors- the child is actually enacting the ages-old strategy for reducing the odds of social isolation and certain death.

Going it Alone

Children's parasympathetic systems will also adapt to conditions of indifference and neglect. As they begin walking- and become increasingly independent- some parents will ignore their realistic needs for safety. This lack of supervision and support has potentially dangerous consequences, especially when children inevitably encounter physical or emotional harm. When this happens, there is no one around to re-stimulate their nervous systems. At first, the parasympathetic activation that occurs when they are discouraged will make them feel ashamed and guilty that they have done something wrong. Without a reassuring parental response, their nervous systems may remain inhibited for some time. This state of parasympathetic shutdown, however, is not an adaptive response in the long run. Over time, neglected children will learn to re-stimulate their own nervous systems without the help of the parents. They develop the capacity to restrict their parasympathetic responses. Instead of feeling sorry for themselves, they pick them selves up by the bootstraps and re-engage life as best as they can. As an adult, these self-reliant individuals believe that they must always act alone. They often have trouble trusting others and forming relationships. The normal relaxing responses of the parasympathetic do not flow naturally. This makes it difficult to form social bonds and relax into the cycles of intimate contact. In spite of the costs, this adaptive strategy is a remarkable expression of instinctual intelligence that helps individuals to survive in the most difficult of conditions.

Finding the Balance

As a result of this developmental research, many parents are increasingly recognizing the importance of providing their children with a reasonable balance between freedom and appropriate assistance. It's one of the most immediate ways parents can help the nervous systems of children develop in an optimal manner. In these ideal circumstances, the mother allows the child to explore the environment in a manner that is realistic and age appropriate. This means that there is little restriction of the child's movement. The possibilities for free exploration are made possible by providing a safe and secure environment in which the child can play. The parental caregivers, primarily the mother, must have a clear sense of what is physically challenging for the child without placing them in danger. This allows the child to be fully engaged in independent activities without fearing the restriction or disapproval. Another aspect of the mother's supportive presence will be her timely response to her child's occasional struggles. Here, the mother does not rush in immediately to solve every little frustration the child encounters. However, if the child has had a chance to solve their problem on their own and still continues to meet with frustration, the mother's timely support is essential for the child's instinctual development. A healthy sense of autonomous instinctual intelligence requires the accurate recognition that sometimes we realistically need assistance. Humility is not a failing. Being able to ask for help, without being utterly dependent, is a characteristic of an instinctually balanced adult.

The Parasympathetic Signature

As we can see, developmental researchers have made great progress in understanding the forces that shape our parasympathetic responses. This developmental phase has a profound impact on the individual's instinctual capacities throughout the human lifespan. Depending on the nature of the interaction with the mother (and to a lesser degree, the father and/or other caregivers) during this period, individuals develop lasting patterns of instinctual inhibition. These inhibiting patterns will subsequently affect their sense of instinctual functioning *and* relational dynamics well into adulthood. It is important to remember that the adaptive instinctual intelligence of our parasympathetic systems- as well as our sympathetic systems- is primarily shaped by parental interactions. However, it is also influenced by grandparents, aunts and uncles, siblings, playmates, teachers, and even strangers.

For most individuals, their own experiences during the phase of parasympathetic development will fall somewhere between the extremes I have presented. Each individual will have their own unique set of parasympathetic responses. Every one of us has had experiences of dependence, disapproval, shame, and being left alone in scary situations. While there is usually a tendency towards one extreme or another in our developmental histories, each of us has had at least a taste of these experiences. Our *parasympathetic signature* is the result of all our childhood experiences. It determines which specific social cues that will trigger a feeling of shame and an inhibitive restriction of our basic instinctual programs.

The Costs of Adaptation

We now have a fairly clear understanding of the two components of the autonomic nervous system that regulate so many of our body's instinctual functions. We have seen the extraordinary adaptive intelligence of these two systems and how they facilitate survival in the face of life's most difficult circumstances. However, we have also begun to recognize that the adaptiveness of our instinctual responses also has serious consequences. It's evident that the influences of the social environment on the sympathetic and parasympathetic systems create life-long tendencies within our nervous systems. Developmental researchers have shown us that these early experiences influence our relationships, our careers, our sexuality- and every other aspect of our lives. Almost every adult I know struggles with the burnout of stress or the shame of inhibition to one degree or another. In some cases, these early experiences can severely compromise the ability of our parasympathetic system perform its healthy, restorative functions. Without this deep sense of relaxation, endless mental and physical agitation fuels the fires of burnout. This has led some people to believe that human instinctual responses has evolved to be *too responsive* to the social environment and therefore fundamentally limited in its capacity to develop. Or is there another piece to the puzzle?

This is the question that students of human development have been asking in recent decades. And they have come up with some astounding answers. As it turns out, the detailed knowledge of how the autonomic nervous systems develops and functions has been the basis of several breakthroughs in the contemporary applications of instinctual intelligence. This emerging knowledge of the autonomic nervous system is helping us understand how our basic instinctual programs become dysfunctional and distorted. It is also helping humanity unlock the deeper potentials of our instinctual consciousness. The knowledge of the earliest stages of nervous system development is essential for understanding how people are learning to work more effectively. They are able to get more done- without driving their nervous systems to the point of burnout. This emerging instinctual intelligence is allows us to work smarter and with greater satisfaction. It is also helping people to liberate themselves from the paralyzing sense of shame and nagging depression that has held them back of all of their lives.

But before we discuss these amazing breakthroughs, we'll need to confront a hidden barrier. This barrier is what prevents us from embracing the deeper levels of our instinctual intelligence.

Instinctual Intelligence

CHAPTER 8

The Price of Rationality

Did you ever find yourself in a situation where a friend had really pissed you off? For most of us, this is a confusing situation. On one hand, you're just flat out angry- perhaps verging on livid. Or maybe just seriously irked. On the other hand, the rage is tempered by feelings of love and friendship. Still- what she did was unforgivable- and you need to say something to let her know just what an idiot she's been.

Unable to stand it anymore, you storm over her house, ready to let a torrent of venom fly her way. As you march thought the front door, you find her holding her young daughter, who has fallen and cut her knee. It needs stitches. It is not a life-threatening wound, but the young girl's tears tell you she's upset and scared at the sight of her own blood. Your friend looks at you and asks you to help take her daughter to the emergency room.

The Adaptive Intelligence of Inhibition

If you're like most people, you'll hold your anger in check until this small crisis has passed. Later- when the crisis is over and you're alone with your friend- the intense feelings will no doubt return. And then you'll let her have it.

When we look a little more closely at this incident, we can recognize another remarkable feature of our instinctual intelligence: the ability to *self-inhibit* any one of our basic instinctual programs, even when it is in the midst of a full-blown response. This is quite an extraordinary evolutionary achievement and something only humans can do. The capacity of human beings to express their instinctual energies in an increasingly flexible and sophisticated fashion arises from the interaction of cognitive, emotional, and physical qualities unique to the human species. Our enlarged brains possess a greater capacity for remembering past events and imagining what might happen in the future. This enhanced cognitive capacity allows us to consider the consequences of our actions. The memory of past events and the anticipation of future outcomes allow us to adjust behaviors and feelings. The increase of our cognitive capacities also fosters a more sophisticated and flexible expression of our social emotions. This allows us to work cooperatively in groups. All of these evolutionary advances combine to free us from the limited repertoire of our most primitive instinctual responses. In short, our ability to regulate our pre-programmed impulses is the basis for the unique qualities of human civilization and evolving sophistication of our instinctual intelligence.

Developmental researchers now have a clear understanding of how this form of instinctual intelligence develops. In conjunction with the latest discoveries about the autonomic nervous system, this knowledge is modernizing our understanding of how children learn to control their instinctual energies. This new research has also shed light on how this inhibitory control can *negatively* impact the healthy expression of our innate instinctual energy. As we saw in the last two chapters, the adpativeness of our nervous systems can sometimes distort the natural functioning of our basic instinctual programs. As many of us know all too well, the inhibitory capacities of our rational adult minds can rob us of our innate instinctual aliveness. In the process of "growing up" we steadily lose touch with the limitless wellspring of energy, inspiration, and passion we experienced as children. Our desire to be grown-up rational adults often creates a deep-seated hesitancy that holds so many of us back from our full potential.

How does instinctual energy become so rationalized that it becomes downright dull?

We are now closer than ever to finding the answers to this question. We now know how the inhibitory systems of the nervous system actually work. Uncovering the developmental origins of our inhibitory systems is the final piece of knowledge we need to understand how we can regain the energy necessary for becoming a mature- *but instinctually vibrant-* adult.

The Shift to Cognitive Control

As children develop, their natural instinctual impulses come into contact with the existing rules and regulations of the family and outside world. In order to gain the love and approval of their parental caregivers, children must learn to conform to the expectations of the family and the larger culture. Before the age of four or five, children need to behaviorally test their instinctual energies through a process of trial and error. They act on an impulse- and see what kind of trouble follows and how adults react. Keeping a watchful eye on their parents' faces, children adjust their behaviors based on the rewards and punishments of their parents and other caregivers. In this way, they achieve a tentative balance between their innate instinctual impulses and the constraints of physical and social reality. In the previous chapter, we saw how this process begins with the adaptive responses of the autonomic nervous system. But as children reach the age of four or five, this method of developing instinctual intelligence ceases to be effective for the growing needs of the child. Controlling their instinctual impulses based on immediate reactions of parents and other adults does not allow the child to develop their own independent judgment. As children get older, they begin to spend more time away from their parents. Sometime around the fourth or fifth year, the nervous system begins to shift to a more efficient means of regulating instinctual impulses. Due to the development of their cognitive abilities, children can use *thoughts* to control their behavior. This provides them the means to navigate safely in the world, without the constant supervision of adults. In short, it helps them take a big step towards becoming an independent, self-sustaining human being.

The Neurophysiological Basis of Cognitive Inhibition

The development of cognitive self-inhibition is actually the continuing maturation of specific cognitive, emotional, and neurophysiological mechanisms that are established during the first three years of life. As such, it can be viewed as a continuing development of the autonomic nervous system. Starting around the age of 18-24 months, the parasympathetic system is primarily activated by the disapproving facial gestures and vocal expressions of the mother or other caregivers. This is the classic shame response described in the previous chapter. As cognitive capacity grows, children develop the ability to regulate themselves using mental representations of the parental figures that are based on memories and impressions of previous parental interactions. Developmental researchers call this process of forming mental representations of the parents and using them to guide subsequent behaviors *internalization*. By the time children reach the age of four or five, the inhibitory functions of the parasympathetic nervous system can be activated internally by specific representations. The child's cognitive capacities are so developed that he or she can readily recognize potentially dangerous or threatening situations and instantly activate a set of representations that will dampen the level of neurophysiological arousal. The activation of the inhibitory mechanisms of the parasympathetic nervous system can produce immediate effects. These include a decrease of somatic energy, a negative affective state, a narrowing of the perceptual field, and a constriction of several cognitive functions. The parasympathetic nervous system develops as a series of neurobiological systems that downshift the child's state of arousal. Kids at this age no longer need Mom to yell at them. They can inhibit many of their impulses on their own.

The Inhibition of Embodied Energy

The internalization of the social rules regarding the expression of sexual, emotional, and embodied energy initially occurs from the ages of three to six. The process of teaching a child to regulate and control bodily energy begins early in infancy. However, it is with toilet training that we can see the most obvious and lasting impact of internalizing rules regarding the expression of the instinctual functions of the body. As all parents know, young children are incredibly excited about and interested in the functions of their young bodies, especially anything involving urine and feces. As children reach the age were toilet training becomes a necessity, parents become increasingly involved in helping the child to regulate basic bodily functions. However, parents cannot describe exactly how children need to contract certain muscles in the lower abdomen or anus that will stop the flow of urine or the elimination of feces. Parents can only show approval or disapproval for certain *results*. Children must learn how to regulate their bodies in order to produce parental approval. As you can see, the origins of your most refined human qualities of self-control are not exactly noble. But establishing mastery over certain bodily functions is an obvious- and often messy- necessity.

The desire to gain parental approval by establishing control over the primitive impulses of urination and defecation establishes a basic template for future development. In a physical sense, the body of the child is now incorporated into the family system at an instinctual level. Once toilet training is completed, children must disrupt the uninhibited excitement of urination and defecation and impose some control over these natural functions. This type of instinctual control paves the way for subsequent internalization of parental rules concerning sexual energy.

The Social Inhibition of Sexual Energy

The continuing development of the nervous system affords the child an increasing capacity to experience pleasurable sensations in all areas of the body, especially the genitals. Typically, around the third or fourth years, and extending through the sixth and seventh years, the child's natural instinctual energy is often directed towards the exploration of pleasurable activities. These pleasurable activities are organized around the *stimulation* and *display* of highly energized regions of the body- primarily the genitals. This means that not only does the child need and want to experience pleasure for his or herself, but it is equally important that others see and delight in this pleasure. Children at this age have a deep need to have their bodies and their emotional/physical energy acknowledged- and enthusiastically responded to- in developmentally appropriate ways. This is a natural and instinctive evolutionary need. It gives children a chance to get used to the social dimensions of their physical and sexual energy by integrating their actions with the responses of others.

By the age of four, the child's sense of self is becoming increasingly focused on their bodies. At this stage, there is not an elaborate self-concept based on abstract notions about the self. Most of the associations and memories concerning the notion of self have to do with experiences of the *body*. This has important implications for the development and expression of their instinctual embodied energy. For children at this age, the sense of self is primarily derived from their identification with their bodies. Therefore, the responses of their parents and caregivers concerning their emerging sexual and energetic behaviors will have a powerful impact on their sense of self. Unresponsiveness, rejection, disapproval, or aggression by the parents or other caregivers will be experienced not just as a condemnation of some aspect of their behavior. It is experienced right in the heart as a complete condemnation of their entire being. If their bodily energy is ignored, rejected, or abused- so is their overall sense of self.

When the emerging sense of being a sexual energetic person is not recognized in a developmentally appropriate manner, the normal and healthy expressions of human development and evolution are interrupted. The effects of inappropriate parental and adult caregiver responses at this stage of development will have severe consequences for the expression of sexual and other forms of embodied energy throughout life. It will also directly impact how children feel about themselves. Children will automatically internalize rules about what is acceptable and not acceptable regarding their instinctual embodied energy based on the responses of parents, caregivers, and other people in their environment. If others do not value them, they will not value themselves.

The Need to Adapt

The sad fact is that most children grow up in a household environment where their budding sexual and emotional energy is responded to in a less than optimal manner. Under benign circumstances, is it is relatively ignored or quickly hidden away through disapproving looks. In more constrained situations, it is actively suppressed and discouraged. When abusive conditions prevail, the child's emerging sexual excitement is responded to with inappropriate physical contact or violence. Amazingly, the innate instinctual intelligence of human beings will find strategies to cope with this lack of attunement and support. If children could not compensate for the various types of adult insensitivity, their sense of self-worth might become so diminished that their psychological and physical well-being would be severely compromised.

At a very basic level, children at this age are trying to develop a representational understanding of what it is to be "good". They will internalize memories of interactions with their parents that contain the set of behaviors that were responded to in the most favorable manner. From the child's perspective, being "good" means conforming to their parents' expectations and thus receiving praise and acceptance. Encoded in this representation will be a set of idealized images of behavior, speaking, moving, and dressing that will win the approval of others. Using these idealized images as a guide, children learn to inhibit behaviors that are not likely to solicit approval. This helps them navigate more safely in sexual and other social environments. It helps them formulate acceptable ways of expressing their instinctual energy. As we get older, these representations become quite complex, with intricate sets of behavioral patterns that are activated in certain social conditions. The core of our sexual identity -what we experience as desirable about ourselves- is originally shaped by the desire to gain our parents' approval.

Remember that the expression of sexual energy is quite a vulnerable and confusing situation for children. They are cognitively and perceptually hardwired to determine the rules of "right" and "wrong" that will prevent the rejection and disapproval by parental figures. From the child's perspective, being "right" means conforming to their parents' expectations and thus avoiding criticism and rejection. Encoded in this representation will be a set of rules that circumscribe the "right way" of behaving, speaking, moving, dressing, and responding to others. Using these rules as a guide, children will inhibit behaviors that will result in criticism and disapproval in sexual and other social situations. Again, this will help them choose ways of expressing their instinctual impulses that are appropriate within their social environments. This helps keep them safe while allowing them to satisfy their basic needs. As we grow into adolescence and adulthood, we develop even intricate sets of situationally-dependent rules, expectations, and judgments, all designed to prevent sexual embarrassment and rejection. No wonder we feel like pretzels sometimes.

No one escapes this phase of life. Modern anthropological and psychological research indicates that the integration of social rules concerning embodied physical energy into stable, self-regulating personality structures appears to be a universal developmental process found in all the world's cultures. A central feature of the emerging instinctual intelligence of children is their capacity to inhibit impulses and behaviors. This helps them express their instinctual energies in ways that are compatible with the prevailing social rules. Over the course of evolution, this has helped children adapt to all sorts of conditions that might have otherwise threatened their survival. It has helped them escape the wrath of a parent with a violent temper. It has helped them avoid unwanted sexual advances by uncles, brothers, and strangers. It has helped them limit their hunger and share food in times of famine.

In today's world, this inhibitory intelligence is no less important. How many times have you wisely held your tongue when you were frustrated or angry? Perhaps you didn't lash out at the boss when he was being a bonehead. Maybe you didn't get angry with your husband when he was sick, even though he was being a jerk. And how many times a day do we modulate our tone of voice with our children, inhibiting an impulse to yell harshly because what they really needed was kindness and guidance? The key point here is that inhibition does not always mean we just stuff your emotions inside. Inhibition gives us a brief second to pause. In this priceless moment, we can then select more judiciously from a wider variety of possible responses.

Do Adolescents Have Any Instinctual Intelligence?

Contrary to what many parents think, teenagers are actually instinctual geniuses. This may be hard to recognize at times. But if we consider the monumental challenges they face in integrating their instinctual energies with the complex social rules of modern cultures, we might begin to cut them some slack.

As children enter into the seventh and eighth years of life, the steady growth of their cognitive capacities and biological reproductive systems foster changes in the expression of their developing instinctual programs. At this age, they have an increased capacity to understand and respond to the perspective of others. Because they are in school and out of the house with increasing frequency, they are exposed to more complex experiences of other peoples' reactions and responses. These experiences are, in turn, integrated into an increasingly sophisticated and nuanced set of mental representations that guide instinctual behaviors. As children grow through adolescence, these mental representations grow in their capacity to shape thoughts, emotions, and behaviors. The teenage years bring a continuing exploration of social interactions and corresponding adjustments to instinctual behaviors. Every day, teenagers learn a great deal about themselves- based on the responses and reactions of others.

Gathering Social Intelligence

A close examination of a teenager's inner world will actually tell us a lot about ourselves as adults. We might not like to admit it, but it will become painfully apparent that we still organize our instinctual expression based on our experiences as adolescents. The patterns of instinctual behavior we internalize during adolescence are deeply entrenched. Many of our basic adult instinctual programs- especially those concerning our social and sexual behaviors- are formed during our teen years.

With the onset of puberty, physical, emotional, and cognitive changes propel the interest of teens away from parents and family. Instead, they are attracted to peers, friends, and especially to potential sexual partners. All of these changes are amplified by the hormonal surges of puberty. Children of this age are vitally interested in the opinions, responses, reactions, and judgments of other children in their own age group. With a natural human evolutionary drive, children increasingly orient themselves towards the outside world. Their peers become an important social reference point to help them make friends and to explore society and culture outside the bounds of their family of origin. Most importantly, relationships with peers help them begin to explore sexual relationships. There is a deep instinctual need in the human soul to find a comfortable and gratifying position in our local social and cultural communities. The need to feel accepted, appreciated, understood- and most important of all, to simply belong- manifests powerfully during adolescence.

Teens are constantly exposed to new social situations. In order to navigate successfully in these novel environments, they need to learn to adjust their instinctual responses to meet the requirements of unfamiliar social situations. Think of the first day of each school year. As they walk in their classrooms, teens need to scan the faces of all their classmates to see who looks familiar and who looks like a stranger. They have to evaluate the facial gestures of the teacher to determine a relational strategy that will optimize the chances for a passing grade. And, of course, a potential sexual partner might be close by. This has to be weighed against other concerns. They want to sit by their friends and avoid enemies. All of this occurs within the first thirty seconds of entering the room. Teens process all of this complex information to form adaptive social relationships. This social information is stored as complex mental representations that guide instinctual behaviors.

Inhibition Can Be Sexy

At this point in their development, adolescents are learning to regulate their instinctual energy to gain the approval and recognition of others. It's their central preoccupation. The development of regulating skills is a critical phase for developing instinctual intelligence. From an evolutionary standpoint, the investment in one's social adaptation, especially during adolescence, was critical for survival and success in reproduction. Without constant vigilance and effort, one's social and reproductive strategies would not succeed. Considering the short life span of men and women throughout human history, the maturation of cognitive capacities and social knowledge that occurs at the ages of 9 to 12 is just in time to begin one's life as a socially aware adult. Individuals that could not inhibit ineffective or inappropriate instinctual impulses would have significantly diminished chances of social, cultural, and reproductive success. Social adaptation is critical for survival. Adolescents utilize the same parasympathetic mechanisms used by children and infants to inhibit their impulses. While it does not always go smoothly, most teenagers do manage to bring their most lustful, aggressive- and just plain idiotic- impulses under control.

We can see how this inhibitory intelligence is essential for a young woman to get through her first date. First, she has to control her laughter as a young man nervously asks her out. There is likely to be a great deal of stammering, nervous laughter, and irrelevant, if not outright stupid, statements by the young man. If she just laughs in his face, he will probably never speak to her again. If she likes the boy even a little bit, she had better suppress that nervous giggle. Next, she has to decide what to wear. Now- as all women know- this is an ultra-complex process that I could never even hope to address in several books. Let's just say that she has to strike a balance between flirtatious and boring. She will draw on countless mental representations culled from friends, family, magazines, TV, movies, and the internet. In a very basic way, she is sorting through all the behavioral rules regarding sexuality and social responsiveness she has learned since childhood. Her accumulated instinctual intelligence will tell her which impulses to inhibit and which ones to activate. She remembers how her creepy uncle once grabbed her when she was dancing around in a short skirt when she was only five. This memory will likely inhibit her from borrowing the super short skirt her friend just bought. She also remembers how everyone told her she looked so hot in her white sweater. These memories will guide her choices, optimizing her chances for social success.

Later in the evening, she just might have to help her date inhibit some of his impulses as well. If he can hold back his initial impulse to stick his tongue down her throat the first five minutes of the evening, he's off to a good start. For him, striking a balance between expressing his budding sexual desire and just sitting there like a scared little boy will also require the skillful inhibition of certain impulses. This delicate skill is the difference between a total dork and a charming young man that every girl wants to date. Just like cologne, a little inhibition goes a long way for men. If all goes well, these kids will take the first steps of a long journey of sexual exploration that might take them far beyond Las Vegas and into the frontiers of human sexuality and intimacy. However, developing the sophisticated sexual intelligence needed for this journey will depend on how well they incorporate one more layer of inhibitory control into their overall instinctual functioning.

Adult Inhibition

Just as we observed with the childhood and adolescent, adults utilize a variety of inhibitory strategies to guide their instinctual behaviors. Remember, the type of instinctually intelligent inhibition we are talking about does not mean *repression*- we'll discuss that later in this chapter. Granted, one of the fundamental functions of inhibition is to keep us out of danger by not doing stupid things. But it also keeps our options open. As we have seen, inhibition helps us formulate better, more socially attuned ways of expressing our instinctual desires. Without inhibition, we would act on every impulse that enters our minds. This would make it very difficult to form any type of satisfying relationships or meet complex goals that require a sustained long-term commitment. Marriages, families, and careers would be impossible.

As we get older, our cognitive inhibition systems use increasingly sophisticated mental representations to modulate instinctual impulses. There is a key difference between the adult representations and the representations used to guide instinctual behaviors during childhood and adolescence. The adult representations are derived from a more complex set of social and cultural experiences. To be sure, adults still crave the approval of others. However, the primary representation of the "other" is no longer fixated on the parents or a small group of significant peers. At this stage of development, adults internalize a much wider variety of social and cultural experiences to guide the expression of each of their basic instinctual programs. We not only internalize actual experiences- but we also internalize a variety of abstract aspirations, rules, and fantasies.

The Source of Guiding Principles

Adult inhibitory intelligence can reach a very sophisticated level of flexibility and adaptability. A lifetime of accumulated representations helps us formulate behavioral strategies for complex goals that require sustained applications of our basic instinctual programs. Finding a mate, building a house, cultivating artistic mastery, raising children, achieving financial security, developing athletic skill- and every other mature adult enterprise- requires a degree of instinctual intelligence. This instinctual intelligence works on two levels. First, we have to internalize representations that will serve as prototypes of attributes that we wish to emulate and eventually integrate into our self-experience. Often, they are comprised of representations of *idealized others* from whom we want acceptance, guidance, or admiration. We also form implicit rules to avoid the rejection or disapproval of others from whom we seek approval. These representations are derived from a matrix of other people and various qualities that they possess, including:

- individuals with specific professional achievements
- idealized partners for sexual relationships
- relatives that we wish to please
- creative artists
- spiritual leaders
- individuals with established roles within family structures
- specific physical attributes
- individuals with athletic abilities
- specific types knowledge and intellectual capacity
- wealth, prosperity, and social influence

The list is endless and each individual has a unique set of aspirational attributes and relational desires.

These representations are critical for the second level of instinctual intelligence. They act as guidelines to *inhibit* behaviors that are not compatible with these goals. Building a house means that you may have to forgo the purchase of a boat. Getting married means that you cannot pursue every sexual impulse that tickles your fancy. Developing a career means that you have to inhibit the urge to go play golf all the time. Becoming an artist requires that you practice your skills with discipline and forgo the pleasure of spending all your time in museums sitting around and admiring the work of others. Raising children requires that you inhibit so many impulses and personal desires that it would be impossible to list them. Mature adult instinctual intelligence is fueled by goals- but it's honed by inhibition.

The Dark Side of Inhibition

At some point in our adult lives, we begin to wake up to a very sobering fact: the development of the inhibitory aspect of our instinctual intelligence often comes with a heavy price. Somewhere along the line, we begin to notice that we have lost something quite priceless. As children, we had no choice but to give up a portion of our instinctual vibrancy in order to accommodate the rules and restrictions of our families. We did this as adolescents, and we do it every day as adults. When the miraculous energy of a human being is stifled in any way, a piece of our soul fades with it. For some, the loss is relatively small. If our parents were open and encouraging of our innate energy, we end up with a few minor feelings of shame and self-doubt. For others, the aggressive repression of embodied energy results in an endless spiral of inhibition, frustration, and awkwardness. For the majority of adults, the process of having to modify their bodily and sexual energy to conform to the behavioral guidelines of their particular family and subculture resulted in an obvious diminishment of their vital energy. This energy is not just sexual in nature. It includes the full range of dynamic living sensitivity, excitement, pleasure, passion, and spontaneity of human instinctual life. Yes, inhibiting our energy helped us survive. But at what cost?

In recent years, psychologists and other students of human behavior have become aware of a disturbing truth. Increasing numbers of people are living in a constant state of instinctual dissatisfaction. To cope with the demands and responsibilities of the modern world, humans have to live in a state of inhibitory overdrive. We impose control over our instinctual impulses in a very particular manner. *We evaluate ourselves relentlessly.* Many of us are firmly convinced that the only hope of getting what we really want is to compare ourselves to ourselves and impose rules that help us live up to these idealized goals and standards. Some individuals have actually told me they have an image of an entire audience of imagined judges, guides, leaders, and potential lovers. In order to feel secure, most adults feel they have to conform to the idealizations and admonishments of these imaginary judges. They also have to avoid acting in ways that would be seen as inadequate or foolish in the eyes of these representations. This whole game is like performing in front of a large classroom of judges, row after row, rising up like stadium-seating movie theaters. Few adults have the courage to admit that their instinctual aliveness is governed by an endless list of rules and fears. Fewer still would be willing to admit that the flow of their natural energy has been hijacked in ways over which they have no conscious control. We simply think that this is the way life is.

The Mind-Body Barrier

The majority of our inhibitory self-judgments are based on the simple rules of *right/ wrong* and *good/bad* we learned as children. Our self-judgments are the voice of every self-doubt and every fear we had in childhood, where we first learned to inhibit our instinctual energy to gain the love and approval of our parents. This self-doubt keeps us locked into our comfort zones- where our instinctual energies are held at bay- non-threatening and safely subdued. It is also the voice of inhibiting self-judgment that admonishes us when these energies spill over and create a big fat mess. The truth is that our contemporary media cultures play a big role in shaping which types of idealized representations we will seek to emulate. By reinforcing notions of what is not *cool*, the modern media shows us what types of instinctual expressions are acceptable. Buying right into these social rules and ideals, adults internalize these images. And then we use the same inhibitory mechanisms of self-judgment we first learned as children to regulate our instinctual impulses. Back then, we learned it was safer to *think* before we act. In effect, children learn to create a barrier between their bodies and their minds to control their impulses. It allowed us survive and adapt as children, so we believe it will help us thrive as adults. Our self-judgment is what maintains this barrier. We endlessly evaluate our impulses and feelings in our minds, to determine if they are appropriate or not.

In the process, we grow increasingly distant from the living instinctual intelligence of our bodies.

One of the most profound discoveries made by cutting-edge psychologists in recent years is that the barrier of self-judgment drastically restricts our natural instinctual intelligence. This barrier dampens our natural instinctual intelligence by restricting our bodies, our emotions, and our minds. It keeps us locked in an unhealthy cycle of repression and unsatisfying discharge. It keeps us fearing our own power, but then regretting the raw fury of pent up aggression. It keeps us from recognizing our potential as adult human beings. Most painfully of all, this barrier keeps us cut off from the love we seek and the connection we crave. We experience our lives through a secret belief: if we can just figure out how to adjust our physical and emotional energy to fit the situation- then someday we'll be able to experience the full passionate embrace of instinctual satisfaction. For many of us, that day never comes.

Have We Reached the Limit?

What's going on here? Is our instinctual intelligence inherently flawed? Have we reached some limit in our collective human evolution where the rationality imposed by modern cultures has exceeded our capacity to adapt? For some, the endless maze of self-judgment and an instinctual inhibition is simply the reality of adult life. It was, after all, Freud's conclusion that neurotic conflict is as good as it gets. In this view, our self-judgments act as a set of internal guardians against our primal impulses, keeping us safe and our world orderly. The *superego* must rule over the *id*. In this way, civilization- with all its discontents- is preserved. However, a new generation of psychologists and experts in human development are offering us a different view. They have recognized that as these internal guardians can create distortions in the natural functioning of our instinctual intelligence. They create a restraining set of parameters that define what is acceptable for us to experience in terms of our instinctual energy. They not only keep us away from anything we fear, they also leave us stagnant in the habitual cycles of familiarity and safety. These insights lead us to a startling conclusion: *By the time we reach adulthood, these internal guardians act as a very limited and immature form of instinctual intelligence*. They are the basis of our inhibiting self-judgments that see the world through childlike notions of good and bad, right and wrong. They also relentlessly drive us toward burnout and inhibit us through shame. Above all, the internal guardians cut us off from the evolutionary wisdom of our instinctual energy. The world is too big and our potential too vast to be constrained by the fears and restrictions that were forced on us as children.

As we will see in the following chapters, the time has come to reclaim the wise and potent energy of our adult bodies. For within this living pulse lies the essential fuel for the evolution of humanity's instinctual intelligence.

CHAPTER 9

Facing the Facts

Maybe it's just me. Every time I turn on the evening news, I feel a bit disgusted. Just when I think that humans have finally learned their lesson- and that we are about to evolve beyond the need for aggression and violence- I'm reminded of the harsh reality.

I doubt I'm alone on this. I imagine that everyday, millions of people just like me turn on their TVs and long to hear a different story. In my fantasy, it goes something like this:

IN A STUNNING DEVELOPMENT, ISRAELI AND ARAB LEADERS AGREED TO A SWEEPING PEACE AGREEMENT THAT WILL FOREVER ALTER THE VIOLENT CONFLICTS THAT HAVE DOMINATED THE REGION FOR CENTURIES. BOTH SIDES HAVE AGREED TO DESTROY THEIR ARMS AND DISBAND THEIR MILITARY ORGANIZATIONS. THIS NEW AGREEMENT WILL ESTABLISH A JOINT ECONOMIC AND CULTURAL DEVELOPMENT COUNCIL THAT WILL CREATE NEW A NEW EDUCATIONAL AND RESEARCH PROGRAM OF UNPRECEDENTED SIZE AND SCALE. THE COMBINED MILITARY AND DEFENSE BUDGETS OF THE ENTIRE REGION, ALONG WITH THEIR MASSIVE OIL REVENUES, WILL BE USED TO FUND AN EDUCATIONAL SYSTEM THAT WILL PROVIDE STATE-OF-THE-ART FACILITIES FOR EVERY CHILD AND ADULT, COMPLETELY FREE OF CHARGE. THIS NEW EDUCATIONAL SYSTEM WILL BE THE CENTERPIECE OF A VAST RESEARCH PROGRAM THAT WILL ATTRACT SCIENTISTS FROM ALL OVER THE WORLD IN AN ATTEMPT TO SOLVE MANY OF PROBLEMS FACING HUMANITY. THERE WILL BE SEPARATE RESEARCH CENTERS FOR DEVELOPING ALTERNATIVE FUELS, FIGHTING DISEASE, ENDING HUNGER, AS WELL AS A WORLD-WIDE INSTITUTE FOR DIPLOMATIC RELATIONS. LEADERS ACROSS THE GLOBE ARE HAILING THIS DAY AS A TURNING POINT IN HUMAN HISTORY.

What stands in the way of a day like this?

The New Pathways of Change

As everyone knows, the instinctual conflicts that have ruled human history are slow to change. That's why every time we turn on the news we hear more about violence than we do about breakthroughs that will lead the planet to new levels of peace and prosperity. As our weapons become more powerful and oppressed people grow more desperate every year, potential for disaster increases. In our personal lives, we also know the things we need to change. Whether it's a healthier diet, improving a miserable relationship, spending more time with our kids- or just being a nicer person- we all want to resolve our conflicts and improve our lives. We usually know what we need to do. Actually *doing it* is the hard part. Despite the relative wealth and knowledge enjoyed by so many of us, the inertia of our lives can be overwhelming. Plus, the incessant urgency of the thousand and one responsibilities and obligations keeps us in a constant state of distraction. That makes it doubly hard to make the changes that are so sorely needed. Not only is the flesh weak, but who has the time?

Change is not easy, even in the best of circumstances. This is exactly what the best and brightest minds who are studying instinctual intelligence are telling us. Changing our *minds* is simple. Actually changing the way our *deeply entrenched instinctual habits* function is a lot harder. But it is possible. In the first half of this book, we prepared the ground to see how this change is possible. We have a solid grasp what the basic instinctual programs are and how they work. We also have a detailed knowledge of how these instinctual programs develop and how the inhibiting functions of the autonomic nervous system can become unbalanced and distorted. This has allowed us develop a deep respect for the power of our instinctual energy and a penetrating insight into the complex control systems that guide its functioning. This knowledge of the basic elements of our instinctual heritage will help us understand how deep change- both in personal lives and in our collective evolution- is now possible.

In the second half of this book, we're going to meet some of the people working on the forefront of human development that is ushering a new phase of instinctual evolution. These scientists, psychologists, spiritual teachers, and cutting-edge thinkers have forged extraordinary new techniques that can recalibrate the functioning of our instinctual systems. The recent discoveries in the science of recalibrating our basic instinctual programs have emerged from some seemingly diverse disciplines. Evolutionary biologists have stressed the adaptive genius of our instincts. They have described the anatomical basis of the primary systems as well as analyzing the neural networks that formulate innovative responses to novel situations. Clinical psychologists have helped us understand the specific therapeutic techniques that are effective in changing deep-seated patterns of behavior. Contemporary approaches to spiritual development are adding a new precision to traditional wisdom as they incorporate the latest neurobiological and psychological research into their knowledge base. This has resulted in the emergence of a brilliant new synthesis of science and wisdom. This synthesis allows humans to discover previously hidden neurobiological pathways for evolving our basic instinctual programs. More and more people are beginning to utilize these transformative pathways to move beyond the neurophysiological imbalances and emotional distortions that restrict the optimal functioning of our instinctual intelligence. The power to change ourselves and our world is closer than many people think.

A Frustrating Inertia

If we take a broad view of the diverse systems of knowledge that comprise the new paradigm of instinctual intelligence, there is a unifying theme that links them together. They all begin with the fundamental recognition that to actually understand and transform the powerful instinctive forces that shape humans and nature, one has to be very, very *realistic*. Yet, historically, this is obviously one of the most difficult things for humans to do. As I stated in the introduction, no aspect of the human experience has been subject to more self-deception, judgment, misunderstandings, confusion, shame, and conflict than our instincts. They are, at times, praised and admired as we look with awe on heroic soldiers and rock stars. Other times they are relived as we look with disgust on murderers and rapists. And we only have to think back to Bill Clinton and Monica Lewinsky to remember that lying about our secret instinctual behaviors is one of our most fundamental human traits. The rules of instinctual control we learn as "good" boys and girls grow outdated in the adult world. If history has taught us anything, it is that our instincts cannot be repressed, as they will only emerge in more explosive and dangerous forms. However, acting on every impulse that arises leads to chaos, not satisfaction. Where does this leave us?

For most of us, it leaves us somewhere between guilt, denial, and numbness. We feel guilt when our lust and anger spill into our lives and hurt other people. In order not to create too much of a mess in our lives, we can begin to deny the reality of our instinctual energy and desires. This self-deception results in a loss of our vital energy, which can spread like a cancer in our lives. We carry on, driven by a gnawing frustration and a distant dream of a more empowered life. We resolve a hundred times a week that tomorrow things will be different. We admonish ourselves to do better, but it is hard to enact anything but the most superficial of changes. Our dreams of creating real change in our lives- of embracing the full passion and power locked in our DNA- becomes like so many fading New Year's resolutions. The promises we make to ourselves are simply overwhelmed by the vast inertia of our instinctual habits. Superficial changes will not even budge the powerful and dynamic instinctual systems that have been honed by millions of years of evolution. As a result, we modern human humans are left frustratingly stagnant. So many of us have the intuition that there is so much more to our lives, yet it seems so hard to unlock this elusive power.

Getting Real

In the 21st century, we finally have enough objective insight into the nature of human instinctual energy that we can begin to understand it in a realistic way. We are now in a position to use our accumulated knowledge to harness its adaptive intelligence and understand the exact nature of the distortions that create suffering and conflict. This knowledge also gives us a glimpse of the extraordinary potentials locked within this energy. Without this deep layer of insight, it is impossible to transform and evolve our instinctual intelligence. However, we must remember how easy it is for humans to deceive themselves. As I stated above, all the cutting-edge approaches to transforming our instinctual nature stress that to really understand and transform these powerful instinctive forces one needs to be *utterly objective and realistic*.

The insights and wisdom that are arising from the new paradigm of instinctual intelligence will not be effective unless we face the *basic facts* of our modern adult instinctual lives. These facts help us to recognize some very painful realities about which we might otherwise be tempted to sweep under the rug. They expose the conflicts and limitations that restrict the full expression of our instinctual intelligence. They reveal the implicit and subconscious ways in which our instinctual energy gets trapped, blocked, burned out, and otherwise distorted. An objective appraisal brings us face to face with the compromises and deceptions of our adult lives. Unless we are willing to recognize the exact nature of the constrictions of our instinctual intelligence, there will be no way for us to evolve, both as individuals and as a planet. Most importantly, facing the facts of our adult instinctual lives helps us appreciate the extraordinary insights of the new paradigm of instinctual intelligence. We cannot take advantage of the new transformative pathways of this revolutionary paradigm without courageously recognizing the reality of our limitations.

Seven Facts of Modern Adult Instinctual Life

The consensus of all the state-of-the-art thinkers in human development is uncompromising: our instincts cannot evolve unless we understand the precise nature of how they become stagnant. Therefore, let's take an unflinching look at the obvious facts.

1) **Self-judgment restricts our instinctual intelligence by perpetuating a corrosive sense of dissatisfaction and fear.**

The gnawing feeling of dissatisfaction is one of the most familiar features of the inner landscape of most adults. Psychologists' offices are crammed with growing numbers of people who are intensely frustrated by a sobering realization of modern life: no matter how hard they drive themselves to meet their lofty expectations, they inevitably fall short. Countless individuals complain of feeling stuck on a treadmill of striving and achieving, only to have to begin chasing a new set of goals and expectations every day. As we saw in chapter 6, burnout is a very real problem. This not only applies to the standards of professional and economic success that so many individuals relentlessly pursue. It is also driving the passionate desire to meet ideal standards of physical appearance and beauty that seems to drive much of modern culture. When this happens, the basic instinctual programs become hijacked by a wicked self-judgment that berates the individual for not exercising more, eating too much, not going to the gym, and for not having sexier clothes. The voice of self-judgment will criticize their bodies, trying to match some ideal of sexual attractiveness. It might even compel some individuals to get cosmetic surgery. The vicious self-criticism is endless. Recent research indicates that the discrepancy between idealized goals and the reality of our lives will commonly manifest as a secret feeling of discouragement, sadness, and low self-esteem. This discrepancy appears to play an important role in clinical and more moderate forms of depression.

On the other hand, many individuals feel paralyzed by the need to meet the rule-ridden demands of critical self-judgment. These people are caught in the endless struggle to make their reality match the guidelines of perfection to which they aspire. When they fall short, and the standards are not met, they face the consequence of inner ridicule and self-punishment. There is compelling evidence that this sense of failure manifests as fear, threat, worries, and multiple forms of anxiety. This form of self-judgment inhibits the basic programs of the nervous system. When under the spell of self-judgment, people feel too insecure and afraid to express their instinctual energies in healthy and adaptive way. They are afraid to speak out because they might say something wrong. They are afraid to touch somebody because it might be interpreted the wrong way. They are afraid to ask someone on a date because they might be rejected. They are afraid to dance because they might look stupid. The nagging suspicion that they are *simply not good enough* creates a tension that pervades even the most relaxed situations. Many adults in the modern world experience dissatisfaction and inhibiting anxiety to one degree or another. It can be quite difficult to admit how our self-judgments keep us on a treadmill, keeping us sprinting toward the dream of a better future but never outrunning the threat of failure. It can be downright painful to recognize that our efforts to gain the approval of others or avoid being criticized for breaking the rules were first learned in childhood. This striving and this fear still runs our lives. Because we are always caught up in this struggle, it is not easy to recognize that our instinctual intelligence has become stagnant.

2) Anger and aggression are poor long-term strategies for getting what we want.

In the wild, animals frequently respond to life-threatening situations with aggression and violence. In most cases, if their attacks are successful, wild animals do not face any subsequent consequences stemming from their outbursts. They just go on with their lives. However, when humans use anger or overt aggression to meet their needs or to defend themselves, it can have a variety of negative consequences. Animals do not have to consider hurt feelings or jails. As we saw in previous chapters, certain childhood experiences can predispose the nervous system to sympathetically-charged outbursts of emotional and physical energy. In some situations, the only chance we had of getting our needs met was through aggressive demands or temper tantrums. As adults, we can still act this way. When we feel like we are being treated unjustly, we still feel the burning desire to be pushy, rude, or even verbally abusive. A lot of times this angry behavior goes on inside our heads, in an endless bitchy monologue that never really resolves anything. However, sometimes it boils over. We lash out, sometimes with words, sometimes in other hurtful ways. Cruel looks. Cutting remarks. Devastating criticism. There are many ways this viciousness strikes. The people we work with and the people we love often end up bearing the brunt of this fury. Again, it can be very difficult to recognize that our anger is creating problems in our lives because it feels so *justified*. This way of asserting ourselves creates a lot of messy situations in our lives. Others end up distrusting us, and it becomes hard to maintain relationships. Our professional and personal lives suffer, because no one is willing to treat us with affection and respect. It can get to a point where more aggression, manipulation, and anger are the only options left.

3) Repressing the desire to stick up for ourselves makes us feel weak and afraid.

Some people never get angry. When confronted with a situation where they are threatened and intimidated, their nervous systems become inhibited. Even in situations where they are being abused or taken advantage of, they cannot bring themselves to muster up a self-protective response. Granted, not everyone is this inhibited. But we all have our secret fears, situations where we just cannot seem to express our natural instinct to defend ourselves. Maybe we cannot set an appropriate boundary with our teenagers or an ex-lover. We let them walk all over us, without the slightest consideration of how we feel. Sometimes this inhibition just leaves us apathetic to many of the challenges we face as adults. We fail to assert ourselves in our careers, letting a peer or a boss treat us unfairly.

Just like with anger, the childhood experiences of some individuals establish lifelong patterns of inhibition, withdrawal, and apathy. Subsequently, whenever these individuals feel even subtle urges to confront someone about their actions, their nervous systems will produce a freezing response. This causes a suppression of the natural flow of energy. They withdraw into a state of numbness. The freezing response is a primitive reaction of the brainstem that inhibits the nervous system, diminishing the ability to enact life-supporting behaviors and emotions. Recent studies have shown that this inhibition can even suppress immune system functioning. The subjective feeling is one of being too weak to move or even say anything. For children, this inhibition might have been a wise choice if a more energetic response would result in violence or abandonment. However, as adults, habitually inhibiting assertive responses based on memories of the past makes no sense. Yet we do it anyway. Almost everyone has had the experience of feeling angry, frustrated, or hurt- and then saying nothing. In these situations, we swallow our anger. Our only satisfaction is the secret belief that someday the person who hurt or threatened us will regret what they did. Our vengeance will be how miserable they will feel when they see our pain. But we are the only ones who feel sorry for ourselves. I have known people who spent most of their adult lives wallowing in self-pity. They continue waiting in vain for the day that their suffering will be acknowledged.

4) The stubborn belief that we have to do everything ourselves often exhausts our instinctual energy, leading to stress, burnout, and disease.

We all know people that take great pride in never asking anyone for anything. They protect their independence vigorously, fiercely rejecting any notion that they might need help- lest they appear weak. For adults that had repeated experiences of being left on their own during childhood, they have no desire or expectation that anyone will support them in any way. They are afraid to confide in others when they are lonely or scared. Outwardly, they can appear confident and busy, always working on one project or another. But their rigid, hyper-autonomy hides something. In reality, the pain of their early neglect is so acute that they will not risk experiencing it ever again. Therefore, they are experts at not putting themselves in situations where they will be let down, by anyone, ever again.

Everyone experiences this to one degree or another. We all want to feel strong and capable. But, deep down, there is always a fear that we will fail and be abandoned. This fear creates a tension that drives many of our actions. For many of us, we feel like this tension is what protects us, what keeps us going. We all know the sore tightness in our backs and in our necks we get when we are stressed and pushing ourselves too hard. Yet most of the time we just grit our teeth and push harder. This leaves us in a stagnant cycle of exhaustion and stress. How many people do you know that are always working, always sleep deprived, and always pushing their bodies beyond their limits? Why do humans do this? For most of us, we fear not being in control of our lives. We are reluctant to ask for help because we then we are dependent on someone else and we cannot control what they do. Deep within all our nervous systems are some very deep-seated impressions of having felt abandoned and betrayed by caregivers during young childhood. The core of our instinctual consciousness is convinced that any feelings of dependence might lead to the same excruciating pain of isolation and failure.

5) Always depending on others leads to feelings of shame and inadequacy.

Have you ever had days when you just wanted someone to come and take care of everything for you? While your house was being cleaned, you could take a nice long bath. While your breakfast was being made, you could relax and read the paper. While you took a nap, your bills were being paid. Instead of driving to work, you have a chauffer. And when you get to work, your boss informs you that you can retire today, on a salary triple to what you are making now. Ever have a fantasy like that?

Deep within the human instinctual psyche, there is unfulfilled longing for protection, assistance, and nurturance. This sense of wanting someone to protect and care for us is largely unconscious. For some people, it can manifest as a chronic feeling of helplessness and inadequacy. It feels impossible to take action unless another person is there to provide support. This makes it almost impossible to respond with autonomy and confidence to the challenges of adult life. In others, this unfulfilled longing can lead to an unmanageable and destructive tendency toward co-dependence in intimate relationships. Afraid to be on their own, these individuals become experts at manipulating others into taking care of them. Everything from washing the dishes to going to the store to getting a job requires the support of another person. Sometimes the fear of being abandoned is so intense that people are willing to put up with abusive relationships just to avoid the threat of being alone and helpless.

Just like with the other facts of modern adult instinctual life, the deep longing for support and approval is universal. It is a primal need stored within human instinctual consciousness. It was first formed by the complete and utter dependency we experienced during early infancy. As adults, the longing for support and approval can show up in many areas of our lives. For example, many of us feel a particular type of constraint in social situations. It might show up as a fear of asking someone out on a date or a fear of applying for a job. If we look a little more closely, we can recognize that there is something inhibiting the natural instinctual initiative to pursue things we need and want. It is a feeling of inhibiting shame. The inhibition of our nervous system often occurs when we are in social situations where we have to ask for something. As we know, the shame response results in sudden loss of energy, a narrowing of the perceptual field, and the oppressive feeling that we have done something wrong. Before we know what hit us, we have the prickly sensation of being the center of some very *unwanted* attention. We feel ashamed that someone will discover our utter dependence and helplessness. Inside, we feel like collapsing- our bones and muscles are like jelly- too wobbly to support us. We all have situations in our lives that trigger this kind of inhibition of our nervous systems, some of us more than others. Many of us are skilled at forming relationships that prevent us from ever really dealing with our shame. It is easy to become stuck in a stagnant cycle of blaming other people to hide our own fears of inadequacy. If we are always victims of bad luck or *other* people's lack of support, then we can avoid responsibility for our own lives. We all have our secret excuses.

6) Many of our adult behaviors are based on the instinctual responses we adopted during childhood; adherence to these outdated responses prevents our instinctual intelligence from developing and evolving.

The first five facts of modern adult instinctual life point to a very sobering reality: most adults in the modern world meet their instinctual needs and desires using the strategies they learned in childhood and adolescence. Of course, as adults we have developed a more sophisticated veneer to disguise our infantile tendencies. But if we view the situation from the inner workings of our instinctual consciousness, we can still see the basic outlines of our temper tantrums and a secret wish for our mothers to come and take care of us. We still use the same self-judgments and manipulative strategies to coerce ourselves and others gratifying our most basic impulses. On our better days, this inner sea is relatively calm. But as soon as we are tired, or tense, or threatened- the full force of our primal impulses emerges- without warning or forethought. Day by day, the outdated responses of our instinctual consciousness threaten to erode the quality of our lives. We see this erosion in our strained families, our tense professional relationships, and in the war-torn regions of the world. As weapons grow more powerful and conflicts more bitter, we have to acknowledge this fact of modern adult instinctual life. We can no longer rely on our child-like tendencies of blame, anger, fear, and shame- to guide us. The choice is clear: either we go along with the same destructive stagnation or evolve a more mature and refined instinctual consciousness.

This leads us to the last and most important fact:

7) It is possible to develop more mature and refined levels of instinctual intelligence that align our embodied energy with the higher aspirations of the human soul.

In the last three chapters, we have been coming to terms with the fact that our basic instinctual programs can become stuck. This has forced us to confront the possibility that humans have reached some sort of evolutionary dead-end. From this perspective, it can seem like humans reach a point in their adult lives where their instinctual intelligence reaches its full capacity. Our basic programs help us to survive. We can take are of ourselves by putting food on our table and staying safe and warm. We manage to satisfy our sexual urges. We somehow struggle through relationships. But so many of us feel a nagging conflict- a misalignment between the push of our responsibilities and the pull of our instinctual impulses. This *misalignment* leaves us feeling cut of from the deep sources of our innate energy. We are surviving, but not really thriving. Like all living things, our instincts need freedom to grow and flourish. Otherwise, they will become murky like stagnant water and breed reptiles of despair and venom.

Fortunately, the human race is finding ways to grow. Many people have faced these facts and are deciding that they are no longer willing to let unconscious fears rule their lives. They are no longer willing to inhibit their instincts, for they recognize that repression cuts them off from the source of life and happiness. They are no longer willing to give in to anger and aggression, resisting the drive to burn out their nervous systems to get what they want out of life. These courageous individuals are waking up to the possibility that our instinctual intelligence can continue to develop as we grow older, reaching new levels effectiveness, creativity, and wisdom. This evolution brings with it new capacities to work, to love- to passionately embrace life as fully mature adults. We now have enough scientific knowledge and wisdom to align our instinctual energy with the most refined qualities of intelligence, compassion, and joyous exuberance.

In the pages that follow, we'll meet the people taking the first steps into this new phase of human evolution. The more each one of us is willing to follow in the wisdom of their footsteps- and undertake the brave work of aligning our bodies with our souls- the more our world will surely change.

Instinctual Intelligence

CHAPTER 10

The Spectrum of Human Potential

OK. It's obvious something needs to change within the collective intelligence of human instincts. I don't think anyone would dispute the fact that the self-centered, greedy, and violent impulses which helped humans survive for hundreds of thousands of years have run their course. But what is the next step? All this talk of "instinctual intelligence", "refinement", and "evolution" sounds great. However, the world is flooded with well-meaning individuals espousing peace and love. The problem is they rarely offer real substance or systematic research. If we are to bring about an authentic change in the instinctual inertia of humanity, we need something more than good intentions. And we need to answer some very hard questions. What would such an evolutionary change in our instinctual intelligence look like? How would we separate unrealistic utopian dreams from realistic approaches grounded in science and tangible results?

These questions bring us to the very heart of the collective wisdom of our species. In the 21st century, we are in the unique position of being able to analyze the nature of human evolution. We're not just talking about physical evolution of our bodies and brains. We're talking about the evolution of our most human qualities. Culture. Creativity. Cooperation. Consciousness itself. In order to understand how these human qualities evolve, we need an overall map of human development. This map would provide a method for charting out- in a systematic way- the complex developmental dynamics implicit within the human maturation process. Such a map would reflect our accumulated knowledge of how children develop the basic physical, cognitive, and emotional skills needed to function in the world. It would also have to include a deep understanding of how children and adults continue to develop the most refined human qualities of compassion, creativity, and self-knowledge. In addition, it would have to take into consideration specific types of intelligences- such as linguistic skills, logical analysis, artistic creativity, athletic and physical genius, interpersonal communication, and sexuality- just to name a few. And since we are talking about the development of humanity as a whole, such a map would have to include not only scientific knowledge, but also the accumulated, time-tested wisdom of all the world's diverse cultures. With this map, it would be possible to form a clear, empirical picture of what the next step of instinctual evolution might look like.

To some, creating an overall map of human development might seem daunting- even impossible. It would require an extraordinary synthesis of vast amounts of information. It would also require an unbiased evaluation of scientific, religious, and cultural beliefs. It would require a complete reevaluation of the nature of human evolution from a modern, cross-cultural perspective. In short, it would call for a new and revolutionary paradigm of human development.

A Paradigmatic Breakthrough

Throughout human history, the most profound paradigmatic shifts occur when someone is willing to look at things in a new way. It begins with the willingness to question what other people have taken for granted. Great innovators are able to analyze vast amounts of information and discover the underlying patterns of organization that no one else has seen. They help us to see the elegant structures within the chaos. Suddenly, what was once obscure is rendered obvious.

This is exactly what happened in the early 1970s. Researchers in the various disciplines of human development were simply overwhelmed by the flood of information that had been gathered in previous decades. Developmental psychologists, beginning with Freud, had uncovered a great deal of knowledge concerning the psychological growth of infants and children. Object relations theorists studied how infants emerged from a state of symbiosis with the mother and became an individuated human being. At the same time, attachment theorists were exploring how the nature of the bond between mother and child affected the child's subsequent social interactions. Cognitive psychologists were investigating how children develop the ability to recognize objects, form accurate mental representations of external reality, and then manipulate these symbolic representations using logical rules.

While all of this was going on, the fields of adult psychotherapy were creating new frontiers. During the '60s and '70s people in the US and Europe began to question many of the existing cultural norms, including taboos around sexuality and mind-altering substances. In short, they discovered the pleasures of sex, drugs, and rock and roll. In no time at all, experiential therapies were created to help people break out of the social rules and restrictions that had bound them for decades. In California and other cutting edge centers of expansion of human consciousness, people began to express a wide range of feelings and instincts that were repressed both within the individual's psyche and within the overall culture as well. If that weren't enough to create chaos, the '60s and '70s also saw the influx of Eastern spiritual teachings. For the first time, many Westerners were exposed to meditation practices that could engender states of consciousness that expanded the possibilities of human experience beyond anything they had ever imagined. It was a breathtaking time in human history. It was now possible to access the accumulated wisdom of humanity. By the mid 1970s, you could go to any bookstore and find volumes on Western disciplines of child development, psychotherapy, and philosophy on one shelf and the mystical writings of Eastern spiritual gurus on the next. Each one of these streams of knowledge was a piece of a very complex puzzle of what it means to be a human being. In a small town in Nebraska, a young man was spending countless hours absorbing this knowledge and working on this puzzle. Within a few short years, he would introduce a new paradigm that would forever change the way we view human development.

The Developmental Spectrum

Ken Wilber is a rare individual that has always been willing to question what other people take for granted. Within weeks of entering Duke University as a freshman pre-med student, he began to realize there was more to human beings than their biochemistry. He was not willing to accept the prevailing notions that said optimal human health was simply a matter of curing disease. He did not see the point in learning to repair hearts and lungs that were damaged by stress, smoking, and other psychologically driven habits. Clearly, there were deeper causes of illness and disease that Western medicine was ignoring. At a very early age, Ken Wilber realized there was more to the human organism than he was learning in chemistry class. A lot more.

He became fascinated by the mystery of what it means to be human. He dropped out of Duke when he realized he was dissatisfied with Western education and that he was more interested in what Eastern spiritual teachers had to say. He moved back to his hometown in Lincoln, where he enrolled at the University of Nebraska. He continued his studies in biophysics and biochemistry at the graduate level but spent most of his time reading every book about Eastern spirituality and human development he could get his hands on. The more he read about all of these different systems of knowledge, the more he realized that his Western scientific education had not told him the full story. Not even close. Wilber immersed himself in the study of the inner world of human beings. He studied the writings of extraordinary individuals in Eastern cultures who had devoted their lives to understanding the nature of human consciousness. They seemed to offer a vision of human potential beyond the materialism and neurotic suffering that characterized Western culture. For several years Wilber pondered these insights, reading all day and waiting tables at night, making enough money for his rent- and his massive orders of books. In 1977, the world first heard from Ken Wilber. Instantly, people realized he had something extraordinary to say.

Limitations, East and West

Over the course of ten years, Wilber would lay out a model that he called the *Spectrum of Consciousness*, which was the title of his first book that was published in 1977. In this revolutionary model, Wilber described the processes through which consciousness develops over the course of the human lifespan. The notion of development was nothing new, of course. Several Western psychological researchers, most notably Sigmund Freud, Jean Piaget, and Erik Erikson, had described specific stages which all humans pass through as they mature. Freud depicted stages of psychosexual development. Piaget illustrated how cognitive capacities develop throughout childhood and into adulthood. Erikson provided a general outline of the moral and existential challenges faced by humans from infancy to old age. These paradigms of human development did not offer much beyond the vision of heroic struggle offered by existentialist philosophers and psychologists. In this view, the ultimate fate of human development is to acknowledge the inevitability of instinctual struggle and death, and live a life that authentically acknowledged these limitations. Wilber, having studied all these models of human development, recognized their importance. He also realized there was something missing.

Wilber was a voracious student of the Eastern religions that were introduced in the US and Europe during the 1950s and '60s. These Eastern traditions spoke of realms of human consciousness that were free from suffering and states of consciousness that could transcend the limitations of instinctual conflict. These traditions had developed methods for harnessing the energy of the body and meditative practices that brought peace to agitated minds. They offered a moral sensibility that compassionately included all living beings, in contrast to the limited individual and nationalistic moral visions of Western cultures. For the most part, the Eastern traditions were viewed as an alternative to the neurotic Western lifestyle and the dour existentialist perspectives. Westerners began to discover the teachings of these ancient philosophies, seeing them as a way to escape the frustrations and conflicts of everyday life. Eastern religions had suddenly become a big hit.

While the appeal of this type of lifestyle was obvious, by the early 1970s the dysfunctional consequences were becoming readily apparent. Simply sitting around all day and "expanding one's consciousness" did not pay the bills and did not get the kids to school. People began to question the value of the Eastern traditions. Western psychology, beginning with Freud, had always been skeptical of mystical religions. The chaotic events of the '60s seemed to confirm his notion that meditation and mystical experiences brought on by psychoactive drugs were nothing more than a regression to infantile states of consciousness that impaired the adult's ability to function in reality. But what did Western approaches to human development seem to offer? The monstrous brutality of the two World Wars left everyone suspicious of the unresolved conflicts lurking just below the surface of Western Civilization. Through the Eastern traditions, people had a glimpse of what was possible- but that seemed unworkable. No one knew which path to follow.

The Breakthrough

Wilber was keenly aware of the confusion between the worlds of Western psychology and Eastern spirituality. His elegant new Spectrum of Consciousness model made sense of this confusion. Wilber's central innovation was to recognize that both Western and Eastern approaches to human development were equally valuable. There was no need to choose between them. They simply addressed different portions of the total spectrum of human experience. Up until that point in history, no Western researcher had ever systematically included the knowledge cultivated by the Eastern spiritual traditions in their models of human development. Just as importantly, none of the Eastern spiritual traditions had incorporated modern psychological knowledge in their models of human development. Wilber recognized that Western psychological science had made great progress in understanding the early developmental phases. The various theories of psychosocial, cognitive, and moral development provided an empirical framework to understand how humans develop from infancy to adulthood. However, Western psychological sciences had little to say about what happens when we reach adulthood. It was as if that was the end of the line.

Wilber realized that Eastern spiritual traditions focused mostly on adult development. They had cultivated sophisticated practices for transforming "normal neurotic" adults into mature and more enlightened humans. In his broad survey of these traditions, he discerned underlying patterns of development that were designed to help adults explore and understand the more advanced potentials of human consciousness. He saw that just as Western psychological sciences had recognized specific stages of childhood development, Eastern spiritual disciplines implicitly recognized that the development of adults into more emotionally and spiritually mature beings also proceeds in stages. Wilber's genius was to link the stages of child and adolescent development depicted in Western psychology with the stages of adult development discovered by the Eastern spiritual traditions. Suddenly, there was no conflict and no need to choose between the two systems. Wilber recognized the underlying unity of these two approaches to human development. When combined, the two bodies of knowledge form a unified map of the full spectrum of human development, from birth to enlightenment.

In this integrated view, each progressive stage of consciousness has its own intrinsic and indispensable significance. Each previous stage is indispensable for the emergence of each succeeding stage. Wilber calls this a *holarchical* evolutionary pattern. The term holarchical means that each level of development includes the capacities and functions of the previous level, but manifests with newly emergent, coherent properties that supercede the previous system. The new system that emerges at each new stage exhibits higher-order potentials for properties, functions, and capacities. Each stage of development is considered to transcend yet include the previous level. We can see holarchical pattern in human development, where the capacities of the earlier stages- walking, speaking, basic logic, etc.- continue to function at higher stages of development even as new, more sophisticated capacities like athletic skills, writing, and computer programming emerge.

Consciousness and the Instincts

Wilber's model offers a general outline of the developmental challenges faced at each stage of human development. Wilber himself has always stressed that this model provides only a *general* outline, and that there are always more complex details involved at every stage. He has also refined it over the years, making adjustments as new scientific and spiritual knowledge emerged. Nonetheless, this model provides an excellent overall map for understanding the stages through which human consciousness develops. But what does the development of consciousness tell us about the development of instinctual intelligence?

The answer to this question is *quite a bit*. One of the central themes of Wilber's work has been to emphasize the depth of the connection between body and mind. This view, which is prevalent in Eastern spiritual traditions, honors the fact that consciousness is embedded within the human body. In the last two decades, the deep connection between mind and body has become increasingly accepted thanks to the work of authors like Deepak Chopra and Dan Goleman. Many modern psychologists, neurobiologists, and spiritual teachers, Eastern and Western, now embrace this concept. There is a mountain of evidence that proves that what we think can affect the body *and* the state of our bodies affects what we think and feel. Clearly, our embodied instinctual experience is a central feature of human consciousness. As we will see, Wilber's model describes how the complete human - a living, physical, cognitive, emotional, instinctual, social being- passes through each stage of development. Therefore, in a very direct way, Wilber's model provides a clear picture of the full developmental potential of our embodied instinctual consciousness.

The Stages

Wilber's model breaks human development into nine stages, which he groups in three broad phases. He refers to these phases as the *pre-personal*, the *personal*, and the *transpersonal*. Very generally, we can say that the *pre-personal* phase covers the early childhood years between infancy and the age of 4 or 5. Wilber calls it pre-personal because the young child has not yet formed a stable ego-personality that has the developmental characteristics of an autonomous individual. This means that they still require the presence of parents or caregivers to help them regulate their instinctual impulses. The *personal* phase begins with emergence of a stable ego-personality that allows the child to function as an individuated and autonomous person. This self-regulating capacity usually begins to coalesce sometime by the age of 5. As the individual matures, he or she will pass through a few more stages on the way to adulthood. These include finding an appropriate role within the society, developing a sense of one's personal identity, and confronting existential issues like meaning, authenticity, and mortality. This is the level of development that majority of the adults in the modern world attain. For our discussion, it is important to note that the successful navigation of each stage of development within this phase requires the skillful inhibition of certain instinctual impulses. As we have seen in previous chapters, by the time most adults reach this stage, their instinctual intelligence has become stagnant. The *transpersonal* phase represents the development of certain capacities of consciousness that go beyond the skills and perspectives developed in the personal phase. Not all adults will choose (or are able) to pursue this level of development. This is because it requires deliberate effort to transform many of the habitual coping strategies and instinctual behaviors that functioned adequately during the personal phase. Moreover, the more evolved stages and possibilities of human consciousness are not accessible without this re-alignment of our basic instinctual programs. We'll look briefly at each of the stages a little more closely. This will help us to understand how instinctual intelligence develops at each stage.

THE PRE-PERSONAL.

Wilber divides this phase of human development into three separate stages:

1) **Sensoriphysical.** At this stage, the infant's consciousness is focused on the needs of the body. The primary developmental challenge for the infant's instinctual intelligence is to establish a physically communicative bond with the mother. This will ensure that the infant's basic instinctual needs are met. This stage is complete when the infant has developed a perceptual sense that he or she has a stable physical body that is separate from the mother and the external environment.

2) **Emotional.** At this stage, the young child's consciousness is focused on his or her emotional needs for support, contact, and affection. The primary developmental challenge for the child's instinctual intelligence is to internalize a lasting sense of emotional bonding with the maternal figure. This allows the child to maintain a reasonably stable inner sense of self- regardless whether the mother is physically present or not. We discussed some of the instinctual dynamics of this developmental phase in chapter 3 in our exploration of the basic instinctual programs that underlie motivation and autonomous perseverance.

3) **Representational.** This requires the development of the capacity to mentally represent the presence of the parents and inhibit instinctual impulses that might lead to their disapproval. This stage is complete when children have internalized a sense of socially appropriate behaviors with regard to their instinctual impulses. We discussed this phase of development in chapter 8 in our discussion of the cognitive inhibition of instinctual impulses.

THE PERSONAL.

Once the pre-personal developmental tasks are more or less complete, children progress to the next phase of development, the personal.

4) Rules and Roles. At this stage, the child's consciousness moves beyond the need to conform to the wishes of the parents and must begin to adapt to the more complex cultural rules that exist outside the family. The developmental challenge of going to school is a perfect example of how the child adopts new roles (a student) and must learn new rules (raise your hand to go to the bathroom). This stage of development is complete when the child establishes a stable capacity to learn new rules and take on unfamiliar roles. Like all the skills and capacities acquired at each developmental stage, the ability to learn new roles and rules is used at all subsequent levels of development. However, because these abilities help us adapt to difficult situations and help us feel safe, many people find it hard to let go of the tendency to follow rules later in life. In other words, they always do what is expected of them. This can lead to the suppression of one's own unique expression of instinctual intelligence.

5) Identity. At this stage, the individual begins to move beyond the limited options of the rules and roles offered within a particular cultural setting. Education and exposure to outside social influences- combined with the individual's inner feelings- come together to create a unique experience of personal identity. The individual at this stage begins to question the rules of the family and of their surrounding culture concerning what are acceptable and unacceptable forms of expressing instinctual impulses. At this stage, teenagers seek to emulate the instinctual behaviors of musicians, video-game warriors, athletes, and other cultural heroes. They want to know what is possible-not what is required or expected. But they also want social acceptance and recognition. The enormously popular TV show *American Idol* exemplifies this search for a unique, instinctually satisfying- but socially valued- identity. Failure to complete this level of development can lead to a loss of one's inner instinctual sense of what is valuable and appropriate for one's self and one's life. To complete this stage, one must begin to answer some of the basic questions in life like: Who am I? What will I do? What kind of relationships do I want? Will others value me? How do I want to express my instinctual desires?

6) Existential. At this stage, the individual faces the challenge of reconciling his or her own sense of identity with the profound and meaningful events of life. Here, the individual's needs and desires to explore the possibilities of life are challenged by the larger forces of reality. As we grow older, the limitations imposed by economics, relationships, illness, and death begin to touch our lives more directly. This forces the individual to make a choice between authentically responding to those existential realities or acting as if they did not exist. Developmental psychologists have observed that individuals who consciously embrace the anxiety and terror of human life live profoundly meaningful lives. However, facing these issues is not that easy. Many people tend to use the incessant pursuit of instinctual gratification as a way to avoid the feelings of anxiety and terror. The accumulation of wealth, sexual addictions, and striving for social status are just a few examples of the way many adults become stuck at this stage of development. On the other hand, those who choose to acknowledge full existential dread and terror of life may find themselves paralyzed by the utter meaninglessness of human existence. When this happens, individuals can feel as if they have reached a dead-end, a point at which they can envision no further development.

The vast majority of adults in the modern world have not realistically addressed the developmental challenges of stages 4, 5, and 6. They are still afraid to leave the safety of following the rules, unsure of who they are or what they want to be, or refuse to deal authentically with the profound emotional intensity of existential realities. In this sense, it is clear how the overall development of their consciousness, as well as their instinctual intelligence, has become stagnant.

THE TRANSPERSONAL.

The final stages of Wilber's model were based on his far reaching analysis of several spiritual traditions, including Buddhism, Hinduism, Kabbalah, and Christian mysticism. He observed that practices of these spiritual systems were designed to interrupt many of the cognitive, emotional, and instinctual behaviors that were established during the pre-personal and personal phases of development. This meant that practitioners had to learn to deconstruct many of the basic features of their ego-personalities. In going beyond the personal, these individuals would be able to experience transpersonal dimensions of consciousness. Now, for some, a discussion of spirituality may seem odd in a book about instincts. However, from this transpersonal perspective, the accumulated adaptations and inhibitions of instinctual energy that were vital to the successful completion of earlier stages are now seen as obstacles to further development.

Nearly all of the world's wisdom traditions reflect the fundamental understanding that the ultimate source of the development of human consciousness was not the adaptive struggling of the ego. This understanding has many nuances and methods of cultivation. Within the theistic traditions, individuals seek to surrender into a union with the heart and mind of God. From the Taoist perspective, individuals enter into the stream of Being, joining in the unfolding flow of existence. Non-dual traditions like Buddhism speak of realizing one's true nature as spontaneously co-emergent with the entirety of all manifestation across time and space. Regardless of the specific formulation or the practices used to cultivate this awareness, the underlying principles speak to a deep sense that the manifestations of human consciousness are part of a larger, all- encompassing reality. The wisdom traditions all point to the realization that the evolutionary force inherent within human instinctual consciousness arose form a source beyond any one individual- it was inherent to all creation. Therefore, the central aim of transpersonal development is to help individuals dismantle their accumulated adaptations and inhibitions and open themselves to the deeper sources of consciousness. According to Wilber, this opening can be seen to proceed in three general stages.

Psychic. This is the first stage of transpersonal development. The central challenge at this stage involves adjusting to the release of emotional and instinctual energy that was formerly repressed and inhibited during the previous stages. Various meditative and contemplative practices will begin to alter the habitual adaptive and inhibitory tendencies of the nervous system. Individuals will begin to experience unfamiliar flows of physical energy and the release of long-held emotional memories. This can happen while meditating, doing yoga- or even just taking a walk in nature. This will often result in the eruption of intense anxiety, confusion, and fear. Successful completion of this stage requires that the individual integrate these new levels of instinctual energy and emotional sensitivity into their lives in a coherent and functional manner. It often involves changes in relationships and careers- as well as a total re-evaluation of one's identity and moral sensibilities. Once one has had a glimpse of the deeper origins of human consciousness, the self-centered focus on instinctual gratification that predominates during the personal stages begins to yield to a broader, more inclusive perspective.

Subtle. At this stage of transpersonal development, the central developmental challenge for the individual is overcome the deep instinctual tendencies of attachment. This attachment comes in two forms. The first is a reluctance to give up old patterns of instinctual gratification. While the individual may exhibit many of the capacities of a mature and wise human being, he or she may still be drawn back to the instinctual behaviors of previous stages. Form the transpersonal perspective, this means that the individual still identifies with elements of the ego-personality, and views transpersonal and mystical as passing states of consciousness. In other words, the individual's sense of identity is split. It fluctuates between the desire for the familiar external gratifications of the ego and the inner realization of the ultimate transpersonal nature of consciousness, which is inherently gratifying. The second type of attachment is the clinging to the profound sense of well-being and bliss that can arise as the individual develops expertise in meditation and contemplative exercises. In this case, the individual can mistake these experiences as the complete realization of their particular spiritual path. They become deluded into thinking they have achieved a divine union with God or complete enlightenment. Successful completion of this level involves being willing to explore the extreme discomfort and anxiety that arises from disrupting these tenacious instinctual attachments. These instinctual attachments are deeply imprinted into the nervous system at the earliest stages of development, when the need for instinctual gratification was at its greatest intensity. They form the deepest core of instinctual identity within human consciousness. To re-calibrate these basic programs, the individual must be able to identify with something beyond his or her core self-centered survival instincts. This requires an extremely high level of development of spiritual and instinctual intelligence. The motivation to develop this intelligence arises from a highly evolved moral sensibility that compassionately considers the needs of other living beings.

Causal. This is the final stage of transpersonal development. The central developmental challenge facing individuals is to overcome the fear of surrendering the subtlest attachments that remain deep in the core of their instinctual consciousness. This fear is quite understandable. The surrender of the last vestiges of one's personal self will be experienced with great terror by the survival programs in the core of one's instinctual consciousness. The great wisdom traditions say that to overcome this fear one must leap into the Great Void, where there is nothing to which one can cling. Only then can human consciousness disidentify with the most subtle instinctual impulses of fear and thus realize its ultimate source. It is said that this final union with God or ultimate realization of non-duality does not mean physical death, but rather the complete transcendence of any attachment to life or death. If one has completely disidentified from all of conceptions of existence and nonexistence, there is no fear, only peace.

Wilber's insights into these higher stages of human development provide a persuasive and systematic groundwork for understanding how instinctual intelligence could evolve beyond the familiar sense of frustration and limitation with which we are familiar. Since Wilber introduced this model, scholars in both Western psychology and Eastern spirituality have embraced it enthusiastically. It all seems so clear and so straightforward, almost simple. Could it really be that easy?

The Barrier to the Further Reaches of Human Development

Wilber used his knowledge of spiritual traditions to chart a roadmap of how humans can grow beyond the personal stages of development. However, he observed that there was a central obstacle that severely limited development beyond the existential stage. He referred to this obstacle as the repression barrier. The *repression barrier* is formed by the cognitive inhibition of instinctual energy. Wilber recognized that the successful negotiation of the pre-personal and personal stages of development required the restriction of certain instinctual and emotional impulses. By the time an individual reached adulthood, the accumulated demands placed on the "civilized" adult often creates distortions within the basic instinctual programs. As we have seen, most adults in the modern world fluctuate somewhere between aggression and suppression. Their collective instinctual intelligence is largely stuck at lower stages of development.

For the most part, this barrier was not well-understood or even explicitly recognized in the world's pre-modern spiritual traditions. Wilber was well aware of the realities of spiritual development, both Eastern and Western. Even in the most sophisticated traditions, only a handful of individuals reach transpersonal levels of development. Historically, the idea that the instincts could be a part of the development of consciousness was rarely considered. Most spiritual traditions believed that for the individual to attain some degree of spiritual realization, the body must be transcended. For consciousness to develop into the higher stages of spiritual realization, the individual must learn not to identify with the distracting urges and impulses of the body. Very few esoteric spiritual traditions realistically acknowledged the influence of the instincts. The notion of including them in the overall process of developing a more spiritual consciousness was considered the most difficult and challenging of all practices.

Wilber's model was among the first to recognize the harmful effects of *splitting off* instinctual experiences from the overall development of human consciousness. The recent scandal within the Catholic Church regarding the sexual abuse of young boys by priests is one obvious example of what happens when the instincts are ignored in the context of spiritual development. Wilber had read the traditional accounts in the literature that describe lethargic or undisciplined individuals who were unable complete the arduous contemplative training. It was obvious to him that what they are describing were the common neurotic problems caused by the repression of instinctual energy during the pre-personal and personal levels of development. Wilber reasoned that in order for an individual to enter into and successfully engage the challenges of transpersonal development, they would have to find a way to restore the health and functionality of their basic instinctual systems. Without a secure instinctually intelligent foundation, the development of human consciousness cannot proceed.

Why Meditation Alone Isn't the Answer

Wilber's model demonstrated that the early stages of instinctual development that occur during infancy and childhood are just as important to the development of human consciousness as the adult stages. In a very basic way, Wilber was challenging the age-old notion of spiritual traditions that the body had to be transcended for the development of consciousness to occur. This insight helped to explain why most Western individuals weren't becoming enlightened, despite years and years of meditation practice- and the direct guidance of some very accomplished spiritual masters. The accumulated repression and distortion of instinctual energy was like a ticking time bomb. Individuals reported extraordinary experiences of bliss and insight while meditating. But as soon as they got off the cushion, their neurotic behaviors and feelings of aggression and anger would return. Observing this over and over, Wilber came to a radical conclusion: meditation alone does not address the behavioral and emotional problems caused by the inhibition of instinctual impulses.

Wilber's insight into how the repression and distortion of instinctual energy impacted spiritual development created quite a stir. Students and devotees of various Eastern traditions accused him of denouncing these great spiritual traditions. Throughout the 1980s, Wilber published a series of articles and books carefully dissecting the problem. It is not that mediation was an ineffective means for developing human consciousness. It is. But it was far more effective when an individual's instinctual energies were not creating conflicts. In other words, the transpersonal stages of consciousness development could only proceed if the individual's instinctual energies were more or less aligned with the higher aspirations of the contemplative mind- peace, compassion, and wisdom. If the individual's instinctual impulses were secretly raging with insatiable desires of violence, lust, and aggression, meditation practices would make little if any difference. Wilber, and his colleagues like Jack Engler, began to recognize that Western psychological approaches, especially psychotherapy, were ideally suited to address the problems posed by the repression barrier. Today, it is widely recognized that both psychotherapy and meditation practices are vital for realistic transpersonal development. Most modern transpersonal and spiritual teachers agree that the higher stages of human development require that the individual intelligently harness the adaptive energy of the basic instinctual programs.

Academic researchers investigating the role of instinctual regulation in early human development have validated Wilber's theoretical insights. Developmental psychologists have established that the capacity to regulate emotional and instinctual impulses is the basis upon which all subsequent cognitive, emotional, social, political, and artistic development occurs. Cutting-edge research is also demonstrating that skills and abilities found at the highest stages of human development involve the cultivation of a very sophisticated and refined instinctual intelligence. This research is beginning to shed light on the refined nervous system regulation techniques utilized by advanced spiritual practitioners. Transpersonal development does not mean simply sitting around and meditating all day, wearing robes, and looking peaceful. As we will see in the final section of this book, the intellectual, social, moral, physical, spiritual, and creative abilities of individuals that have cultivated advanced levels of nervous system regulation give us a clear picture of the possibilities of human evolution on this planet.

Turning Toward a Deeper Source

Ken Wilber's Spectrum of Consciousness model has had profound implications for numerous fields of study- developmental psychology, psychotherapy, religious studies, spiritual development, philosophy, systems theory, and consciousness studies- to name a few. Many professionals in mind-body health and wellness have embraced its basic notions of integrating Eastern and Western approaches to human development, and the effectiveness this approach is beginning to be confirmed by empirical research. The basic notion of the inherent value of both Eastern and Western traditions is now common among young adults who growing up in an increasingly globalized society.

Over the years, Wilber has continued to make important contributions to the understanding of how human consciousness evolves. In recent years, he has developed what he calls *Integral Theory*. Integral Theory is a powerful new paradigm that allows us to appreciate the full scope of the evolving universe, of which human consciousness is just one aspect. Expanding on the Spectrum of Consciousness model, Integral Theory reflects the understanding that the universe is capable of generating increasingly sophisticated self-organizing structures on many levels. In this perspective, the evolution of the material universe also manifests in increasingly complex levels of organization. One distinct type of this evolution can be seen in the development of *individual* biological organisms. Integral theory demonstrates the underlying connection between the complexity of self-organization of biological substrates of living creatures and the complexity of their subjective consciousness. In this way, the Integral model recognizes the equal importance of consciousness and neurobiology for developing a comprehensive understanding of all living organisms, especially humans.

Wilber's integral also model recognizes the importance of *collective* and *systemic* forms of evolution. This includes the dynamic evolution of elementary particles, stars, galaxies, solar systems, and planetary environmental systems of the material universe. The subjectivity of living beings- humans in particular- also evolves in collective self-organizing systems. This shared subjectivity is the basis for our social interactions, ranging from the most basic forms of biological resonance to highly sophisticated global cultural and political institutions.

The great contribution of Integral Theory is that it equally embraces the two primary realms of phenomena- the objective and the subjective. Without privileging either realm, this inclusive perspective allows us to embrace knowledge from both our interior and exterior worlds. It also allows us to appreciate the paradigms of science and spirituality in a manner that does not lead to conflict or dogmatism. This allows us to see, from a totally modern perspective, the foundations of human instinctual intelligence. In this view, the evolution of matter and the evolution of consciousness are not regarded as two distinct phenomena. Therefore, the development of the biological substrates that structure our basic instinctual programs is not inherently separate from the development of our subjective consciousness. Nor are these two realms separable from the matrix of our collective socio-cultural organizations and complex physical environments.

Through the Integral model, we can recognize the human body as the most complex form of self-organization in the known universe. As such, it is the repository of the adaptive intelligence of life, a living matrix of matter and awareness, evolving with every breath. This perspective, while grounded in modern evolutionary science, is in accord with the profound spiritual insights of the world's wisdom traditions. Our instinctual intelligence is an integral expression of the evolving universe. Knowing this, we can begin the journey of opening our instinctual consciousness beyond the strict identification with personal, and toward the ultimate source of all life and creation that transcends individual limits.

Another Dead-End?

Wilber's brilliant models offer a map of the evolutionary possibilities of human instinctual consciousness. They provide us with a glimpse into the world of ancient spiritual traditions, and their methods for cultivating profound levels of instinctual intelligence. But this leads us to an important question. Is the knowledge of these ancient traditions useful- or even relevant- in today's world? In the past, practicing a spiritual tradition meant years and years of arduous meditation in isolated conditions. The monks, nuns, yogis, and other spiritual masters who maintained these practices had little or no responsibilities and commitments. Many people in the modern world sincerely desire to cultivate deeper levels of instinctual intelligence and spiritual insight. However, they have families they love, careers to which they are committed, and worlds of adventure to explore. Most of us simply don't have the time to meditate for eight hours a day, week after week, and year after year. Does this mean that the evolution of our instinctual intelligence is reserved for a chosen few who are willing to devote all their time and energy to esoteric spiritual practices?

Or is there another- more direct way- to evolve our instinctual consciousness?

CHAPTER 11

Surrendering to a Deeper Wisdom

Polar bears.

That's right, polar bears.

Who would have thought that some of the deepest insights into the nature of human instinctual intelligence might come from these furry white giants?

At this point, you might be wondering what polar bears have to do with the evolution of human instinctual intelligence. After all, we were just talking about esoteric mediation practices and the highest potentials of human development. Most people think of polar bears as furry beasts, perhaps sometimes cute- but quite dangerous. At first glance, these massive and often violent creatures would seem to have little to do with the refined human qualities of compassion, intelligence, and creativity.

In previous chapters, we have seen the many ways that our individual and collective instinctual intelligence can reach a plateau of developmental stagnation. We have also glimpsed into the possibilities of how our instinctual consciousness can evolve. But accessing these possibilities solely through the practice of ancient spiritual disciplines seems impracticable given the realities of modern life. How will humanity step into a more instinctually intelligent future? And what do polar bears have to do with it?

In order to envision the instinctual future of humanity, we must first take a step into the past. Through this glimpse into the past, we will discover that an innate wisdom of our animal ancestors is buried deep within us. Re-awakening this dormant wisdom provides the final push that human consciousness needs to break the cycle of stagnation. Our modern knowledge of instinctual intelligence is ready to be combined with the mysterious eternal wisdom that has guided life on this planet, as well as the evolution of the universe, for billions of years. This integration of the modern and the eternal is already happening, as individuals all over the world are using this matrix of knowledge to build pathways to a more instinctually intelligent future. One of these paths to the future runs right through the North Pole, where our distant animal cousins are helping us re-connect with the original source of evolutionary wisdom stored deep within our bodies.

Unlikely as it may seem, polar bears actually provide the critical link in our investigation of the evolution of human instinctual consciousness. They can help us to understand how humans began to diverge from their animal roots, and in the process, lost touch with a vital neurobiological capacity. Reawakening this capacity provides an indispensable key to unlocking the continuing evolution of humanity.

Adaptation and Divergence

Modern neuropsychology has yielded precise descriptions of the biological basis of human instinctual intelligence. Within the last decade, advances in technology have allowed researchers to understand how the brain records past experiences and then uses this stored information to guide future instinctually based behaviors, emotions, and thoughts. This research has revealed the extraordinary capacity of the brain to store detailed memories of extremely stressful and emotionally intense experiences. This knowledge allows us to understand how humans have successfully adapted to the endless challenges of life on earth. The ability of our brains to record information about life-threatening situations is what allowed our ancestors to survive- and thrive.

The Advantages of Instinctual Regulation

Over the course of millions of years, the ancestors of *Homo sapiens* were faced with a changing environment that constantly threatened their survival. Individuals who were born with slightly larger brain capacities than their generational peers received an advantage in terms of survival capability, environmental adaptation, and mate selection. Consequently, the genetic line of proto-humans that eventually evolved into *Homo sapiens* developed progressively expanded neurocognitive capacities. The region of the brain that saw the greatest increase in size, complexity, and neuronal connectivity was the cerebral cortex. The cerebral cortex is the region of the brain where we record and process extensive amounts of sensory, perceptual, emotional, and cognitive data. The capacity to store information and anticipate future consequences provided humans with alternatives to the limited variety of pre-programmed behaviors and perceptions afforded by the more primitive instinctual centers of the brain.

From a neurobiological perspective, the evolution of the cerebral cortex allowed humans to regulate experiences of instinctual arousal in a way that other animals could not. In previous chapters, we have seen how the neural networks centered in the frontal lobes function as a top-down control mechanism that can modify the activity of the amygdala and the instinctual response regions of the brainstem. These cortical networks contain information about dangerous places and situations, escape routes, interpersonal relationships, and behaviors that were helpful in past life-threatening situations. These bits and pieces of mnemonic associations function alongside the innate instinctual impulses giving humans a wide range of options to formulate behavioral, emotional, and cognitive responses. This is what gives humans the capacity to modulate the expression of the basic survival instincts and social behaviors. In short, the cerebral cortex works in association with the emotional and instinctual centers of the brain to optimize our chances for survival and adaptation.

From this evolutionary perspective, it is easy to see the importance of recording information and experiences that could enhance the odds of survival. Individuals who had greater capacities to modify their instinctual responses in light of previous experiences had a clear advantage in terms of survival, social adaptation, and reproduction. The most adaptive humans were the ones that could best remember what happened in the past and use that knowledge to guide their instinctual responses in the future. As our brains grew, humans diverged further and further from their animal roots. This changed the course of human evolution, and led to the extraordinary advances of civilization. However, when we begin to look a bit more closely, we can see the capacity to modify our basic instinctual programs caused us to lose touch with a vital part of our innate animal intelligence.

The Storage of Traumatic Experiences

To understand how human instinctual intelligence began to diverge from its animal roots, we have to have a basic understanding of how the human nervous system records extremely stressful events. Experiences that have a high level of emotional and instinctual significance are recorded in detail within the brain. Sensations of pain, fear, anxiety- any type of intense nervous system arousal- are sharply imprinted on the limbic system. The limbic system is one of the primary brain regions where emotional memories are stored. As we have seen, the neural networks centered in the amygdala are at the core of this system. Numerous other sensory, perceptual, and cognitive impressions associated with the emotionally intense event are recorded in other areas of the brain, especially the cerebral cortex and the hippocampus. This recording process insures that when similar dangerous or threatening circumstances are encountered, the entire nervous system is activated in an attempt to avoid or effectively respond to any perceived environmental challenges. This works fine in most situations. However, when an individual perceives that his or her life is threatened by an *overwhelming force,* the nervous system goes into a kind of frozen shock. This is exactly what happens when a Navy SEALs candidate is pushed too far. The human nervous system has a last-ditch survival mechanism that is triggered when all other basic survival responses- including fighting or running away- are ineffective. This freezing response is the most primitive of all our instinctual survival programs, rooted in the dorsal vagal complex in the medulla. Its activation will immediately reduce the individual's heart rate and blood pressure, and totally inhibit movement in voluntary muscles. In the face of overwhelming threat, freezing may be the only adaptive response.

Psychological researchers that study the impacts of trauma on the nervous system have discovered this freezing response can be triggered in a variety of situations. For adults, the freezing response can be triggered by accidents that cause severe physical injury, such as automobile crashes and falling. Violent attacks by wild animals and other humans will also commonly evoke a freezing response. It is seen in situations of sexual assault, bombings in wars, and physical abuse. Natural disasters, illness, and the death of loved ones can also totally inhibit the other survival responses of the nervous system. Humans do not have to be the direct victims of a physical attack for the freezing response to be triggered. Witnessing horrible accidents, abuse, and torture are profoundly stressful events that can trigger an inhibitory freezing response. This *vicarious traumatization* was experienced by many people in the US and other regions of the world then the World Trade Center was destroyed in 2001. The freezing response is triggered quite easily in children, because their immature physical development often makes the fight or flight response impossible or ineffective. Children are vulnerable to the same the types of experiences that trigger the freezing responses in adults. In addition, children that experience emotional abuse, neglect, or abandonment will frequently respond with this type of nervous system inhibition. Infants are even more vulnerable. Current research in infant neuropsychology suggests that intense inhibitory responses will inevitably occur during the first year of life, even when parents are attentive and loving. Researchers have recently discovered that a variety of seemingly less stressful events and situations can also provoke freezing responses, depending on the individual's mood, mental state, and physiological condition.

This state of frozen shock is one of the worst experiences a human can endure. The primary outflow of the dorsal vagal complex in the medulla provides parasympathetic input to the stomach and intestinal tracts. This increases the production of digestive acids and increases intestinal motility. At the same time, the extreme activation of the stress response causes areas of the midbrain and brainstem to send sympathetic outflow to the gastrointestinal system, which inhibits digestive processes and intestinal motility. The net result of this is a state of extreme physiological distress involving inescapable nausea and severe visceral and somatic dysregualtion. This paralyzing state of misery will totally inhibit all motor movement- leaving the individual stuck in a state of frozen agony.

Avoiding the Terror

We know a lot about the neurobiological and psychological impacts of traumatic experiences thanks to the work of Bessel van der Kolk and his colleagues. For over 30 years, Van der Kolk- who is the Founder and Medical Director of the Trauma Center in Brookline, Massachusetts- has carried out detailed research that demonstrates how these memories subsequently influence the functioning of the nervous system after the traumatic event has occurred. He has explored how the details of the traumatic event are registered in the limbic and cortical networks. Individuals who have experienced traumatic events can remember where it happened, who was there, what it sounded like, what it felt like- even what it smelled like. The human brain has evolved to evaluate incoming sensory information through the filter of past events. Our associative perceptual networks are sensitive to any type of environmental cue that may signal danger. These perceptual networks are especially sensitive to any environmental cues that were associated with life-threatening events and traumatic experiences that occurred in the past. *Any* type of sensory experience directly or indirectly associated with the traumatic event- sounds, voices, faces, locations, objects, smells- can automatically activate cascade of nervous system survival programs. In an evolutionary sense, this response is quite adaptive, as it instantly activates automatic survival oriented behaviors. It no doubt insured the physical survival of many brave individuals who explored new territories and encountered extreme danger and hardships.

But here is where the larger brains of human beings become a liability. The extreme horror of the traumatic freezing response is deeply imprinted on the nervous system, especially in our expanded limbic and cortical regions. Those who have experienced it will do anything to avoid having it triggered again. However, the massive associative connections of the human brain make this difficult. When these individuals sense the slightest hint of anything associated with the previous traumatic event, their nervous systems will automatically employ a variety of behavioral responses to prevent a return to the frozen state of terror. Their daily lives are often interrupted by the sudden uncontrollable arousal of their nervous systems. This can be experienced as uncontrollable anxiety, intrusive memories, inappropriate behaviors, and irrational avoidance of situations that are incorrectly perceived to be threatening. The effects of traumatic experiences are now clinically recognized as a specific set of nervous system adaptations collectively referred to as Post Traumatic Stress Disorder (PTSD).

Dissociation

Over the course of several decades of clinical and experimental research, van der Kolk and his colleagues discovered something quite remarkable. They observed that the brain also stores memories of the *internal* experiences associated with the traumatic experience. This internal storage system includes details about autonomic nervous system activation patterns and other biochemical responses. Memories of the inhibitory freezing responses are also recorded. However, because these memories are so terrifying- and disruptive- they are largely isolated from the individual's conscious awareness. The tendency to *isolate* memories of traumatic experiences is a central characteristic of PTSD. These isolated memories can be understood as a form of *state-dependent* traumatic memory recall, which only become active when stressful external events- or internal memories called *flashbacks*- activate the neural networks in which they are stored. Van der Kolk's research led to the development of innovative psychotherapeutic techniques for treating PTSD. It also provides us with a vital piece of information concerning the evolution of instinctual intelligence.

Following van der Kolk's groundbreaking insights, researchers discovered that the dissociative symptoms of PTSD are primarily associated with abnormal functioning in the interconnected networks between the orbitofrontal cortex, anterior cingulate, hippocampus, and amygdala. The internal memories are stored in these networks comprise what van der Kolk calls *distinct ego states*. The biological substrates of these distinct ego states are *functionally discrete* neural networks. These networks are centered around the over-arousal of the amygdala, producing a unique set of sensory, perceptual, emotional, and cognitive processing characteristics. These networks, while functionally coherent, are markedly different from the individual's normal personality and self-regulating characteristics. Much of the time, these isolated networks lie dormant. However, when they are triggered, they will produce the same nervous system responses that were experienced during the initial traumatizing event. The re-activation of the freezing response can cause a variety of effects, ranging from moderate anxiety to powerful aggressive impulses. At its most intense levels, individuals experience paralyzing cognitive, emotional, and somatic inhibition- a dreaded terror and bleak constriction of their life energy. The state of blank frozen agony wipes out everything else in the individual's consciousness. This phenomenon is referred to as *dissociation* by clinical psychologists.

The Isolated Amygdala

Emerging research in the field of trauma clearly indicates that certain traumatic experiences lead to the decreased ability of the orbitofrontal cortex to control the arousal level of the amygdala. Experiences of abuse, assault, and social abandonment induce the growth of over-arousing amygdaloid-hypothalamus connections. These horrific interpersonal experiences radically alter the individual's social instinctual intelligence by restructuring the regulating neuronal connections between the orbitofrontal cortex and amygdaloid-hypothalamus circuits. The memories of social interaction stored in the orbitofrontal cortex no longer sooth- they further escalate amygdala arousal. Recent research also suggests that traumatic experiences negatively impact the appraisal functions of the hippocampus, a brain region directly involved in the storage of the factual memories needed for accurate reality testing. The hippocampus also serves as a primary inhibitor of the amygdala, by providing enhanced perceptual discrimination via its cortical connections. Hippocampal-cortical networks produce more refined cognitive and emotional appraisals of external stimuli than the crude appraisals of the amygdala. Based on this evidence, we can see how the reality testing functions of the hippocampus and social intelligence of the orbitofrontal cortex is altered by traumatic experiences. Without these two instinctual controls, the amygdala dominates the functioning of the nervous system. In this unregulated state, the amygdala will activate fight or flight programs in an irrational attempt to avoid a stimulus that is *mistakenly perceived* as a threat. In some cases, it becomes hyperaroused, and it will activate the dissociative freezing response. The unrestricted activation of the amygdala severely limits the adaptive functioning of the individual's instinctual intelligence.

Van der Kolk's study of the psychological and behavioral consequences of traumatic experiences led him to an inescapable conclusion: the basic survival programs of the human nervous system- *especially the primitive freezing response*- function rather poorly in the modern world. Humans seem especially prone to slide into the dissociative freezing response, and they are even more vulnerable to having it inappropriately triggered in non-threatening situations. Most animals do not appear to suffer the ill effects of life-threatening events the way humans do. They are able to shake off the effects of dangerous situations and go about their business. It was as if the evolution of human instinctual intelligence had suddenly left us unable to cope with the challenges of modern life. This seemed puzzling to many researchers and clinical psychologists. Had humans left some part of their innate instinctual intelligence behind in the animal kingdom?

The Wisdom of the Polar Bear

This was the question that Peter Levine had been pondering for some time. Levine had earned a Ph.D. in physiology during the '60s- a time when the study of the effects of trauma was in its infancy. In his work, he had begun to notice how certain individuals responded to stressful situations. He noted that their responses seemed out of proportion to the reality of the situation. With his training in physiology, he could detect changes in the autonomic nervous system responses of his clients. He observed how they would become anxious or agitated in response to seemingly inconsequential stimuli that others ignored. As he investigated more closely, he began to uncover an even more interesting phenomenon. Beginning in 1969, Levine grew increasingly intrigued by the tendency of these individuals to become fixated on specific perceptions, feelings, or thoughts. This fixation was somehow related to the anxiety they were feeling- but Levine couldn't quite put his finger on it. His patients would often repeat themselves or direct the discussion over and over again to a specific topic. Their compulsion to repeat themselves left them caught in some kind of mental and emotional vortex. Slowly, and almost by accident, Levine began to piece together what was happening.

He realized that these individuals had experienced some kind of traumatic event in the past. Because the event was overwhelming to their nervous systems, they had gone into an inhibitory freeze response. Levine came to realize that their inhibitory freezing response had prematurely shut down their natural fight or flight programs. Their compulsive behaviors and anxiety were subconscious attempts to discharge the powerful instinctual energy that had been inhibited by the freezing response. Over the next decade, Levine began to develop an intuitive method that could guide people out of the frozen loop of incomplete discharge. His technique allowed traumatized individuals to complete the fight or flight survival responses that were shut down by the freezing response. His clinical method, called *Somatic Experiencing,* has been successful in treating thousands of individuals who suffered from varying types and degrees of PTSD and related psychological disorders. Many of his students have gone on to develop specialized psychotherapeutic techniques designed to treat specific types of nervous system imbalances caused by a wide variety of traumatic experiences. Levine's contributions to the understanding and clinical treatment of trauma, along with his colleague Bessel van der Kolk, are monumental. Together, they have provided insight into a previously hidden dimension of the nervous system that is radically changing our modern understanding of instinctual intelligence.

Why Can't We Just Shake it Off?

As Levine was developing his Somatic Experiencing technique, he was haunted by a nagging question. Why is the human nervous system so vulnerable to the after-effects of traumatic experiences? Animals face life-threatening situations every day. Almost every time I look out into my backyard, I see squirrels clinging from treetops to avoid falling. I see birds dive bombing these same squirrels to keep them away from their precious eggs. Raccoons are frantically avoiding aggressive dogs by scurrying up trees or hiding in holes. Field mice freeze to avoid detection by the passing hawk. Yet, once the danger has passed- the mouse resumes its search for food as if nothing ever happened. On the other hand- if I almost fell from a tree, or my children were attacked, or I were chased by a giant dog four times my size, or swept away in the claws of a giant pterodactyl- I would be freaking out! I would be calling my friends, telling them about these harrowing events. It would be hard for my nervous system to settle down for a few hours- or days. Weeks later I would still probably freeze in my tracks and break out in to a cold sweat every time I heard the bark of a dog or the tweet of a bird. And I would probably go see Peter Levine to help me discharge my nervous system energy in a healthy way.

While I was there, Dr. Levine could explain to me why humans are more vulnerable to the after-effects of traumatic experiences. He himself stumbled upon the answer in one of those rare "a-ha" moments about which every scientific researcher dreams. Back in 1982, he was watching a National Geographic documentary about polar bears. The video followed a research team that had captured a polar bear in the wild. They sedated the bear and carried out some standard research tests. Within a short time, they released him back into his native habitat. As soon as the bear woke up, Levine noticed something amazing. The giant beast staggered to its feet and appeared to have trouble breathing, as if it were is a state of shock. Suddenly, it began shaking. This shaking was quite intense, almost violent, and lasted a few minutes. As suddenly as it began, it was over. The bear was breathing normally and resumed its usual routine of searching for food as if nothing had happened. As he was watching this brief sequence, Peter Levine felt a flash of inspiration. He instantly recognized an innate form of instinctual intelligence in the polar bear's shaking.

Levine immediately grasped that the polar bear was discharging the trapped energy of the fight or flight survival programs that were interrupted when it was captured and sedated. This was an extraordinary insight that would forever transform his approach to treating trauma. He realized that the nervous system of human beings had not entirely lost this basic neurobiological capacity. He was seeing this type of shaking and nervous system discharge in his clinical work with traumatized individuals. But he could see that this process was *not spontaneous or natural in humans*. It became obvious to him that the strange behaviors he was observing in his clients- the compulsiveness, repetition, and anxiety- were an attempt to discharge the trapped energy of the fight or flight survival programs that were inhibited by the freezing response. Levine reasoned that the evolutionary development of the human nervous system was preventing the full discharge. Here's why: The civilizing ability to modify our basic instinctual programs acted as a brake on the primal drive to discharge frozen energy. Unlike the polar bear and other animals, humans are wary of surrendering control of their nervous systems. The inhibitory mechanisms of the orbitofrontal and hippocampal networks will do what they can to avoid re-experiencing the shock and terror of the nervous system activation associated with the traumatic experience. Levine could see that the nervous system intuitively tries to discharge the energy and return to a state of balance. However, as the discharge process begins, the individual mistakenly interprets the experience of this energy as a *threatening anxiety*. Instead of surrendering to this wave of instinctual energy, they try to inhibit, suppress, or otherwise control it.

The Frozen Self

Humans have retained the innate drive to discharge the frozen energy of their instinctual programs. For years, Levine had observed that his clients were constantly placing themselves in situations that were similar to the original traumatic events. Women who were sexually abused as children were working as prostitutes as adults. Soldiers who had witnessed unspeakable violence during wartime were seeking out violent confrontation years after they returned to civilian life. Clearly, these were not random behaviors. Levine realized that they were trying to recreate a situation where their nervous systems could finally complete the fight or flight responses that were originally inhibited. In an unconscious way, traumatized individuals subconsciously hope that this time they would be able to defend themselves or run away. They would take themselves to the edge- but since they did not understand what they were doing- they could not complete the discharge cycle in a healthy way. Sometimes, they would shut the cycle down and revert to the freezing response when the anxiety became too intense. Other times the energy would spill out with aggression and violence. This did not effectively discharge the energy. It only re-traumatized the individual, leaving them mired in shame, confusion, and regret.

Now it all made sense. Levine realized that his Somatic Experiencing therapy systematically and effectively guided individuals through the discharge process. His clinical techniques skillfully regulated his clients' anxiety and helped their nervous systems navigate the discharge cycle. By engaging the process with conscious awareness of what was happening, his clients were able *to complete* the healthy instinctual actions that were interrupted during the traumatic event. This discharging completion allowed them to return to a state of nervous system balance. Their natural instinctual intelligence could function without fear and confusion. Levine's work proved that the adult nervous system- including the instinctual regulating centers of the brain- are far more plastic and malleable than we previously thought.

In the last decade Levine's students, most notably Pat Ogden, have begun to refine Levine's basic insights into comprehensive psychological treatment paradigms. Ogden's Sensorimotor Psychotherapy Institute now trains therapists all over the world in the latest clinical techniques for mitigating the neurological and emotional residue of traumatic experiences. These discoveries open up worlds of possibilities for the development and evolution of our instinctual intelligence.

The original insights of van der Kolk and Levine also put us in position to understand the primary barrier to the personal development and collective evolution of human instinctual intelligence. This barrier is what cuts us off from our animal origins and causes our nervous systems to become caught in a cycle of stagnation. It is also what stands in the way of the evolution of human consciousness. It's so familiar and so basic to our daily experience that we do not even recognize the way it restricts our life.

If we follow the clues, it will become obvious. The world's wisdom traditions have stressed that this restrictive force is the root of all our suffering. Ken Wilber's spectrum of consciousness model showed that transcendence of this restrictive force is necessary for reaching more advanced levels of human development. Bessel van der Kolk's research on the neurobiological basis of dissociation demonstrates how this restrictive force is intensified by traumatic experiences. The wisdom of shaking polar bears shows us how we can begin freeing ourselves from the restrictive force. In this freedom, we can begin to sense the mysterious origins of our instinctual intelligence, an intelligence that was present long before humans walked the earth.

It's all around us. All we have to do is step outside the box.

CHAPTER 12

Stepping Outside the Box

Deep in the soul of every human being burns the instinct for freedom. We all have the intuition that there is so much more to life, so much more intelligence, passion, and creativity than we let ourselves acknowledge. And yet, the sticky glue of the *restrictive force* keeps us bound, leaving the vision of freedom tantalizingly out of reach.

Hameed Ali knows more about the restrictive force than anyone alive today.

Hameed Ali is the founder of *The Diamond Approach*, a cutting-edge paradigm of human development. During the last 30 years, Ali (who writes under the pen name A.H. Almaas), has developed a sophisticated understanding of how the restrictive force obscures the extraordinary potentials of human life. In the process, he has gained a detailed understanding of how to help people step outside the box of the restrictive force.

The Final Piece

We are on the verge of putting it all together. The final stage in our investigation of instinctual intelligence is finally here. By examining Ali's work in the Diamond Approach, we can now step fully into the 21st century, right out into the leading edge of the evolution of human instinctual consciousness. On this leading edge we will witness a true convergence of knowledge, where all of the various strands of previous discussions- evolution, neurobiology, spiritual development, clinical psychology, and of course, polar bears- all begin to organize with a clear and elegant precision. We will also witness how this integrated knowledge is creating a diverse matrix of effective methods for developing instinctual intelligence. This matrix is spreading across the globe, through state-of-the-art science. It is also spreading more directly, through human contact and intuition as each one of us slowly but surely learns to step outside the box of the restrictive force.

The Dawn of a New Spiritual Sensibility

Hameed Ali always had a profound respect for all of the world's wisdom traditions. From a young age, he was aware that these esoteric practices could bring about extraordinary states of consciousness. When he was just in the beginning stages of his exploration of spirituality and psychology, he realized many of these ancient methods for refining and expanding human consciousness were restricted to a privileged few. Most of the spiritual masters of these traditions had made superhuman efforts to dedicate themselves to their quest. From Buddha to Jesus, these highly realized individuals had left all worldly desires and obligations behind it the pursuit of spiritual attainment. The vast majority of "non-spiritual" people continued with their daily lives, working and raising children. To Ali, this division of life into "spiritual" and "non-spiritual" made little sense. He had met a wide variety of people who had experienced extraordinary states of expanded consciousness. Some were overtly spiritual. Some were atheists. Others had expanded their consciousness through drugs. He himself had experienced deeply expanded states of consciousness simply sitting around watching TV. It became obvious to him that human beings could experience all sorts of expanded states of awareness, regardless if they considered themselves spiritual or not. In addition, this division of life into spiritual and non-spiritual seemed to go against the fundamental beliefs of the wisdom traditions that envision all humans as manifestations of the same divine source. Theistic traditions describe this source has the creativity of God, while Eastern traditions might refer to it as the play of divine consciousness. If all living things are emanations of the same divine source, how could one person or one activity or one culture be more "spiritual" than another?

Who is More Spiritual, a Monk or a Soccer Mom?

Ali was onto something. At the time, he was a student at the University of California at Berkeley, working towards his Ph.D. in physics. Berkeley in the 1960s was a flashpoint of the expanding human consciousness. It had every type of spiritual practice, psychotherapy, wild music, mind-altering substances, and alternative lifestyle imaginable. Ali grew increasingly fascinated by the mysterious potentials of human consciousness. He realized that the answers he was searching for could not be found by focusing exclusively on the scientific investigation of matter and fundamental particles. Putting aside his pursuit of a Ph.D. in physics, he focused his brilliant analytical mind on the nature of human consciousness. He sought to answer some very basic questions: What was the nature of the living consciousness of human life? What were the potentials of this living consciousness? Are these potentials available to everyone, or just dedicated practitioners of esoteric traditions?

The '60s were a turning point in Western civilization. Young adults were rejecting the dogmatic rigidity of the religious traditions that had dominated Western cultures for several centuries. In the US and Europe, people were exposed to the teachings of exotic spiritual traditions of the East. At the same time, music, art, and culture were awakening a sense of instinctual passion and freedom that was long suppressed. From this sense of freedom and limitless potential, a new sensibility was emerging. People were craving a more spiritually oriented lifestyle, but did not want the moral restrictions of orthodox religious traditions. They wanted the opportunity to explore the depths of their consciousness, but they were not willing to become monks or nuns. In this new world, humans were waking up to the fact that building a career, getting married, playing music, having sex, or driving your car was no less "spiritual" than praying, meditating, or becoming a priest. Even taking your kids to soccer practice can be an utterly sublime and transcendent experience. It was as if, all at once, people throughout the world began to realize that every aspect of life could be infused with a profound joy and satisfaction. Today, more and more individuals are embracing an organic spiritual sensibility that is rooted in the living passion of their bodies and the activities of daily life. Who says you cannot have profound insight into the depth of your consciousness and still raise children?

Ali was personally aware of this emerging spiritual sensibility right from the start. But he also noticed something very important: many of the traditional spiritual teachings that were available to Westerners were not designed to address the issues faced by individuals living in the modern world. In his extensive study of traditional spiritual practices, he noted that they were usually practiced in isolation, far away from the trials and tribulations of daily life. These "spiritual" individuals would have to meditate or perform other contemplative exercises for thousands upon thousands of hours. While these methods occasionally produced an enlightened sage here or there, most practitioners made only marginal progress. Few could maintain the arduous discipline needed for the advanced levels of training. Those that completed this rigorous training developed extraordinary capacities of concentration and insight into the workings of the human mind. However, these supposedly "enlightened" individuals did not seem to have much insight into their own emotional and instinctual behaviors. Throughout the '60s and '70s, many Westerners encountered spiritual teachers that seemed to have great abilities to experience transcendent states of consciousness- but almost no ability to control their instinctual impulses. Many of these gurus were widely known to have serious drug and alcohol problems, inappropriate and dangerous sexual relationships, and abusive attitudes toward their students. Devotees turned a blind eye to these blatantly dysfunctional behaviors, naively thinking that these gurus possessed a profound wisdom that "ordinary" individuals could not recognize due to their "unenlightened" condition. It was painfully obvious that some of the students of these teachers were developing similar traits.

A New Approach to Human Development

To Ali, it was clear that most modern Westerners, even the most sincere practitioners, were having a lot of trouble applying the esoteric insights of their spiritual practices into their daily lives. Their teachers would talk about love, peace, and compassion- all of which sounded wonderful. Then the students would come home to screaming children and stressed out spouses and the stack of bills waiting to be paid. Teaching people about love, peace, and compassion really did not help them find any peace or balance in their daily lives. It just set up some expectations of some idealized state of peaceful consciousness that seemed far removed from the realities of the daily world. Most people found it impossible to apply these teachings where they were needed most. In a very basic sense, their entrenched emotional and instinctual conflicts overwhelmed the good intentions of a more peaceful and spiritually oriented life.

As he began to investigate the situation further, Ali realized that he would have to acknowledge an obvious fact: living a spiritual life in the midst of the modern world was a considerable challenge. In fact, it was proving to be far more difficult than being a socially isolated spiritual practitioner in a pre-modern culture. If people wanted to have it all- live as normal people in the world and develop themselves spiritually- then it was obvious that the spiritual practices of the past were not going to work. Like Wilber, Ali recognized that traditional spiritual practices were not designed to address deep-seated emotional and instinctual conflicts. After all, it was just plain common sense. If a spiritual teaching were to be really effective in transforming the person's life, it would have to meet them *right in the middle* of the day-to-day emotional and instinctual conflicts which all adults experience. The sensibilities of this modern age required a new and innovative approach to human development. It became clear that this approach would have to have a sophisticated knowledge of both psychological dynamics and spiritual insight. He saw that if individuals included the psychological understanding of their emotional and instinctual conflicts from the start, it would be easier to integrate their spiritual insights into their daily lives. From this fundamental insight, the Diamond Approach began to take form.

The Diamond Approach begins with a simple fact: In order to make steady and sustainable progress on any path of spiritual development, the individual needs to address the most obvious and practical aspects of their life situation. This usually means dealing with some very basic emotional and psychological issues. In previous chapters, I have described this developmental plateau as a specific phase of life when the development of our instinctual intelligence begins to stagnate. This stagnation is not seen as unsolvable problem, just a basic fact of life. Ali saw time and time again that if these basic conflicts were not resolved, they would quickly undermine the individual's spiritual development. For instance, if an individual has a problem controlling his or her anger, then it might be difficult to find steady employment. Always having to search for a new job is time consuming and stressful. The person would have little time, energy, or money to devote to any kind of self-development. The prevailing sensibility at the time was that the individual should seek out psychotherapy to resolve this basic emotional conflict. Once this was accomplished, he could begin to follow a spiritual practice with more likelihood of success. Clearly, there is a major drawback to this approach. Most people have quite a few emotional and instinctual conflicts. If they waited to resolve them all before beginning any type of spiritual exploration, they would spend the rest of their lives in therapy.

Beginning with the Instincts

Ali, with his penetrating insight, recognized this fundamental problem. The dichotomy between psychological and spiritual development was based on a mistaken assumption about the nature of human spiritual realization. The ultimate development of human consciousness, according to most of the traditions, was associated with some kind of radiant inner peace, a sort of mystical equipoise of wisdom, transcendence, and deep understanding. "Spiritual enlightenment" was more or less equated with the attainment of this radiant inner peace. The prevailing notion was that individuals could only attain this spiritual state if they dedicated their lives to it, suffering years of discipline and hardship. Ali had questioned this assumption from the start. From his study of physics, he knew that the innate intelligence of the universe was elegant and efficient. Why should the development of human consciousness be any different? He quickly realized that comprehensive spiritual realization was not just the attainment of a single insight that required years upon years of suffering and discipline, after which one might taste a glimpse of inspiration or enlightenment. Rather, it was actually the systematic realization of an *entire spectrum* of qualities. Like a light passing through a prism, the potentials of human consciousness have many distinct facets and refined qualities. The Diamond Approach refers to these distinct qualities of refined consciousness as *essential aspects*. The fact that human consciousness can develop a diverse range of *distinct* refined qualities has profound implications for our understanding of instinctual intelligence, as we will see below.

As the Diamond Approach began to touch the life of more and more students, a distinct symmetry began to reveal itself. As students began to explore and understand their basic emotional conflicts each type of emotional or instinctual conflict was directly related to a specific essential aspect. Ali saw that these conflicts obscured the functioning of particular essential aspect that was inherent within the individual. The exploration of the psychological origins of the conflicts and distortions was an elegant and efficient pathway to profound levels of spiritual realization. For example, as individuals explored and resolved their conflicts around anger, the essential aspect of *Strength* would begin to function in the individual's life. Instead of getting angry and then having to deal with the awkward consequences of an aggressive outburst, the Essential aspect of Strength would allow them to assert their needs in a more intelligent and graceful way that was naturally attuned to the situation. Strength, like all essential aspects, arises as a part of human consciousness, but it also pervades our feelings, thoughts, bodies, and behaviors. There is no contradiction between the internal experience and the external expression. The natural capacity to assert one's self without anger was one step on a path of realizing the full range of potentials of human life. If individuals were no longer hampered by angry outbursts, then they could function a bit more smoothly in life. This would help their relationships, their careers, and just about every other dimension of their lives. They could think more clearly and behave more intelligently- and thus end up having more time and energy to continue their self-exploration.

Over the years, the Diamond Approach systematically helped individuals to investigate each and every type of emotional or instinctual conflict that was arising in their lives. Issues around relationships, sexuality, money, creativity, power, joy, survival, intelligence- every conceivable sphere of human activity- were welcomed by Ali. He helped his students to see that every type of conflict was an opportunity to realize a specific Essential aspect. In this way, Ali realized that addressing the deep-seated instinctual conflicts helped them enter into the transpersonal stages of human consciousness as described by Wilber. This was a radical change to the traditional spiritual methods that usually sought to ignore instinctual conflicts or required 20 to 30 years of sophisticated mediation techniques to integrate them into a refined spiritual awareness. With the contemporary methods of the Diamond Approach, students systematically resolved more and more of their basic psychological issues. Their spiritual realization was slowly but steadily integrated into every aspect of their lives. This was an elegant and efficient means of dissolving the instinctual stagnation and repressive barriers that limited transpersonal stages of development. Step by step, individuals could resolve psychological conflicts and develop a living, realistic, and *sustainable* experience of their most sublime human qualities. The realization of Strength could pave the way for the realization of Compassion, Will, Joy, Power, Peace- an infinite range of qualities. Ali himself has stated that there seems to be no limit or endpoint to the human potential. He sees the process of human development as being like the creation of a multifaceted diamond. The realization of each aspect adds another refined surface through which the Essential nature of existence can radiate, facilitating the recognition of one's self as an integrated and luminous being. This is why it is called it the Diamond Approach.

The Diamond Approach is only one example of the amazing new paradigms of human development that are emerging all over the globe. Many of these new paradigms are beginning to recognize that the most powerful and efficient pathway for developing human consciousness is through the instinctual dimensions of human experience. The exploration of instinctual energy is emerging as the most realistic and immediate method to bring about lasting personal transformation- and insure the collective evolution of humanity. These cutting-edge approaches to human development have discovered sophisticated techniques for helping adults break out of the stagnation that limits the growth and maturation of instinctual intelligence. However, if this knowledge is to become more widespread and impact humanity as a whole, it needs to be understood from a scientific perspective. In other words, we need to know how the process of transforming instinctual consciousness *actually works on a biological basis*.

The Emerging Science of Nervous System Recalibration

To understand the effectiveness of the cutting-edge techniques developed by Hameed Ali in the Diamond Approach, we have to return to our analysis of the effects of traumatic experiences we began in the last chapter. Remember the *dissociative freezing response* described by the trauma researchers van der Kolk and Levine? We saw how traumatic experiences are stored in the nervous system in isolated neural networks. These isolated networks contain memories of the traumatic experience, as well as information about the internal neurobiological responses that were activated during the traumatic event. As we know, traumatic experiences leave the nervous system in a state of hypervigilance, predisposing it to activate these networks at the slightest perception of danger. Because the nervous system is so hypervigilant, even a totally non-threatening stimulus can trigger the dissociative freezing response. This is what happens to individuals suffering from PTSD. When these networks are activated, they slip into a *distinct ego state*. This distinct ego state is characterized by the activation of specific neurobiological networks that are dormant when the individual is in a normal state of consciousness. Understanding how traumatic experiences create an *isolated, neurobiologically distinct identity* is the key to understanding how Ali's methods of transforming instinctual consciousness actually work.

Self-images

In his study of developmental psychology, Ali could see that the nervous systems of young infants and children are highly impressionable because the neuronal connections in their nervous systems are still forming. From the infant's subjective perspective, almost all of the early interactions with parents and caregivers are *instinctually significant* interpersonal exchanges. The interactive experiences are infused with considerable affective arousal. Almost every interaction with caregivers will result in the recording of a specific pattern of instinctual responses in the infant's developing brain. Ali observed that the process of recording the impressions of instinctually intense experiences continues throughout childhood, adolescence, and into adulthood. Because of the intensity of these experiences, the way a developing child's brain records these early instinctual experiences is *basically identical* to the way the adult brain records experiences of trauma. This means that the impressions stored in the brain's limbic and cerebral cortex structures will create isolated, neurobiologically distinct neural networks. These networks will be activated when similar interpersonal situations are encountered. This is just like the activation patterns of the neural networks that store the responses to traumatic experiences.

In his psychological and spiritual work with adults, Ali could see that the imprints left in these networks guide the individual's moment-to-moment emotional, perceptual, and cognitive experiences. They shape how adults instinctually respond to external and internal stimuli. This is especially true for interpersonal relationships, which often activate instinctually driven responses based on our earliest infantile and childhood experiences. Ali began to see how these accumulated memory networks exerted a profound influence on the individual's adult life. He recognized the specific ways in which they prevented the development of psychological clarity and mature spiritual realization. It is obvious that they also severely limit the development of the individual's instinctual intelligence. Ali described these isolated, neurobiologically distinct neural networks as *self-images*. These self-images function just like the *distinct ego states* described by van der Kolk.

The activation of the networks that comprise self-images is implicit. They operate just below the threshold of conscious awareness. When a self-image is active, individuals experience their awareness through the filter of these memory networks. Individuals literally experience the present moment through an implicit *image* of themselves that was formed in the past. If you were to close your eyes, the activation of a self-image would make you *feel* as if you were a small helpless child. This experience is similar to the activation of the networks associated with traumatic experiences. Self-images make the adult behave, think, and feel like they are still participating in the actual reality of a survival-threatening situation that occurred during childhood. Ali recognized that the primary barrier to unlocking the extraordinary potentials of the transpersonal stages of human consciousness were the restrictive influences imposed by self-images. One of his greatest accomplishments was to develop a precise method through which this restrictive influence could be reduced and even eliminated.

The Clinical Dynamics

Over time, Ali developed a specific technique to help his students in the Diamond Approach to systematically dissolve the restrictive influences of these self-images. It is usually carried out in a private session between himself and individual students, in a setting that is similar to a psychotherapy session. As the individual is examining a particular emotional, instinctual, or psychological conflict (usually some combination of the three) he or she will commonly experience vivid sensations, perceptions, images, and memories related a particularly stressful event in the past, usually in childhood. Depending on the age when the event took place, it is possible to ascertain the particular developmental stage in which the self-image was formed. The individual's attention is directed to the self-image. In most cases, the activation of the neural networks that comprise the self-image will cause the person to feel small and child-like. At the same time, feelings of anxiety and helplessness will also arise. This results from the activation of the memory networks in which the freezing response was recorded in the nervous system. The re-activation of the freezing response is often difficult for individuals to tolerate. They might begin to dissociate or want to change the subject. The technique requires that individuals continue to their direct attention to the embodied sensations of the frozen self-image. Teachers of the Diamond Approach will often remind students that the self-image is only a memory and that re-experiencing these childhood fears of weakness and despair will actually allow the nervous system to disengage these restrictive neural networks.

As the self-images surfaces in the student's awareness, a threshold is reached. The key element of Diamond Approach technique is to simultaneously direct individuals' attention toward the experience of their bodies as it is *actually perceived* within the real-time adult perspective. Without losing conscious awareness of the frozen childlike self-image, part of their attention is simultaneously directed to their adult bodies. This accomplished by having the students pay attention to their adult-sized arms and legs, gently sensing their muscles, breathing, and simply being aware of their actual size and strength *as it really is* in the present moment. When the self-image of the small frozen child is seen in comparison to the experience of adult physical reality in the present moment, something astonishing begins to happen:

The frozen self-image- along with the restrictive fear and anxiety- begins to dissolve.

The *Simultaneous Awareness* Technique

This type of deep neurobiological transformation is certainly not limited to Ali's work in the Diamond Approach. Similar techniques are also seen in cutting-edge treatments for healing trauma, such as those developed by Levine, van der Kolk, Pat Ogden, and others. It also happens naturally and spontaneously in the contexts of intimate relationships, when we hold our trembling lover. It can also happen in the artistic process, athletic endeavors, and in deep spiritual contemplation. Both the Diamond Approach technique and the new psychotherapeutic techniques for treating trauma empirically demonstrate that there is an innate capacity of our instinctual intelligence to clear out neurobiologically stored memories and behavioral patterns that restrict our ability to respond adaptively to the challenges of life. The critical element in many of these nervous system recalibration techniques is the *simultaneous awareness* of the self-image and the adult physical reality in the present moment. There is growing clinical evidence from contemporary researchers that indicates that if the two are not held in conscious awareness at the same time, the frozen self-image does not dissolve and its associated neural networks remain intact. Merely recognizing the self-image and its associated memories does not seem to alter nervous system functioning. *The simultaneous awareness of the self-image and the adult body is essential.* When this contrast is experienced, the innate instinctual wisdom of the human body will begin to reorganize the nervous system by dissolving the neural networks that comprise the frozen self-image. This liberates the functioning of the basic instinctual programs, allowing them to regain their natural responsiveness.

---

* Ali offers a word of caution concerning the use of these techniques. He has stressed that his psychological and spiritual techniques were developed for adults with healthy nervous systems that have developed a normal adult level of self-regulation and are thus capable of dissipating anxiety. As of yet, the techniques used in the Diamond Approach have not been scientifically tested on individuals who have severe physical and nervous system abnormalities, developmental delays, serious physical illnesses, or mental illness. These conditions may render their nervous systems temporarily or permanently unable to tolerate intense negative affects that arise during this process. Many somatically trained therapists working with individuals that have experienced trauma use the basic principles of the simultaneous awareness technique. Pat Ogden, founder of the Sensorimotor Psychotherapy Institute, has written extensively and trained therapists in several countries on the clinical dynamics of treating trauma, especially the simultaneous awareness technique, which she calls "dual processing".

How it Works

Modern science provides us with a neurobiological basis to understand how these nervous system recalibration techniques actually work. There are two central principles that that we need to consider in order to gain a full appreciation of how these techniques can transform the functioning of our basic instinctual programs. As we consider these two principles, notice how all of the evolutionary threads that were presented in earlier chapters begin to weave together. We can now begin to see the precise neurobiological processes that underlie the evolution of human instinctual consciousness.

1) Because humans evolved as social animals, recalibrating our basic instinctual programming requires establishing new memories of non-threatening interpersonal interaction.

We know from earlier chapters that the neural networks centered in the orbitofrontal cortex stores memories of instinctually intense experiences, especially those of an interpersonal nature. As we saw in our discussion of PTSD, one of the primary characteristics of the dissociated freezing response that characterizes PTSD is the lack of orbitofrontal inhibition of the amygdala. This is not caused by a lack of neural connections between the orbitofrontal cortex and the amygdala. The orbitofrontal cortex does not inhibit the amygdala because its functioning is influenced by the dissociative freezing response that was formed during the original traumatic event. In the original traumatic event, there *really was* an overwhelming threat from which the individual could not escape. In addition, in the face of overwhelming threats, the individuals feel abandoned, as if no one is there to help fight the attacker or to assist with an escape. It is now thought that one of the central therapeutic healing mechanisms that takes place in psychotherapeutic treatments- including those designed to treat PTSD- is the encoding of new positively charged memories of interpersonal emotional contact derived from the interaction with the therapist. These new memories are stored in the orbitofrontal networks. They will gradually begin exert some control over the amygdala, lessening the likelihood that it will jump into a hyperaroused state.

Accumulated impressions of non-threatening interpersonal contact allow fear to be replaced by trust. The individual no longer feels overwhelmed and abandoned. The networks that store the memories of external threats are gradually destabilized as experiences of more relaxed and loving human interaction are recorded. This process also affects the hippocampus. Positive human interactions contribute to the re-activation of hippocampal inhibitory connections with the amygdala and the lateral hypothalamus. This raises the activation threshold of the individual's arousal responses to low intensity or non-threatening stimuli. This model is now considered to be an increasingly accurate neurobiological description of the effects of psychotherapy and PTSD treatments. It has been confirmed by recent neuroimaging studies that conclusively demonstrate that a lack of right orbitofrontal cortex modulation of amygdaloid hyper-reactivity is a primary feature of PTSD emotional dysregulation symptoms.

2) The restoration of the adaptive functioning of our basic instinctual programs requires the destabilization of self-images of being weak and helpless that lie at the core of the dissociative freezing response.

We also know from previous chapters that the orbitofrontal cortex networks play a major role in the dissociative freezing response. The freezing response activates memories of internal body states that are stored in the orbitofrontal cortex and adjacent brain regions. The activation of these internal, embodied memories creates the subjective impression of being weak and helpless. The self-image of the dissociative freezing response consists of a matrix of impressions of feeling small and defenseless in the face of an overwhelming threat. State-of-the-art research can help us understand the neurobiological basis of the nervous system recalibration techniques used by Ali in the Diamond Approach. We now know that the treatments for PTSD developed by psychologists like Levine, van der Kolk, and Ogden are designed to systematically integrate dissociated memories of the freezing response into conscious awareness. They use techniques similar to those used in the Diamond Approach. These techniques help the individual tolerate feelings of being weak, helpless, and overwhelmed while simultaneously directing attention toward the *here and now* capacities of the adult body.

When the self-image and adult physical reality are experienced simultaneously, the neural networks that comprise the frozen self-images seem to lose their functional coherency. It is as if the new experiences of having an emotionally and instinctually resilient body *overwrite* the old memories of being weak, helpless, and frozen. The orbitofrontal cortex now "knows" that the individual has an adult body that can experience its instinctual energy, free from the restriction of the dissociated freezing response. The subconscious self-image of having a weak and defenseless body is dissolved by experiences of having a strong, instinctually resilient adult body. The dissolution of the weak and defenseless self-images also appears to re-activate hippocampal inhibitory connections with the amygdala and the lateral hypothalamus. If the individual's nervous system is no longer operating under the belief that it is small and defenseless, the individual's sensory and perceptual systems are more capable of evaluating *the reality* of external threats. As a result of these neurobiological changes, the neural activation patterns of the frozen self-image no longer function as a distinct ego state with maladaptive sensory, perceptual, affective, and cognitive characteristics. Often, when the simultaneous awareness technique is used in clinical settings, the frozen instinctual energy that was inhibited is discharged. This allows the interrupted defensive actions to be completed. The adult nervous system is now liberated from the ghosts of the past- and free to respond to the reality of the present moment.

Dissolving the Restrictive Force

Although Ali has a sophisticated knowledge of modern psychological science and neurobiology, his training in quantum physics and relativity taught him to look for the fundamental forces that govern the universe. This allowed him to take his psychological knowledge one step further. He had observed, in a very systematic way, how the steady accumulation of self-images during infancy, childhood, adolescence, and adulthood influence the overall development of the individual. It was obvious to him that the accumulation of self-images is what the psychological and spiritual traditions referred to as the *ego*. Western psychology had focused on the development of the ego as central means by which an individual could *function* in the world. The development of the ego was the source of the interpersonal skills, defense mechanisms, emotional regulation, and reality testing operations that allowed the person to successfully navigate the challenges of day-to-day living. In this view, the self-images that comprise the ego also provide a coherent sense of *identity*. By recognizing his or herself as the subjective center of these accumulated experiences, the individual can derive a sense of self that has emotional significance and stability over time. Just like Wilber, Ali recognized that the development of the ego's functional and self-identification capacities were absolutely necessary for the overall development of the human being. They both observed that the development of the adult ego marked a completion of the *personal* stage of development. They also could clearly see that the development of the ego imposed restrictions on the individual's transpersonal and spiritual development.

Self-images accumulated during infancy, childhood, and adolescence constrains individuals' ability to function in the world as an emotionally and instinctually mature adult. The neural networks that underlie the self-images restrict the operation of their natural instinctual intelligence. These networks impose specific neurobiological restrictions on their capacity to function with a full, unrestricted sense of strength, compassion, determination, joy and power. They also limit the way people feel about themselves and how they recognize themselves. One of the great innovations of the Diamond Approach is the understanding that this restricted sense of identity was exactly what the world's great wisdom traditions had been describing for centuries as the central barrier to authentic spiritual realization. The matrix of accumulated self-images acts as a *restrictive force* that causes the individual to think and act as if they were an isolated entity, totally cut off from the rest of the universe. In the Eastern traditions, the attachment to this isolated sense of self is seen as the primary barrier to development of consciousness and profound spiritual realization. In the theistic traditions, the clinging to an isolated sense of self blocks the submission to God's will- and the ultimate union with the divine. From the perspective of the Taoist traditions, the belief that one is an isolated individual is recognized to be the restrictive force that prevents the joining with the Way of the Ten Thousand Things.

The Dissolving Capacity of Instinctual Intelligence

Ali, relentlessly inquiring into the fundamental forces of reality, realized that the dissolution of self-images was not just a neurobiological phenomenon. He saw something even more fundamental. The dissolution of self-images is a natural expression of the deeper intelligence the universe. As we know, animals have the innate ability to discharge their frozen instinctual energy. The same instinctual wisdom that flows through the trembling muscles of the polar bear is what dissolves the restrictive force of the self-images in humans. Ali recognized that this dissolution is a naturally occurring aspect of human consciousness- and, therefore- a natural and inseparable part of the universe.

Many of the world's wisdom traditions acknowledge this dissolving essence as a phenomenological and ontological reality. Some spiritual traditions refer to this dissolving essence as *emptiness* or *the void*. The Buddhist tradition is known for its highly developed philosophical and experiential understanding of emptiness. Some schools in the Tibetan Buddhist traditions view emptiness as an absolute nothingness. Other Eastern spiritual traditions view the void as the unmanifest nature of the universe from which all things mysteriously arise. Many of the contemplative practices of both Buddhist and other Eastern traditions place a great deal of emphasis on cultivating a deep experiential awareness of this mysterious, ineffable void. It is said that even a brief glimpse of this emptiness begins to remove distorting influences from the individual's consciousness. In short, it *dissolves the restrictive force of the ego*. Theistic traditions do not emphasize the emptiness aspect of the dissolving essence. However, we might understand the notions of God's infinite grace and forgiveness as a direct manifestation of this dissolving capacity. God's power to heal the human soul is based on the cleansing away of the guilt, shame, and suffering of past sins. In most of these traditions, it is said that the mercy of God is infinite, and that no action- no matter how horrible- can be cleansed from the soul of the both the perpetrator and the victim. The submission to God's grace can dissolve the restrictive force of the ego.

In a more modern sense, we might simply say that part of the innate instinctual intelligence of the universe is the capacity to cleanse the nervous systems of living beings.

Spontaneous Expression

The profound insights of Hameed Ali and the Diamond Approach offer new possibilities for living an instinctually intelligent life in the modern world. More and more people, following a wide variety of paths and using different techniques, are discovering the same fundamental truths about the innate capacities of instinctual intelligence. The human nervous system is so marvelously plastic that there are infinite numbers of ways that it can be cleansed of inhibiting neural impressions. It possesses unlimited points of intervention where the restrictive force of the ego can be disrupted- thereby restoring the capacity of our basic instinctual programs to operate with freedom. As a species, we are slowly learning how to gain some freedom from the perceptual, emotional, and cognitive restrictions imposed by the matrix of self-images. We are evolving out of the instinctual stagnation that has limited the human potential for so long. As we begin to reconnect with the deeper origins of our instinctual intelligence, *all* of our basic instinctual programs can operate with more flexibility and intelligence. When this happens, the neural networks of the basic instinctual programs work in the balanced and adaptively responsive manner in which they evolved. One obvious benefit is that the nervous system can make more realistic appraisals of the outside environment, thus preventing the inappropriate activation of fight, flight, or freezing responses. Our growing knowledge of how to treat PTSD and other psychological disturbances is already changing the course of human evolution, one brain cell at a time. The restoration of the body's natural instinctual intelligence makes life a whole lot easier. But that's just the tip of the iceberg.

Being Selfless in the Modern World

The emerging science of nervous system recalibration provides a sophisticated method for the realistic integration of the instinctual energy of the human body with the highest aspirations of the human soul. When we step outside the box of the restrictive force, we are able to experience ourselves- and our bodies- as part of the living universe. Within this freedom, we are able to re-connect with our animal origins and the ultimate source of our instinctual intelligence. This freedom carries with it some profound implications. To begin with, if the human body is truly an inseparable expression of the instinctual wisdom of the entire universe, then we have the access to the same forces we have seen operating since the very inception of the universe. Within each human being is the same majestic power of creativity that gave rise to the Big Bang. Within each human being is the same organizing intelligence that shapes the mathematical precision of galaxies and solar systems. Within each human being is the same spontaneous brilliance that exudes from light. Within each human being is boundless unfolding dynamism that sets all of creation in ceaseless motion. And within human consciousness is the same eternal awareness that witnesses and experiences the boundless participation of life.

As we begin to recognize that the true nature of a human being *is* the unrestricted participation in the intelligence of the universe, a deeper dimension of our social instincts also begins to arise. Our hearts open to the fact that we are made of the same fabric as our fellow humans, as well as all living beings. It is true that we are all composed of atoms that were originally formed inside of stars. But our connection runs even deeper than that. In the Buddhist tradition, it is said that when the inherent emptiness of the universe dissolves the egoic matrix of self-images- even just a little bit- we begin to be aware of the suffering of all beings that are still trapped by the restrictive force. From this awareness, a tiny bit of compassion for all living beings spontaneously arises. As we become less identified with the restrictive force of the ego, human consciousness begins to recognize itself as a seamless part of the larger fabric of all creation. Being selfless in the modern world means that we feel a natural and choiceless responsibility to all living beings- including the planet and its living ecosystems. Because we were born in the form of a particular type of being- a human being- we have a natural and innate connection to our fellow *Homo sapiens*. The more each human being liberates themselves from the restrictive force of the ego, the more the natural instincts of compassion and responsibility will influence the course of our collective evolution.

The Spectrum of Instinctual Intelligence

So, what happens to our instincts when the restrictive force finally begins to dissolve?

In a very direct way, the natural intelligence of the universe begins to operate through the living instinctual experience of the human being. When this universal intelligence begins to infuse the living reality of the human world, each of our instinctual systems is free to express themselves with a spontaneous wisdom that is inherent in their evolutionary design. Our self-protective instincts are freed from the distortions of anger and fear. We feel a strength that allows us to assert our needs with courage and clarity. Our social instincts no longer get caught in the web of jealousy, envy, and co-dependency. Instead, we feel a natural connection to all living things that is smooth and loving. When our instinctual energy is aligned with the true evolutionary wisdom of the universe, it becomes easier to support ourselves and others. We feel a natural confidence to persevere in the face of difficult challenges and a capacity to fulfill our responsibilities with a graceful consistency. The evolutionary force of the universe also infuses the human being with an inexplicable joy and delight with the pleasures of our embodied senses. A playful passion replaces the repression and stagnation that used to wilt our lifeforce. Freeing us from our darkest fears, the innate instinctual wisdom of the universe unleashes the extraordinary power of the human being to face into the deepest mysteries of existence. As it returns to its source, the human soul breathes a profound and silent peace.

This evolution of our individual and collective instinctual intelligence is not just a bunch of beautiful words and idealistic dreams. It's actually happening.

CHAPTER 13

Assertive Strength

Now that we have a sense of *what* a more evolved instinctual intelligence might look like, we're going to explore *how* to this knowledge is being applied. To do this, we have to answer some very basic questions: As our instincts evolve, how do they become more intelligent? What is the nature of this intelligence? How can this intelligence be used to make our lives more efficient, healthier, and more satisfying?

To answer these questions, we first need to understand that each one of the specific instinctual systems we have studied in previous chapters has its own unique forms of intelligence. The notion of multiple intelligent instinctual systems is somewhat analogous to the notion of *multiple intelligences* that has been advanced by Harvard psychologist Howard Gardner. However, there is one important difference. The different forms of instinctual intelligence are not directly associated with specific skills. In other words, increasing your instinctual intelligence will not make you a math genius, linguistic expert, star athlete, or a master of the other types of intelligence described by Gardner. The various types of instinctual intelligence that we will be examining in the last section of this book are more of an embodied wisdom that can be utilized in a variety of situations. In that sense, we can come to understand instinctual intelligence as a set of core nervous system capacities that act as a kind of master intelligence that underlies all types of human development. The wisdom inherent in our embodied instinctual intelligence can be applied in our work and professional careers, as well as relationships, creative endeavors, raising children, athletics, and spiritual development. In the deepest sense, these types of evolved nervous system capacities can enhance every aspect of our lives.

The Heart of our Instinctive Intelligence

The first and most obvious example of these types of intelligence can be seen in the qualities of our evolved self-protective instincts. Normally, these instincts are associated with aggression and violence. And let's face it- violence and intelligence aren't exactly synonymous. Quite the opposite. Violence arises when we lose touch with our humanity and intelligence. When we think of the sheer power of human aggression, our initial response might be a visceral cringe. Given the history of human civilization, it is easy to see why this gut reaction might seem painfully honest, if not inevitable. We keep a wary eye on this volatile instinctual energy, knowing that it has a tendency to boil over. Every continent on this planet has a trail of blood that flows from the misuse of our aggressive impulses. In many ways, aggression and violence are signs that intelligence has failed.

Yet, at the same time, it is possible to recognize deeper wisdom within our aggressive impulses. In our clearest moments, we have all experienced a desire to be confident and capable. We want to feel like we can protect ourselves and our loved ones from harm. We want to feel like we can accomplish whatever we want to do. We want to feel empowered to take risks and engage life in a bold, expansive dance- wherever our dreams may take us. Deep down, we know there is a source of life within us, a source that spirals back to our truest selves. Brave, bold, and confident, the resurgence of this fearless energy is always ready to spring into action. This burst of assertive energy is at the heart of our instinctual intelligence. It is what gives us the courageous wisdom to engage the adventure of life.

The First Step Takes Courage

At first glance, it's not easy to see courage as a form of intelligence. However, without courage, the entire enterprise of enhancing and evolving our instinctual intelligence would be impossible. Sure, I could fill the whole last section of this book by laying out the latest breakthroughs in neurobiological research and nervous system recalibration techniques. But I would be lying if I said it were possible to make much use of that technical knowledge *without first awakening your courage*. It takes a lot of guts to change the status quo. Evolving the instinctual intelligence of humanity is not just a matter of applying scientific facts, therapeutic techniques, or a set of spiritual insights. It is a human enterprise- one that calls out for the awakening the most exquisite of human qualities of bravery and daring. Without these qualities, the commitment to enhancing and evolving our instinctual intelligence will be easily overwhelmed. The clandestine forces of ignorance and apathy will make easy prey of anyone afraid to activate innate boldness encoded in each cell of our bodies.

How do we awaken this courage? This as the first question we need to answer to enter the next phase of evolving our instinctual intelligence.

Facing Into our Fears

The simple truth is that our courage is often choked by some knot of anger, or drained by the silent shroud of fear. The gnawing dissatisfaction of our unexpressed protective energy wears us down, leaving us irritable and ineffective. As we have seen, the strongest influence on the development of our instinctual tendencies arises from our early relationships with our parental caregivers. These influences shape our adult attitudes and beliefs about our instinctual aliveness, implicitly dictating what is safely expressed and what must be held back. To understand how we can break free of these habits, we need to learn to apply our growing knowledge of instinctual intelligence we developed in previous chapters.

To begin with, it can be helpful to understand how the basic instinctual programs were recognized, supported, encouraged, and valued during childhood. This gives us a powerful tool to free ourselves from the inhibiting self-images stored in our nervous systems. We know that the natural self-protective programs can become inhibited. This often occurs when very young children reduce the arousal levels of their sympathetic nervous systems in response to the immediate needs of the mother and other family members. Damping down the nervous system leaves a debilitating self-image of being weak and helpless.

The nervous system recalibration techniques described in previous chapters demonstrate how the inhibiting influence of this self-image can be disrupted. In a simplified example, we can observe how a skilled therapist might help an individual direct his or her conscious attention to the feelings of weakness. By focusing on the feelings, thoughts, and images of weakness, it is possible to recognize the self-image of a young child. At first, we might begin to remember situations where it was not safe to assert ourselves. When the neurobiological networks that mediate this self-image are activated, the individual image feels small, fearful, and collapsed- both emotionally and physically. This self-image is of a young child that was punished for trying to separate from the maternal caregiver. This punishment took the form of being abandoned, rejected, or simply ignored. When children are left alone after initiating the separation, their nervous systems *initially* react with frustration and arousal. But within a short period of time, their nervous systems will go into a state of inhibitory shock. The absence of love, touch, and reassurance triggers an instinctual response of sympathetic inhibition. Just like the freezing responses that are activated during traumatic experiences, the nervous system is imprinted with a self-image. This self-image is what restricts our sympathetic systems- *as well as our capacity to feel courageous*- as adults.

At first, it will be difficult to tolerate the feelings of weakness that arise as the self-image is activated. They will bring up feelings of worthlessness and anxiety. The weakness and anxiety feels like a threat to the individual's instinctual well-being. This is where it is helpful to have an experienced and compassionate therapist who can gently guide the individual into places where he or she might otherwise be afraid to go. At this junction, the therapist would direct attention to the actual feelings of strength and vitality within the individual's adult body. The contrast between the childlike self-image and the strong adult body will begin to dissolve the self-images of weakness and smallness.

How We See Ourselves

Although this is a relatively simplified example of how the process actually works, it allows us to recognize a basic principle of instinctual intelligence: How we view ourselves determines how we express our self-protective instincts.

Not long ago, I read a story about a remarkable 38 year-old woman in Syracuse, New York. One afternoon she was sitting in her motorized wheelchair waiting for a bus. She has cerebral palsy and is unable to walk or drive. Suddenly, out of nowhere, a teenage boy grabbed her purse from under her arm and ran off at top speed. When I first read this, my reaction was one of pity. I thought to myself, "poor woman...a helpless victim of our violent culture." What I read next surprised me.

Without hesitating, the woman engaged her wheelchair and took off after her assailant. She chased after him for two blocks, dodging patches of snow and cracked holes in the sidewalks.

"I wasn't really scared. I was more angry. I felt violated", she reported. She bravely followed the young man until he ran between two houses and she could no longer keep up with him. She proceeded to a nearby business and called the police. Based on her detailed description, police apprehended the purse-snatcher within a half an hour. He had already purchased a flashy new cell phone with the money he stole and was caught with several personal items that were in the purse. I am amazed she had the presence of mind to remember the precise details of his clothing and other physical characteristics. Not only was she physically bold, but her mind was observant and clear.

"He thought he could take advantage of me because I am disabled." she added later. "I think he saw me as vulnerable." Nothing could be further from the truth. Clearly, this naïve young man did not count on the fact that our heroine did not have a self-image of being weak and vulnerable. If she did, it was instantly immolated by the surge of self-protective energy. This courageous woman was not going to allow herself to become a victim. To me, she a perfect example of the indomitable force of evolution that protects and affirms life. This intelligent energy has tremendous potency, regardless of our physical stature.

Freedom from Self-images

When the self-image of weakness has been dissolved, we feel liberated, capable of feeling any emotion that arises. Our innate impulse to assert ourselves is no longer blocked. Neurobiologically, we can see that the frozen self-images of being weak are encoded in the orbitofrontal networks. When activated, they exert too much inhibitory control over the limbic and autonomic regions that regulate the sympathetic nervous system. This inhibition chokes off the sensations from the heart and belly. The disruption of the frozen self-image allows the impulses of the lower regions of the brain to exert themselves in accord with their design. This is a classic example of the *bottom up* integration that characterizes an evolutionary advancement in the functioning of our instinctual intelligence. Information from lower regions of the brain and the body are free to enter into the individual's conscious awareness. Liberated from this habitual restriction, the entire nervous system is recalibrated. The individual will experience an entirely new *sympathetic signature* that is more actively shaped by the sensations of the heart and belly. The sense of being an empowered adult helps us to draw on the deep instinctual resources available to us in any situation. If we wish to transform our fears into the mature assertive strength of an adult, we have to allow this potent energy to inform us.

Our resources include the capacities for self-reliance. This gives us the courage to separate from relationships that no longer serve our interests. We are not afraid to feel alone. This is important. *Really important.* Remember that the feelings of weakness implicit in the self-image were originally imprinted on the nervous system as a result of feeling threatened. At a basic level, if we acted aggressively toward our parents in response to feeling threatened, we risk the loss of their love and potential social isolation. This is a very primal fear. As children, we learn to inhibit our sympathetic nervous systems to secure our social bonds. When we are free from the fears of loneliness and isolation, a feeling of *independence* arises. This is totally different from feeling abandoned. When we are no longer experiencing ourselves through the self-image of a young child, we realize that it is up to us to defend ourselves and protect our life-energy. No one is going to magically come and defend us from every threat.

The capacity to live one's life with courage and independence is particularly important for surviving in today's modern economic environment. Corporations are no longer the stable and reliable sources of employment and security they once were. The ability to function as an *independent entrepreneur* is a new and indispensable requirement for lasting economic security. To thrive in this challenging environment, one needs a fairly evolved degree of self-protective instinctual intelligence. It provides the assertive yet balanced energy we need to take on any challenge that arises. Not only can we take care of ourselves more efficiently- we have more courage to confront and challenge anyone who is not aligned with our life goals. The intelligence of our self-protective instincts can be summarized as follows:

> At the core of our instinctual intelligence is a courageousness that is the heart of the human spirit. This courage is a form of intelligence in that it gives us the capacity to *know* that we can deal with the challenges of life. This knowing goes beyond words and concepts. It is a deeper and more direct form of intelligence that allows our gut instincts to inform our thoughts and actions. It gives us the confidence to overcome the inhibitory effects of our self-judgment and inner fears.

The courage that arises from coming into contact with our hearts and belly is not just a powerful emotional experience. It awakens a deep intelligence. Opening our hearts tempers aggressive impulses with a natural wisdom that takes the reality of other people's well-being into account. This may seem unbelievable at first. But it's not so far fetched. Think of the people you love. You don't have to "figure out" how to love them with some complex set of calculations. Your concern for them arises spontaneously; it's naturally woven into your feelings and actions. Even in complex situations, you automatically take their safety into consideration without thinking about it. Your instinctual intelligence effortlessly includes them. But how do our protective instinctual systems "know" exactly what to do?

A Precise Design

I was out watering my lawn this morning when I felt a sharp pain on the top of my foot. I instantly dropped the hose and reached down into the top of my shoe. My hands dug into my laces, untying them and loosening the tongue at the same time. The top of my foot exposed, I began frantically sweeping the skin. All of this happened in less then a second. Only then did my mind put together the stinging sensation and the small buzzing creature that flew out of my shoe. I had been stung by a bee.

Separating Protection from Violence

Now, I'll be the first to admit that on the grand scale of the instinctual universe, this is a pretty trivial incident. However, it does reveal something quite fundamental about the nature of our self-protective impulses: *they can act with great precision.* Far from the messy and violent menaces they are often portrayed to be, our self-protective responses can express themselves with an economical precision and elegance that we rarely recognize. Using this precision, we can examine the hidden intelligence behind these responses. This will help us discriminate its life affirming wisdom from the ugliness and destruction often mistakenly attributed to our self-protective instincts.

One of the first steps of enhancing our instinctual intelligence is to separate the life-supporting actions of self-protection from the impulses of anger and violence. The innate function of our self-protective instincts is to defend the physical health of our bodies. When I felt the stinging sensation on my foot, my first impulse was *not* to kill the bee. It was to stop the pain. This is a *huge* distinction.

There is a physiological basis to this distinction. As we saw in the first chapter, the neuroarchitectural design of the human self-protection system can generate a wide variety of flexible responses to changing environmental conditions. We know that at the core of this system are the primal structures of brainstem and limbic regions. The basic circuits between the amygdala, the hypothalamus, and the periaqueductal gray (PAG) region of the midbrain are always involved in self-protective responses. As we saw above, these networks are activated automatically, providing the *bottom up*, instantaneous assertion of our protective needs. We have also seen how the basic impulses of assertive energy are modulated by the frontal lobes and the hippocampus. These structures help to refine our perceptions of reality and produce more flexible and sophisticated adaptations to an infinite variety of changing environmental conditions and situations. They exert a *top down* control over the limbic and autonomic regions. Modulating neural information also flows from the orbitofrontal and prefrontal corticies to the core of the midbrain and the brainstem. The result is a complex interactive network of excitatory and inhibitory circuits. They continuously adjust their responses to each other, as well as responding to the moment to moment changes in the external environment. When their functioning is not altered by a frozen self-image, the bottom up and top down circuits strike a creative balance that produces flexible and highly intelligent responses to any challenge that arises.

The distorting influence of anger

As we can see, the networks that comprise our self-protective instincts form an incredibly complex and intelligent system. When we talk about enhancing and evolving our instinctual intelligence, we do not mean altering the basic design of these systems. Our focus is on *clearing out the influences of frozen self-images* that limit the capacity of these systems to function in a precise way. From this perspective, we can begin to see how the neural networks of frozen self-images obscure the precision of these systems by imposing a distorting influence of anger and violence.

The self-image of being under constant threat exerts an overstimulating influence on the limbic and midbrain regions. These self-images are encoded during early childhood, when experiences of abuse or neglect predispose the nervous system higher levels of sympathetic activation. The self-images of always having one's well-being a risk will chronically overactivate the core brain regions that mediate protective responses- namely the amygdala, hypothalamus, and the PAG.

As a result, they will exert too much *bottom up* influence on the entire nervous system. This is exactly opposite from the top-down inhibition that suppresses protective responses.

The self-image of anger

At the core of this self-image is a small child that can only get its needs met by whining, complaining, and being angry. As adults, when tend to feel resentful when this self-image is activated. Because the sensations of resentment and anger are unpleasant, adults develop behavioral strategies to discharge this aggressive energy. The problem with this strategy is that it does not really effectively sooth the nervous system. Plus, this childlike expression of aggression creates and exacerbates interpersonal conflicts. We end up feeling dissatisfied. Plus, other people are pissed off. It's a surefire lose-lose situation.

Why doesn't getting angry soothe the beast inside us? The insights of Peter Levine and Hameed Ali provide a direct answer to this question. Levine observed that some of his clients would reenact dangerous or violent situations in an attempt to discharge the self-protective instinctual energy that was suppressed in the original traumatic event. However, when they would simply discharge the energy, all that really happened was the networks that comprise the aggressive self-image became hyperaroused. Instead of dissolving, they were reinforced. A critical element was missing. These individuals were only aware of the self-image of being under attack. In a very direct physical sense, these individuals were not in touch with reality. Remember that Ali stressed the importance of the simultaneous awareness of the self-image *and* the reality of the one's body and surrounding environment.

Ali found that the key to dissolving the hyperarousing self-image is to help individuals feel this energy *without acting on it*. Usually, we want to discharge our angry impulses in some way or to talk about our feelings over and over. In order for hyperarousing angry self-image to dissolve, it is necessary to feel the intense arousing emotions without discharging them. It is not easy to tolerate the feelings of boiling heat, frustration, anger, or rage. An experienced therapist can offer guidance and a supportive presence that makes the process manageable. By simultaneously placing one's awareness on the sensations and feelings of the physical body and the external environment, the self-image can dissolve. New inputs are introduced to the neural networks that were hyperactivating the self-protective responses in the amygdala, hypothalamus, and PAG. The perception of an adult body that is not under threat, coupled with the perception of a safe external environment destabilizes the old networks. This is a classic example of *top-down* integration that recalibrates the individual's sympathetic signature.

More intelligent, more precise

So, how does this top-down integration enhance our instinctual intelligence? The answer, quite simply, is that it makes it more precise. It makes our nervous systems more intelligent by increasing perceptual accuracy and the cognitive assessment of external reality. It also increases the precision of our assertive responses. We are able to protect ourselves without becoming aggressive and violent. We know exactly where the line of self-protection ends and where the escalation into violence begins. Consider the bee that crawled into my shoe. When I was stung, I felt a reddish flash of arousal through my body- as if an electric current had suddenly jolted my muscles.

My automatic impulse was to remove the irritation from my skin. I had no thought- or even a mental image- of wanting to attack or harm the bee. *I didn't even know what was causing the pain.* My first instinct was to protect myself. It was not to inflict pain on someone or something else.

After I brushed the bee off my foot, it fell to the ground. As it was buzzing and sputtering on the grass, I felt a surge of heat, emanating from the back of my neck and into my face and chest. Sympathetically aroused, I was perceptually primed to detect the slightest indication a further threat. I was ready to stomp on the bee. It was spinning in circles on the ground, buzzing and sputtering. I could see it posed no further threat. I walked away, wanting to take care of my foot. Killing the bee would not protect me any further. The threat had passed. I could still feel the heat and arousal. But my higher brain regions were signaling that there was no more threat. My self-protective systems had produced a protective response without escalating into unnecessary violence. We can now see how useful this form of evolved self-protective intelligence is:

Our innate instinctual intelligence is inherently precise. When they are free from fear and anger, our self-protective instincts act with clarity and economy. This type of instinctual intelligence functions in a very efficient manner. It integrates our refined cognitive capacities with our primal impulses- allowing us to assert our needs and desires without creating unwanted consequences. This instinctive intelligence also allows us to treat our bodies with respect by not stressing them beyond their healthy limits.

This understanding allows us to discern the key differences between violence and intelligent self-protection. First of all, the degree of sympathetic activation affects the way we see things. A full-blown sympathetic arousal escalates into an activation of the hypothalamo-pituitary-adrenocortical (HPA) axis. This primes the nervous system for a natural unrestricted blast of fury. There is no top-down regulation of the primal self-protective responses. We don't even know if the external environment has changed and the threat has disappeared. We are literally blind with rage. We can also discern the difference in our bodies. When we feel angry, frustrated, or violent, there is usually a feeling of irritation that *lingers* in the belly and chest. This is caused by the release of glucocorticoid cortisol, which helps the body adapt to the stress of intense metabolic activation. But it continues to circulate in our bloodstream long after the immediate danger has passed. It continues to arouse the sympathetic system. This is the underlying cause of burnout that is so prevalent in the modern world. Our minds won't let go of the situation and this frustration makes our bodies feel prickly and harsh. We want to push those irritating feelings outside of us by discharging the energy at everyone and everything that annoys us.

In contrast, when an undistorted self-protective response arises, there is no sense of irritation. Our bodies feel warm and energized, but inside this feeling is a perceptual clarity alert responsiveness. The bottom-up integration gives us a smooth surge of energy. The top-down integration allows us to respond to changing external conditions instantly. Our bodies feel protected, the heat of our assertion will give us the energy to clear away obstacles and interference. Because of the balanced neuroarchitechture of our self-protective systems, our arms and legs will not feel violent or clumsy. Instead, we are agile and alert. Our energy is not over the top, but we will completely capable of "amping" up our assertiveness if conditions call for it.

Sharper Minds

The integrated precision of our self-protective programs establishes a foundation for enhancing our instinctual intelligence. It provides a dramatic boost to our thought processes. It literally makes us smarter. When the sympathetic system is activated in a balanced way, a cascade of excitatory effects is activated through the sympathetic-adrenomedullary (SAM) axis. This is primarily due to optimal levels of corticotrophin being released into the nervous system. Overall, the activation of the SAM axis enhances the perception of the external environment. Even low-level stimuli evoke an orienting response and attentional focus. In a potentially dangerous environment, this attentional focus helps to further identify and evaluate any other potentially threatening stimuli. In our everyday lives, the balanced activation of the SAM axis will make our thoughts feel more crisp and clear.

This balanced arousal of our nervous systems does not escalate into a hyperarousing HPA stress response- so our energy and clarity does not come at the expense of burnout. Our minds see possibilities and solutions, instead of fears and threats. There is a sense of expansion, as if our minds, bodies, and feelings have been freed from an invisible set of constraints. When there is no restrictive self-image to block its presence, we feel a sense of capacity and effectiveness that can competently respond to the situation at hand. It feels like our instinctual energy is *doing the work for us*- we are actually riding a natural surge of energy. We feel bold and assertive, but in a natural, unforced way.

Some people have described this form of instinctual intelligence as "knowing" exactly what to do as we are doing it. There is no sense of doubt or deliberation. This heightened state of awareness arises from being totally in the moment. Athletes, musicians, surgeons, and other professionals that need to execute flawlessly in demanding situations often refer to this state as *flow*. As we learn to trust this natural flow, we feel as if our minds extend directly into the situation at hand and allow us to participate fully. We know intuitively what to do, and we are not afraid to do it. Our minds feel supple and energetic- totally capable of organizing and effortlessly understanding the most complex situations.

This more intelligent and reality-based instinctual energy will begin to present new possibilities for action, thinking, and feeling that we have never imagined were possible. We feel like we can freely align our instinctual energy with our responsibilities, as well as our dreams. We know what to do without endlessly having to figure it out and weigh all the options and consider everyone's feelings and assuage our inner doubts. Our minds feel capable of cutting through the riff raff without collapsing or becoming aggressive. In general, see can now see how this type of intelligence changes the way we see the world:

At a very deep level, this form of instinctual intelligence imbues our minds with highly evolved capacities of discrimination and analysis. Its balanced neurophysiological arousal of the nervous system allows the human mind to cut through the inertia of old mental and emotional habits. As a result, we can understand reality at more complex levels- bringing more insight to our selves and the world around us.

When this intelligence is allowed to function without restriction, it can be applied to all areas of our lives that require precise thinking. Our ability to think in a clear manner helps us grasp the truth of the situation we are analyzing. We become more objective about our lives, our senses become sharper and more refined. Our minds not only think with clarity- our bodies actually feel and sense with discriminating acuity.

Aligning our Instincts

The integrated functioning of our protective energy is the true engine of our continuing instinctual evolution. It gives us the burst of courage and strength we need to separate from our old patterns of stagnation. It helps us grow into mature, independent adults that can take care of ourselves. It also gives us the mental clarity and focus we need to begin the challenging process of aligning our instinctual energy with our life goals and deepest aspirations. When we live our lives in alignment with this assertive energy, we have the capacity to rise to the challenges of life with courage and self-confidence. We might find ourselves doing things we never dared to try before- like taking a class in martial arts or starting a new business. This integrated alignment is the next step of the evolution of our instinctual intelligence- and the basis for increasingly profound levels of satisfaction, effectiveness, and delight. Freed from restrictive self-images, we no longer deliberate about trying to be good or avoiding being bad. We act spontaneously, letting the self-protective wisdom of the universe flow through us, trusting its natural intelligence.

In that sense, we can see the evolution of our instinctual intelligence as the alignment of our self-protective instinctual energy with the natural individuating wisdom of the universe. It is as if the assertive, individuating energy of all creation is acting through our individual human organism. The tenacity of this self-asserting force cannot be suppressed. It is present in all living organisms. It is an extension of the processes behind eternal formation of individuated structures of the material universe, such as in the discrimination of matter into atomic particles. Within our self-protective instincts is the essential organizing intelligence that relentlessly shapes the ocean of matter into distinct planets, stars, and galaxies. It is the natural capacity of our instinctual consciousness to act in a way that preserves and defends our precious life. The energy of self-protection makes us unique individuals. From this eternal perspective, we can sense the sacred life-sustaining intelligence that exists in each living creature.

CHAPTER 14

Real Connection

Oprah Winfrey gets it.

Look into her eyes next time you see her interviewing someone on her TV show. You can viscerally feel that she understands where the person is coming from. Oprah has a highly developed form of instinctual intelligence. She oozes empathy. You can see it in her face, her emotions, and her gestures. It's in the way she leans forward ever so slightly to listen. It's in the way she shares her reactions with her audience. Her being reflects what her guests are feeling, magnifying the most private of emotions to millions of viewers. Oprah allows you to step into her skin. Sure- what the guests are saying might be interesting- but it's Oprah's reaction that moves us the most. That's why people all over the globe keep watching.

Oprah is a new breed of women that is leveraging her highly developed social intelligence into unprecedented personal success and social influence. But how does she do it? Is it luck? Some mysterious secret? Or can our knowledge of instinctual intelligence help us to understand exactly how Oprah became a billionaire *and* an enormously powerful agent for enlightened social action?

Empathetic Intelligence

The capacity to form intense social bonds is one of the essential things that makes us human. The neurobiological systems that underlie our instinctual consciousness have evolved in response to the need for deep and lasting connections with other human beings. Infants cannot survive if their instinctual needs for connection, love, nurturance, and empathy are not met. As adults, we can learn to shut these needs down and pretend they are insignificant or childish. But to grow into mature instinctually intelligent adults, the capacity to feel love and connection is indispensable. Our instinctual intelligence cannot evolve without it.

Now, in many ways, this may seem obvious. But if we're honest- many of us experience a lot of confusion when it comes to love and connection. I'm not just talking about romantic love. I'm talking about the entire spectrum of human interaction. Parents. Children. Siblings. Spouses. Lovers. Ex-lovers. Neighbors. Friends. Colleagues. Animals. Strangers. Maybe someday extraterrestrials. All of these types of relationships present unique opportunities for connection. Everyone has had moments within relationships that were open and easy. And we've all had those moments where making any kind of heartfelt connection seems utterly impossible. Sometimes we want love from people who are completely unwilling to share their feelings. Other times, another person may desperately want and need our help and friendship- and we feel too empty and closed off to really care. The truth is that *real connection*- deep rich satisfying unconflicted contact with other human beings- is not that common. We all crave it, but few of us know how to get it. Fewer still know how to embrace it with their entire hearts and bodies.

I want to make clear at the outset that the mysteries of the human heart can never be reduced to a simple neurobiological model. However, if we apply our instinctual intelligence to understand some of the basic principles that subconsciously guide human interaction, we might be able to unlock a few of these mysteries. To do this, we're going to examine the social skills of a true master- Oprah Winfrey. Studying her highly evolved sense of social intelligence can help us identify the implicit instinctual processes that guide her interpersonal expertise.

Emotional Self-Protection

The truth is that by the time we become adults, we have built up many walls and layers of protection to dampen our feelings. These layers of protection prevent the optimal functioning the instinctual energy of our social bonding systems. These unconscious conflicts severely limit our ability to function with instinctual intelligence in all types of relationships. As parents, we have a hard time balancing love and discipline. As spouses, these conflicts prevent us from being loving and affectionate. As friends, our ability to be genuinely empathetic and supportive can be compromised. There are infinite ways that these instinctual conflicts can interfere with our relationships.

What's at the root of all these walls and barriers? The most primal of all human instincts- the desire to avoid pain. Almost always, the protective barriers we build up around ourselves are based on this innate desire. In one sense, emotional self-defense is normal and healthy. It's also a byproduct of our evolutionary heritage. This strategy has helped humans survive for thousands of generations. Back in the days of saber-tooth tigers, if you sat around feeling all sensitive and vulnerable, you probably didn't last long in those hostile conditions. On the other hand, if you learned to suck it up and get on with the hunting and gathering, then you ate well, avoided the saber-toothed tiger, had lots of sex, and eventually became the great great^{10,000} grandparent of the person reading this book.

One thing that Oprah reminds us of over and over again is that our vulnerability is an indispensable and exquisite part of being human. Due to the nature of life on this planet, our bodies, our hearts, and our minds will experience suffering. No one can escape it. Some of us have more than our share, while others seem to have less. Our bodies are mortal and can be hurt. Friends and loved ones die, sometimes in the prime of life. Our hearts are breakable. Eventually, our minds give way to old age and exhaustion. Our instinctual systems do their best to keep us from every harm and disappointment, but in the end, our lives will inevitably be touched by sorrow, loss, and grief. These are the facts of life, over which we have no control.

Most of the time, adults use self-judgments and protective defenses to reduce the possibility of experiencing discomfort and pain. Our protective defenses are always busy warding off any potential for vulnerability by keeping us numb, distracted, or just too busy to ever really feel heartache and pain. In terms of sheer survival this makes sense- remember that your ancestors *did not* get eaten by the saber-toothed tiger. But in the modern day world the tendency to avoid experiencing pain is often what creates difficulties in relationships in our lives. In an attempt to protect ourselves, we often create barriers to real love and intimacy.

The Instinctual Basis of Social Success

Most of us know all about protecting ourselves. We know why we do it. We know that it really wreaks havoc on our relationships. We even know when our bitterness and unresolved feelings poison our intimacy. But what can we do about it? This is exactly what Oprah began asking her viewers back in the mid '90s. Her show was already well-established. She knew she had a predominantly female audience that was interested in exploring these juicy but often bitterly complex topics. She also knew that she herself had an instinct for melting people's emotional barriers and getting them to connect with her. Somehow, she wanted to help people get past their protective barriers and learn to engage in healthy relationships- be they intimate, familial, or professional. Oprah sensed that it would be possible to translate her own social intelligence into a format that would touch the lives of her viewers in a more direct way. She knew that, if successful, this approach would take her show- and her own skills- to a new level. Let's look at some of the basic ingredients that Oprah used to make this happen.

One of the things that Oprah knew right from the start was that social connection and communication is a *deeply instinctual process*. Our primal needs for empathetic interpersonal contact are regulated by the periaqueductal grey (PAG) region of the midbrain. As we have seen, the PAG is involved in processing our instinctual responses to the basic needs of pain relief, temperature regulation, and security- as well as social bonding. At a fundamental evolutionary and neurobiological level, these primal instinctual needs are intimately related. They share many of the same basic nervous system architecture and regulating systems. Now Oprah may have never heard of the periaqueductal grey region, but she sure knows how to put people at ease. She knows that for the social bonding instincts to function properly, individuals need a basic level of security and comfort. She also knows that their self-protective mechanisms will relax if they are not anticipating pain and social conflict. Oprah intuitively uses this bit of instinctual intelligence create an instinctual bond with her guests. Before they know it, she has them relaxed and taking openly – even when she was asking them some *very* uncomfortable questions. In doing so, she demonstrates the importance of *empathetic resonance* for developing instinctual intelligence:

> Empathetic resonance is a particular type of instinctual intelligence. When we are truly interested in understanding another person's experience, this innate intelligence allows us to "feel" what the other person is experiencing. This form of instinctual knowing is the basis for developing social and moral intelligence- helping us to form the lasting social bonds of friendship, intimacy, and community.

Empathetic Relaxation

How does Oprah do it? How does she create a bond with people so quickly? How does she get them to lower their defenses? The secret, in part, can be found in the activity of her *mirror neurons*. Mirror neurons are specific types of cells in the brain that allow humans and other animals to generate internal feelings and physiological states that directly correspond to another person's behaviors, emotions, and instinctual states. In other words, our brains are equipped to help us understand the actions, intentions, and feelings of other people. Our brains accomplish this by activating individual neurons (as well as specific neural networks) in such a way that the other person's experience will be mirrored in our own nervous systems. This mirroring is not an exact duplication of the other person's neural state- but it's close enough to inform us directly about what's going on *inside* of the individual across the room. According to the latest research, mirror neurons in the limbic regions generate a feeling of emotional attunement. The mirror neurons in the cortical regions provide more nuanced and refined information about the motivational and conceptual orientation of another individual. Neurons on the somatosensory and motor regions give us an inside feeling of the movements and physical state of the person we are observing. Taken together, the mirror neuron systems in the human nervous system form an essential component of our social instinctive intelligence. They allow us to form real connections to the hearts, minds, and bodies of our fellow humans.

For most of us, we consciously or unconsciously resist our natural empathetic awareness of the suffering of other people- even though our mirror neurons are activated. We dampen this mode of intelligence in a variety of ways. Sometimes we block these feelings by distracting ourselves. Other times, we use internal judgments- labeling others as dumb, stupid, inferior, or lazy. Or sometimes we just feel sorry for them. Rarely do we let their experience of suffering *empathetically resonate* within our own body. This is one of Oprah's greatest talents. She has a rare ability to allow her nervous system to be empathetically open to other people's emotional and instinctual experiences. In some ways, the capacity for empathetic resonance comes naturally to her- as a result of what she has experienced in her life. Because she was pregnant at 14, she does not respond with moral lectures to a young mother's plight. She can resonate with fears and guilt and shame and uncertainty that women in this situation feel. Because she lost her own infant only two weeks after it was born, her nervous system can recognize and *tolerate* the pain of someone who has lost a loved one. Her acceptance and resonance allows her guests to share their feelings without the fear of shame and rejection.

Oprah's masterful social intelligence lies in her capacity to allow her mirror neurons to activate intense emotional and instinctual responses in her own body. Her guests intuitively feel this resonance. This resonance has a very specific effect on their nervous systems. It helps them feel more *relaxed* and *secure*. Their PAGs sense that their basic needs for social acceptance and safety are met. In this way, Oprah's empathetic attunement triggers the release of brain neuropeptides in her guests. The release of opioids and oxytocin bring feelings of pleasure and relaxation. This is the basic instinctual response program that is established during infancy when the mother empathetically responds to her infant. Her guests- as well as her audience- intuitively sense that Oprah *gets* what they are talking about and what they are feeling.

Awakening Compassion

Now we have an idea *what* Oprah does when she works her magic. But *how* did she learn to do it? Unquestionably, Oprah had a lot of innate intelligence when it came to connecting with other people. But there's a lot more to it that the skills she was born with. Oprah worked hard to get started in radio and television. She worked hard to find opportunities to enhance her skills in the early phases of her career. Most importantly of all, she worked to develop her instinctual intelligence after she had already made it and was a multi-millionaire. It was at this point- sometime in the early '90s- that she would have to develop an even more resilient instinctual capability. The challenges of fame and fortune tested her in a very dramatic way. One challenge in particular would give her the opportunity to evolve her instinctual intelligence and catapult her show to a whole new level.

In 1993 Oprah was under a lot of stress. She was being sued for libel by the American Beef Association in a highly publicized trail. The implications of the trial were enormous. Not only was there a huge financial risk- $230 million dollars- but something even more valuable was on the line: Oprah's credibility. If she lost, she would be seen as a cheap sensationalist, someone who was willing to lie and slander other people just to improve her ratings. It would be devastating to her career.

In this situation, it would be only natural to feel defensive. If someone is calling you a liar and suing you for millions of dollars, it's hard not to take it personally. You're primal instinctual responses would be aroused. Under this level of stress, it's hard to keep one's cool. It's a situation that calls for a sophisticated instinctual intelligence. This is why she hired Dr. Phil McGraw, a psychologist and trial preparation expert to help her prepare for the trial. Using his PhD. knowledge of psychology, McGraw had developed an extensive knowledge of how people respond the under stress of high stakes legal proceedings. He knew that trials could be won or lost based on how the instinctual responses of the parties were interpreted by the jury- regardless of evidence or legal maneuvering. In a sense, McGraw had made a name for himself by helping his clients develop instinctual intelligence that improved their chances of legal success.

Speaking the Truth

McGraw, like any good psychologist, knew that juries can detect when someone is hiding something or not being truthful. It's an innate human skill that allows us to detect small discrepancies between what someone is saying and the instinctual inflections of their bodies. It's largely an unconscious form of cognitive evaluation. We don't know exactly *how* we know that the story someone is telling isn't quite truthful. We just know. Once the members of a jury begin to doubt someone's credibility, it's nearly impossible to change their minds. It can radically alter the complexion of a trial and change the way juries view evidence. For McGraw, the challenge was to make sure that the jury would see Oprah's integrity. To do this, he would have to help her refine her already highly developed instinctual skills.

How did he do it? Well, we can only imagine what went on the days and weeks that they were preparing for the trial. But we know that Dr. Phil was not coaching Oprah how to lie. Quite the opposite. He was helping her to speak the truth. In order to this truth to resonate with the jury,

Oprah had to clear out the distorting imprints stored in her instinctual systems. In other words, if Oprah came across as defensive or uncertain, the jury may think she was hiding something. Remember- it was Oprah's credibility that was on the line more than anything else. Simply presenting a self-image of her credibility would not work. Rather, she had to *instinctually embody* her conviction in her own professional skills and her own personal integrity. Think that was easy? Consider what Oprah had to go through. She had to navigate two types of instinctual dysregualtion that could cost her the trial.

Turning Anger into Courage

The first type of dysregulation she had to overcome had to do with the self-protective instincts. If these systems became overheated, that she could come across as aggressive. She had to avoid taking on a posture of defensiveness that smacked of arrogance and superiority. In neurobiological terms, it would be easy to see how the response of defensive aggressiveness could arise. It's a natural protective stance our nervous systems learn when we are young children. In order to protect ourselves from feelings of vulnerability and anxiety, we develop a pretty tough exterior.

You would think that she had gotten used to defending herself. At each step of her professional career, Oprah had to overcome racial and gender discrimination. She had acquired a high degree of self-protective intelligence. But now the stakes were higher than ever. As we have seen, it's these kinds of high pressure situations that can overactivate certain self-protective neural networks. This overarousal of the defensive systems can lead to outbursts of aggression and anger. As we saw in the last chapter, the anger and aggression indicate the activation of a self-image of a small child that can only protect itself by whining, complaining, and being angry. We feel resentful when this self-image is activated. Oprah had a lot to feel resentful about. She had endured years of sexual abuse as a child and as a teenager. This kind of violation often results in the inhibition of aggressive- even violent- self-protective responses. These inhibited responses can smolder hidden for years- until they are triggered by intensely stressful conditions. If Oprah came across as too agitated- too bitchy- the jury would surely react negatively.

Only Oprah knows exactly what she was thinking or feeling at the time. But I would bet that there were moments during the trial when she was pretty pissed. Dr. Phil knew that an angry outburst on the witness stand could doom their defense. In a sense, his job was to hone Oprah's self-protective instincts so they would function in an elegant and balanced manner. As we know, this cannot happen if the nervous system is full of hyperarousing angry self-images. So, during their pre-trial preparation, he needed to have Oprah feel- completely and fully- the feelings boiling frustration, anger, and rage. Being a skilled psychologist, he knew that encouraging her to feel the full intensity of these instinctual responses was necessary to bring out the full intelligence of her self-protective instincts. At the same time, he had to prevent her from simply discharging the energy. That would just solidify the self-image of an angry young girl who was abused and molested. As we know, the key part of dissipating the overarousing self-image is to pay attention to one's adult body while simultaneously feeling the full activation of the anger and aggression. I can just imagine Oprah seething with rage and resentment that she had been sued- and all the injustices she had experienced in her life. At the same time, Dr. Phil was forcing her to answer complex questions and practice staying in touch with the jury. Talk about trial by fire!

Clearly, whatever they did as part of Oprah's pre-trial preparation, it worked. She discovered a deeper sense of courage that she had ever known before. It is said that her performance on the witness stand was a brilliant display of instinctually calm assertiveness. In some ways, preparing for a trial was a perfect setting for Oprah to recalibrate her nervous system and hone her instinctual intelligence. She would use what she had learned wisely as her career advanced.

Frozen and Alone

The other type of instinctual dysregulation that threatened Oprah's legal defense was that the stress of the trial might cause Oprah to freeze up. By all accounts her initial reaction to the lawsuit was one of shock and fear. The pressure of a cross-examination by an aggressive attorney can activate inhibitory networks that severely restrict the adaptive intelligence of multiple instinctual systems. An effective lawyer will try to solicit this inhibitory response. They will they will do this by making defendants feel social abandoned claiming that no one believes them or supports what they are saying. A person can feel pretty isolated up there, alone, on the witness stand. When this happens, individuals might suddenly begin to feel a paralyzing insecurity- like they are the victim of an overwhelmingly dreadful experience. This occurs because the neural networks that underlie the frozen self-image of a small, frightened child have been activated. These networks carry the residue of intense emotional pain, usually imprinted by experiences of abandonment and social isolation. Usually, they lie dormant, protected underneath layers of defensiveness and anger. When activated, individuals literally experience themselves as having the fragile nervous system of a child. Unable to bear this, they begin to dissociate, losing touch with their adult instinctual capacities.

Here is the challenge Dr. Phil faced: He recognized that Oprah, like all human beings, might slip into a dissociative freezing response on the witness stand as a form of instinctual self-protection. Ordinarily, we look to the comforting presence of others to help calm our anxiety when we feel alone and isolated. It is essential to understand how deeply this instinctual tendency is ingrained into human consciousness. As infants, we are totally dependant on our mother and other caregivers. They sooth our pain and empathetically regulate our nervous systems. This forms a direct impression on the nervous system. At a very deep level, we believe that our emotional pain can only be soothed by the comforting presence of another human being. If there is no one there to comfort us, we go into a state of inhibitory dissociation to block the pain. Dr. Phil knew that Oprah had to go to the witness stand alone. He couldn't go up there and hold her hand and give her support. He also knew that no amount of pep talks and confidence building could guarantee that Oprah's nervous system would not slip into some level of inhibitory shock. In order to prevent this from happening, he would need to help Oprah access a deeper source of instinctual comfort. We can use our knowledge of instinctual intelligence to understand how this process actually works.

Allowing Compassion to Break Through

The first step is to recognize a basic fact: *A child's nervous system cannot bear extreme levels of emotional pain and suffering*. The effects of severe, traumatic emotional despair are simply too great of a threat to the young child's survival. Therefore, our instinctual regulating systems have evolved multiple inhibitory mechanisms to help children cope with debilitating effects of overwhelming stress and grief. In previous chapters, we saw how the nervous system establishes dissociative networks in response to this intense level of emotional and physical despair. This protects their bodies and nervous systems from devastating behaviors that lead to malnutrition, psychoimmunilogical breakdown, and social isolation. But here's the problem: As adults, our nervous systems still believe we are small children physically incapable of tolerating deep emotional, existential pain. This belief goes all the way down to a cellular level. For Oprah, her nervous system still held memories of being left alone as a child. She often felt abandoned because her mother worked several jobs and lavished attention on Oprah's siblings, often ignoring Oprah in the process. If these networks were activated when she was on the stand, she would be unable to act with the full clarity, precision, and natural self-protective balance needed for an effective defense. She would lose her connection with the jury. In other words, she would not come across as a mature, thoughtful, and honest professional. Worse yet, if she were feeling victimized and abandoned, she could get bullied by an aggressive lawyer and end up making statements that would undermine her defense.

The next step is to understand that, as adults, our nervous systems are capable of experiencing extreme states of grief, despair, and emotional pain. We no longer need the defenses we developed as children. This is of course, easier said than done. No doubt at some point in the process, Dr. Phil must have reassured Oprah that she was a full grown adult and that her nervous system could actually tolerate the suffering and painful feelings she had been avoiding all her life. By helping her tolerate the feelings of the frozen self-image- while simultaneously directing her attention to the support of her adult capacities- she was slowly transformed. As we have seen, this technique disrupts the inhibitory neural networks that underlie the frozen self-image. When the self-image dissolves, the innate instinctual quality of *compassion* emerges:

Compassion is an indispensable form of instinctual intelligence. It gives us the ability to experience the intense emotional feelings of sadness and grief. The innate intelligence of compassion allows our bodies to endure the heartbreak of loss and disappointment that are inevitable in human life. It also helps us recognize, tolerate, and share the suffering of others with grace and wisdom.

Healing and Cleansing

As many spiritual traditions have long known, compassion has the miraculous capacity to rise up, when we least expect it, and sooth our soul in our darkest hours. This loving compassion is the *true empathic intelligence* of our instincts. It is the quality of instinctual intelligence that allows us to bear our deepest wounds. It gives humans the capacity to tolerate the overwhelming pain of our suffering, as well as that of others. When this level of instinctual intelligence is blocked, it feels as if we are unable to tolerate the threat of suffering both in ourselves and in others. Without compassion, there is a sense that if we allow ourselves to experience the hurt, we will be completely devastated and incapacitated. Again, this is because we had experiences in our early childhood that were simply too painful for our immature nervous systems to endure. Many people become stuck in this contracted posture of protective dissociative dullness, making them unable to respond empathetically to their own or other's suffering. In order to allow the instinct of loving compassion to function, we must consistently remind ourselves that we are no longer children. Our adult nervous systems are capable of tolerating feelings of abandonment and despair in a way that children cannot.

The empathetic kindness inherent in our instinctual intelligence has profound healing capacities. One of the extraordinary qualities of this loving compassion is its ability to calm our nervous system when levels of fear and despair appear to be reaching intolerable proportions. The sense of self-kindness that emerges at these critical junctures is the indispensable elixir that supports the difficult work of developing our instinctual intelligence. We cannot grow into instinctually mature adults without recognizing the truths of our human vulnerability. At times in our lives when we are at our most vulnerable, the innate intelligence of our compassion has the capacity allow us to feel pain, loneliness, and suffering. The embodied physical manifestations are well-known in all spiritual traditions. There is a felt sense of the chest opening, as if the heart is breaking open and a comforting balm pours forth. It actually feels like pure mercy gently flowing through our hearts. This soft energy supports the pain and grief with unconditional acceptance, allowing it to permeate the body in an open and unrestricted manner. Just when we thought we could bear no more, our hearts beak open and we are bathed in unfathomable love and kindness.

The flow of compassion has a type of cleansing effect on sensation and perception, in that the painful emotions are embraced without defenses or denial. Free from defense, our hearts are stretched in ways previously thought to be unbearable. Instead of pain, we feel an inexplicable yet profound wave of comfort. The most difficult part of allowing compassion to flow through us is that we fear the hurt will overwhelm us. It takes some level of trust to simply let go and surrender to our fear and pain. Anyone who has seen Dr. Phil do his thing over the years knows that he has the gentle talent for helping people access their own inner sense of compassion. It can arise in a variety of ways- forgiveness of someone who has hurt us, tearfully acknowledging the grief of an unexpected death or illness, or honestly facing the disappointment of lost love. Over and over, audiences have seen that when the quality of compassion touches someone's heart, they embrace the instinctual desire to heal a hidden pain. The barriers to living a fuller life begin to melt right in front of our eyes, softened by the kind hands of compassion. It's often a magical and intensely moving moment. There can be no doubt that Oprah went through our own moments of fear and grief during that trial. She had to confront her worst fears of pain, abandonment, and loss. While those tender moments were for her soul alone to witness, the results were obvious.

Her nervous system was cleansed of the inhibiting networks that could have triggered a freezing response. When she took the stand, her natural instinctual grace began to flow with integrity, courage, and compassion. This clearly resonated with the jury. They returned a unanimous verdict dismissing the lawsuit. Many of the jurists were so enamored with Oprah they became life-long fans of her show. The change in Oprah was palpable. Not only was the stress of the trial over- she was transformed by the experience. The next season, her show began to reflect the instinctual wisdom she had developed during her trial.

Finding Real Connection

One of Oprah's greatest contributions has been to help countless numbers of women- and men- become most honest about their emotional lives. Over the years, her shows have help people face some very difficult truths. One of the most consistent themes has been to help viewers understand how they cover up feelings of loneliness and emptiness through dysfunctional behaviors. We have seen people who have racked up hundreds of thousands of dollars in credit card debt, spending exorbitant sums of money to avoid dealing with some deeper emotional conflicts. We have also seen guests who try to regulate their anxiety through rigid control of their diets. We have seen her help thousands of people explore the difficulties they face in living more balanced lives. She has also tackled wider social issues like education, sexual abuse, and poverty.

Though it all, Oprah has helped people tell their stories. She has made it safe for so many more people to be honest about the challenges they face without feeling ashamed or embarrassed. Behind the scenes, we can see the sophisticated instinctual intelligence that has emerged in Oprah's work during the last few years. She has introduced us to many of the soft spots of the human heart by focusing on a very specific type of human suffering. In a broad sense, she helps people recognize the *addictive-* and highly destructive- behaviors in which they are trapped. She has made this into a fine art. She has the compassionate, yet forceful wisdom to help her guests confront some very painful truths behind their self-destructive and addictive tendencies. What she has shown us over and over is that these addictive behaviors are an attempt to avoid an underlying sense of emptiness and emotional pain.

Oprah does not try to "cure" the person or "fix" the problem. Her contribution has been to bring the realty of human suffering out of the shadows. But what gives her so much credibility with her audience is that she is willing to disclose her own struggles and conflicts. In part, Oprah is able to do this because of her evolved capacity for empathy. Oprah has also developed a deeply embodied sense of compassion, the exquisite form of instinctual intelligence that many of the world's great wisdom traditions revere as the most refined of all human qualities. She shares her own feelings and vulnerabilities. Because of her openness, her audience doesn't feel like they are getting a lecture when she expresses her knowledge of a particular problem. They feel like Oprah is their friend. In a very palpable way, the audience feels what Oprah is feeling. Oprah is a master at making *connection*.

Looking for Connection in All the Wrong Places

Part of Oprah's skill is helping us understand what real connection means. Most of the time, we think it is having an intimate sexual partner, a devoted spouse, a loving family, a supportive community, or a loyal friend. But there's more to it than that. Often, we believe that the special connection we are seeking can be found in someone- or something- *outside of ourselves*. This misguided belief is what sustains our addictive behaviors and blocks the evolution of our instinctual capacity for real connection. To understand this evolved sense of connection at an instinctual level, we'll have to explore two of the most common types of addictive behaviors that keep our nervous systems locked in a cycle of craving. This addictive craving is what obscures our instinctual consciousness from a direct and consistent experience of real connection.

1) Addiction to Craving

Throughout this book, we have seen how our basic relational tendencies systems are shaped by parental interaction during infancy. We have also seen that there is overwhelming evidence that early interactive experiences of soothing and instinctual satiation form the basis of how we go about getting our instinctual needs met as adults. These early relational experiences have lasting impacts on the neurobiological substrates that mediate social relationships, including the level of opiate activity that promotes social seeking and engagement of meaningful relationships throughout our lives. These deep-seated instinctual tendencies are centered around a basic pattern of escalating frustration and *incomplete* satisfaction. Let's look at an obvious example of this pattern.

We can see these basic instinctual tendencies in the way we relate to food. Because the gratification of eating carries deep infantile instinctual associations with the presence of a maternal caregiver, many adults eat food to dispel feelings of loneliness. Hidden within our eating patterns are nervous system regulating behaviors that are tied to our basic motivational and seeking programs. Many adults have not-so-secret eating patterns that create addictive patterns of arousal and relaxation. This is not limited to individuals with eating disorders. It's more basic than that. This addictive pattern focuses our instinctual and emotional energy on food as a way of blocking feelings of loneliness. Seeking out and consuming food directly alters our internal mood. People use drugs and alcohol for the same reason. New research into addictive behavior clearly indicates that the use of heroin and other opioids draws on many of the same neural circuits that underlie social bonding and connection behaviors.

Here's how craving blocks intolerable feelings of longing and loneliness: When we begin to anticipate a reward of a mood altering substance, our nervous systems begin to experience a sensation of craving. This craving is a combination of desire, anticipation, and seeking with a dose of inhibition thrown in. We really *want* it- yet we know we *shouldn't*. The secret satisfaction we crave might be unhealthy, inappropriate, or illegal. Our nervous systems become aroused by the thought of seeking out something we really want- but that is difficult or even dangerous to get. The important thing to see is that the source of addiction is usually not the mood altering substance- it's the nervous system arousal caused by the *anticipation* and *seeking* that is addictive. Most of the time, the dopamine-fueled arousal of desire, anticipation, and seeking will create a highly addictive feeling of frustrated craving that can last for hours. Our minds are *totally focused* on thoughts and images of the sweet reward and strategies for seeking it out. We will often delay the actual consumption of the substance for a while to experience of anticipatory craving just a little longer. But here's the critical point: When our nervous systems are locked into the sensation of craving, it is so *compelling* that we don't pay attention to anything else. Whether it's food or drugs, the focus on acquiring and consuming mood altering substances dissipates the feeling of social isolation. In most cases, when we finally consume the substance there is only a fleeting satisfaction. What really happened was that the engrossing preoccupation with craving *temporarily blocked* the unwanted feelings of loneliness and emptiness.

2) Addiction to the Promise of Connection

Why are feelings of loneliness and emptiness so hard to tolerate? Every human being ever born experiences some degree of frustration and deprivation during the early phase of infancy. Our nervous systems are left with a lingering instinctual imprint of not being able to obtain satisfaction from our mothers. It is as if the deep cellular memories of the infant are filled with agitation, frustration, and dissatisfaction. Recent research has shown that many of these memories are stored in the right orbitofrontal cortex, forming the central node of an inhibitory neural network. When activated, this inhibitory network restricts our innate social bonding systems. This inhibition is a form of instinctual self-protection. As infants, the frustration and pain of not receiving the warmth, touch, nourishment, and loving contact we need is simply too frustrating and painful to tolerate. It's a matter of survival. Better to shut down these basic instinctual desires than to risk life-threatening levels of nervous system agitation and arousal.

The frustration and anguish of these early states of deprivation have a very particular impact on our instinctual capacities for connection and satisfaction as adults. Our desire to surrender into a deep, relaxed interpersonal connection will be met with a subversive instinctual resistance. Whenever feelings of connectedness and satisfying relaxation are anticipated, we will find a way to inhibit further connection because this level of intimacy is associated with the anguish and frustration of early infancy. Here, we can see how we secretly protect ourselves against these agonizing feeling: We create the addictive illusion that there is always someone out there who has what we want, but we are somehow unable to get it or connect with them. This sense of frustrated craving leaves us constantly on the *verge of satisfaction*. We fantasize endlessly about the connection we long for. Usually it is an exciting sexual partner. Sometimes it is the desire for a close friend or a powerful business partner. For other people it can be the perfect home or a sublime vacation in the tropics. But this satisfying connection always seems to elude us. Even if we think we have found what we want, we never feel quite satisfied. The next day, we begin the same pursuit, hoping that today will be different- that today our efforts will finally pay off and we'll find the *real thing*. It's as if some part of us wants to keep our most compelling fantasies at a distance, where we can continue to chase after their promise without the risk of disappointment.

Underneath the Craving

If we look honestly and objectively at our adult lives, we will see that we have many of these *almost satisfying* situations. For many of us, our landscape is filled with the irritating promise of a perfect love, great sex, the ideal job, the right house, the seductive body, or the looming artistic breakthrough. Underneath it all is an insatiable addictive feeling of *always-being-on-the-verge-of-satisfaction*. It's the same feeling of craving that draws us compulsively toward mood altering substances. Focusing in on the sensation of pure craving is difficult, because it is so agonizing. Most of our day is spent trying to discharge or satisfy it. For many of us, it's simply a way of life. However, if we keep our attention on the *embodied feeling* of the frustrating craving, we open the door to a deeper sense of connection.

If we can sustain our attention long enough on these feelings of craving, we will find the self-image of a small infant, desperately afraid of being abandoned. This young helpless infant desperately wants to bond and merge with the mother to gain a sense of support and connection.

As this self-image is exposed, we will see how our nervous system desperately tries to avoid feelings of aloneness and abandonment. And for good reason. The nervous system impressions formed during infancy tell us we cannot tolerate these gut wrenching and heart breaking feelings of social isolation. We need to patiently remind ourselves that we can, as adults, experience aloneness. This helps us to sustain our attention on the feelings of agitation, frustration, and loss. It requires great courage and compassion to let ourselves feel the depths of the aloneness and raw agitating neediness that lurks in the core of our instinctual fears. If we are willing to take this brave journey, we will open our instinctual consciousness to a breathtaking dimension of connection and contact.

The self-image of an abandoned infant is the core of the addiction to craving. This frozen self-image compels the nervous system to operate on the belief that it is better to be always searching for someone to meet our needs than to be alone. For an infant, this is absolutely and existentially true. But for adults seeking to develop a mature instinctual intelligence, the persistent belief that we actually need someone or something to give us a sense of connection obscures a deeper truth:

> Real connection is a natural expression of an evolved instinctual intelligence. As this intelligence is refined, we begin to awaken to the deeper understanding that the ultimate source of connection is not just with other people- it is a direct connection to *reality as a whole*. This awakening helps us to embrace the extraordinary possibilities of human life, allowing us to recognize our innate connection to the vastness of all creation- including the depth of our own souls.

This is exactly what Oprah has been trying to tell us all these years. She has shown us it is OK to sit home at night and read a book- even if we feel lonely. She has shown us that confronting our addictive behaviors is ultimately more fulfilling than a sweet dessert or another affair. Most importantly of all, she has given us the priceless knowledge that being truthful with ourselves is the direct path to the ultimate source of true connection. And that's the true gift of the countless guests who have appeared on her show. The very modern act of exposing one's deepest vulnerabilities in front of millions for people is another manifestation of instinctual intelligence. Consciously exploring one's inner anguish while *simultaneously* having to deal with the realities of being on a television set is a rather unique way of destabilizing self-images of being alone and abandoned. It might not be for everyone- but it obviously works. The transformative effects on the guests- as well as on the viewers- are palpable. I imagine Oprah will be the first one to acknowledge that being truthful with ourselves is difficult. But in the long run, it's the only way we can experience the unparalleled satisfaction of becoming instinctually mature adults.

Ultimately, this exquisitely satisfying connection is not dependent on any other person. It is a natural state of our instinctual consciousness, experienced free of the impressions of our frustrating childhood experiences. When we experience real connection, we feel as if we are melting into a vast warm pool, totally relaxed and totally cared for. Our need for companionship is satiated, although no one else may be present. This state has been described by many spiritual traditions as merging into the infinite loving embrace of the universe. Theistic traditions describe this as the perfect union with God. The embodied sense is one of a sweet warm dissolution of separating boundaries. Our hearts are open and undefended and we feel a sense of interconnected support from our bodies and our environment. This melting feeling pervades our inner and outer experience, and we feel as if we are merged into a state of warm loving grace. There is no sense of being alone, or of the possibility of aloneness. The golden melting connection feels like it is everywhere at the same time.

Limitless Connection

The instinctual intelligence behind this real connection is helping to awaken the collective wisdom of humanity. This form of collective intelligence is guiding the creative web that connects human consciousness- in both physical and nonphysical ways. It's happening all over the planet. Perhaps you've recently encountered it the last time you were on the Internet googling some item of interest. The internet company Google creates software that helps individuals and businesses search efficiently and intelligently for information in the vastness of cyberspace. When you type in Google search, you arrive at the gateway to instant knowledge and connectivity. Google's search engine helps connect humans to other humans and vital sources of knowledge. This accelerating connectivity is sweeping all over the globe and transforming every culture it comes in contact with. But that's not the only form of connectivity Google specializes in.

As a company, Google demonstrates the emerging business reality that interconnectedness is essential for economic survival. This web of interconnection extends externally to other companies, with whom Google shares technological, strategic, and economic interests. Just as importantly, it extends internally. Google depends on the innovations of its talented workforce to produce new products. Google's founders, Larry Page and Sergey Brin, recognized early on that innovative ideas for new software applications are emerging everywhere. They can come from consumers, engineers, and some guys just playing around in their basements. In order to turn the grass roots surge of creativity into profitable ideas, Google cultivates innovation from the bottom up. This is a sharp contrast from the traditional business models where creative ideas were originated by top executives and then implemented by lower-level managers and technicians. This state-of-the-art business design is a model of interconnection. Anyone and everyone in the company is encouraged to talk to everyone else. Small groups and committees are always meeting to share ideas, thoughts, sketches, solutions- even dreams and whims of inspiration. The most promising ideas are selected for further study. Sometimes parts of one project are adapted to solve problems on another idea-in-progress. The key behind this interconnected creativity is the free exchange of information within the company. In this design, top executives have to trust that this interconnected intelligence will produce profitable ideas worthy of further funding and development.

Interestingly enough, Google has begun a massive research project to further analyze the human genome. They are using the unprecedented processing power of their computer networks to support ongoing research and then distribute this knowledge to researchers all over the world. By contributing to the scientific knowledge and well-being of the human species through the investigation of our DNA, Google is a living example of the innate connective intelligence guiding the human evolutionary matrix. The results of this great experiment in interconnectivity help us to perceive the reality of the inseparable fabric that permeates living beings, material systems, and the natural environment.

The Connection of Compassion

If we feel connected to ourselves, other people, our natural environment- even the entire universe- then it is impossible not to be aware of the feelings of others. Ultimately, compassion and connection are like two sides of a single piece of paper. This deep sense of connection and compassion makes it impossible to feel that we are isolated, alone and incapable of meeting our needs. It gives us the courage to reach out and put our compassion into action. We no longer have to meet our needs by addictively chasing after the promise of connection to that special someone. We can fulfill our needs for connection in ways we might have never considered. Oprah's ANGEL NETWORK is a perfect example of the living integration of compassionate connection. This network allows people from all over the world to contribute time, energy, money, and other resources to solve some very real problems. Whether it is helping catch sexual predators, building houses for hurricane Katrina victims, or just giving a few dollars to a worthy cause, Oprah has found a way to help people build a deeper sense of connection to the world. In doing so, she opens the door to the extraordinary potentials of an evolved instinctual consciousness:

As our capacities for compassion and connection evolve, it becomes possible to recognize the underlying unity of the entire universe. There is a deep, ineluctable intelligence within this unity that is the basis for our instinctual intelligence, as well as all other forms of knowing. The more we learn to trust that each of us is an inseparable part of this underlying unity, the more compassion and wisdom can infuse our instinctual consciousness.

And one last note- real connection does not mean that we no longer need other human beings. On the contrary. The more we embody the evolved instinctual intelligence that underlies our true interconnectedness, the easier it becomes to form real relationships with others. Intimacy becomes smoother and richer when it is no longer restricted by the hidden fears of loneliness. Who knows, you might even meet the real person of your dreams while volunteering for one of Oprah's *ANGEL NETWORK* projects. Connection is all around us. All we need is the willingness to embrace it.

Instinctual Intelligence

CHAPTER 15

Determination

Long before the days of Oprah and Dr. Phil, before the discovery of evolution and neurobiology, even before anyone had ever heard of Sigmund Freud, human instinctual intelligence was evolving. Our modern terminology may make it seem like instinctual intelligence suddenly emerged in the last couple decades. Nothing could be further from the truth. It has always been silently guiding the evolution of life on this planet. It's been a long, slow journey and we've come a long way since the first stands of DNA began to self-replicate. Sure, we've learned some things over the years- and the understanding of the process has become considerably refined. Back then, people had different names for it. People that underwent the difficult journey of instinctual evolution were said to have Fortitude. Perseverance. A sense of destiny.

To see how instinctual intelligence has been quietly working behind the scenes, we're going to take a trip back to the past. 150 years ago, humans knew next to nothing about the nervous system. We didn't know about the effects of trauma, nor did we know anything about the basic principles of autonomic regulation. No one had heard of psychotherapists. Back then, people had to rely more on their gut instincts and intuition. When they were frustrated, or feeling down, they couldn't watch a movie or surf the net to find the latest research on whatever was ailing them. They had to slog through some of the most difficult quagmires of human existence with little or no guidance. They had to face directly into the unknown.

In the past, developing one's instinctual intelligence called for a particular kind of bravery. A person would have to have the courage to peer directly into the mystery of the human soul, facing the demons of tragedy and loss. And, if they were fortunate enough to come out with a more intimate understanding of their true instinctual intelligence- it would require the most resolute determination to forge a life consistent with this knowledge. Moreover, using this knowledge to lead others through a time of profound cultural change and instinctual chaos would be the ultimate test. It was difficult back then- as it is now- to get people to side with the better forces of human nature. This challenge would ask nothing less than a willingness of the individual to align his own determination with the deeper wisdom that has intelligently guided the evolution of life. You had to have an unbreakable determination to face this lonely crossroads. This is exactly where Abraham Lincoln stood on a February night in New York City in 1860.

Crawling Out of Depths of Despair

Lincoln's life-long struggle with depression and his heroic perseverance during the Civil War are well known in American history. What many people don't know is the profound struggle he went through before he became president. In 1846, Lincoln was elected to the House of Representatives. He served an admirable term. However, he declined to seek re-election because he had pledged not to run again as part of his election campaign. Despite encouragement, he held true to his word and returned to Illinois to practice law. The next year, his son, Eddie, died after a long illness. The death of his son sent him into the depths of despair. This was not the first bout of intense depression and melancholy that Lincoln had experienced. Several years earlier, two broken engagements had triggered serious episodes of depression that lasted several years. Even in less stressful periods of his life, Lincoln was said to be morose individual, frequently slipping into sudden spells of gloom and withdrawal.

Getting Over "Just Getting Over It"

Lincoln's strong work ethic told him he must keep going and work hard at all costs. He worked tirelessly at his law practice, hoping that by staying busy he could avoid falling further into the vortex of depression. It is not hard to imagine what Lincoln was experiencing. Many of us live in a perpetual state of busyness, trying to stay one step ahead of our silent, encroaching fears. In overscheduled lives, we rarely stop long enough to consider that we might be overlooking an opportunity to develop our instinctual intelligence. The modern world is full of individuals who pride themselves on their independence. They rigorously avoid the help, intimacy, and support of others. This independent stance takes a lot of vigilance and energy to maintain. As we saw in previous chapters, the hyper-individualist adult often had repeated experiences of maternal neglect or rejection during childhood. The nervous system adapts to these conditions by suppressing parasympathetic activity. At the core of this rigid autonomy is a self-image of a small child that is wary of feeling dependent on others in any way. This self-image is maintained by neural networks that encoded experiences of having felt abandoned and betrayed by caregivers during young childhood. These networks are activated when they detect any situation that might lead to the same excruciating pain of isolation and failure.

After his son died in 1851, something was changing deep in the core of Lincoln's instinctual consciousness. Outwardly, he showed some obvious signs that his basic instinctual programs were undergoing a relentless transformation. Many of his friends remarked that Lincoln often appeared very stiff, his arms and legs were often rigid. From a modern perspective, we know that a lack of parasympathetic arousal will leave an individual in a state of sympathetic overcharge. The neural networks that underlie this frozen self-image will create a great deal of tension throughout the body. It is as if a plate of armor surrounds the body, making it impervious to sensation or intimate contact. The rigidity is an attempt by our persevering instinctual programs to enhance the likelihood of survival. Internally, this rigidity gives us a feeling of support that was missing during our childhood, when we first learned to go it alone. The rigid self-image is trying to make us feel strong and capable. Its basic impulse is to keep our nervous systems activated and to maintain life-sustaining behaviors like eating, resource gathering, and staying warm. In the modern world, many of us grow so accustomed to a pervasive physical tension that we regard it as an unalterable fact of life.

An Instinct for Security

Lincoln intuitively sought out ways to recalibrate his nervous system during these dark times. One of the things he credits for helping him through his cycles of intense despair was the companionship of friends. Although many admitted that his company was at best uncomfortable- and often downright depressing- Lincoln often pleaded with friends and acquaintances to stay and talk with him into the wee hours of the night. He wasn't dependant on them for support. Lincoln was more than capable of being alone for extended periods of time without even noticing no one was there. Rather, his awakening instinctual intelligence knew that he needed the company of friends as part of his healing process. He was not ashamed to ask for help.

Lincoln, like others in his day, followed a simple folk wisdom that that recommended humor as a way of keeping up one's spirits. Taking this advice to heart, Lincoln would force- sometimes with great awkwardness- his friends to listen to his backwoods jokes and humorous stories. Form a modern perspective, we can see the instinctual intelligence behind Lincoln's actions. Like most farm boys growing up on the American frontier in the early 1800s, Lincoln had to become self-reliant at a fairly early age. His mother died when he was nine, and his father was a harsh disciplinarian. Neurobiologically, we can surmise that his orbitofrontal cortex was not full of memories of warm interpersonal contact. More likely, it was full of memories of being alone and being told to gather firewood in the cold Kentucky winter so he and his family would not freeze to death. Recall that the periaqueductal grey (PAG) region is where the most primitive instinctual responses to temperature, pain, and social isolation are produced. When we fear these basic needs for security might not be met, the natural tendency is to activate our resource gathering and environmental control programs. We work harder. We become more guarded and more tense. When we perceive the world through the lens *of scarcity*, we feel like we might not get what we need. We carefully monitor the state of our resources and even begin inhibiting our impulses to eat and expend energy. Think of this resource conservation mode as a slightly more evolved form of the hibernation cycle seen in some animals.

By asking his friends to keep him company, Lincoln was literally encoding new memories that would re-program his nervous system. In modern neurobiological terms, we can see how the social contact literally recalibrated his orbitofrontal cortex and his PAG. Their smiling faces informed his nervous system that his basic needs for security- warmth, protection, and social contact- were available. His self-image of a poor and cold little boy growing up in conditions of extreme material scarcity and social isolation was destabilized. His PAG could relax and his instinctual intelligence could evolve.

By seeking out help, Lincoln was learning to let go of the deep instinctual tendency to *control* his external environment. He had an incredible practical wisdom about his instinctual needs. Without any real psychological knowledge, Lincoln found a way to engage in *reality testing*. Modern psychologists use reality testing in a variety of clinical modalities as an effective tool in the treatment of a variety of mental disorders. In a very basic way, Lincoln was using reality testing to destabilize encoded memories that told him the world was harsh and lonely. By challenging this deep-seated, but incorrect, instinctual notion, his nervous system learned that external reality can be supportive. Lincoln was learning an advanced lesson in instinctual intelligence: that asking for help when we need it allows adults to actually become *more* independent and autonomous. Knowing that our instinctual seeking systems can function – that we can feed ourselves, get to work, find a place to live, and seek the intimate personal connections we need-gives us confidence that we can support ourselves on the journey of becoming a mature adult. This helps us see an essential principle that can help us face the challenges of developing our instinctual intelligence:

> An innate capacity of our instinctual intelligence is to gather the resources we need to support our growth and development as human beings. This not only includes the determination to get up and go to work each day- but also to acquire the knowledge, understanding, and supportive allies we need to help our instinctual intelligence evolve.

By encoding new memories of interpersonal connection and support, Lincoln was overwriting memories of aloneness stored deep within the instinctual regulating centers of his brain. Clearly, his friends knew something was wrong- it was widely acknowledged that Lincoln suffered from some unknown "nervous affliction". Lincoln was no doubt embarrassed about his condition. His great courage was to give up the pretext of "just getting over it" and expose his inner vulnerability. For many of us living in the modern world, we feel that tension is something that protects us. Always being busy is necessary for our survival. Our self-judgments will desperately to hide our vulnerability- from ourselves as well as others. Our fear of being seen as weak will cause us to feel critical and dismissive about the whole notion of feeling anything that even hints of vulnerability. Our cognitive defense mechanisms will encourage us to "get back to work" and to "just get over it". Lincoln's ability to acknowledge his own vulnerability allowed him to survive one of the most profoundly difficult struggles any human had ever had to endure. His willingness to ask for help did not take away the blackness in his heart- it allowed him to explore it with greater intimacy. It was this depth of exploration that carried him to a whole new level of instinctual intelligence on that cold February night in 1860.

The Support of Self-Knowledge

During the years 1851 to 1854, Lincoln plummeted into a vortex of despair that seemed more acute than ever before. His heart and mind wrestled endlessly with profound questions of existence and meaning. He agonized over his purpose in life, feeling that surely he most have some higher calling. He felt less concerned for his personal ambition- but still anxiously driven by some haunting restlessness. His wife would often find him awake in the early hours of dawn, staring blankly into space with a piercing look of anguish and utter hopelessness. In this silent abyss, he seemed to be listening for the whisper of inspiration. In 1854, the inspiration came.

That year the Missouri Compromise was repealed by the U.S. Congress. Upon hearing this news, something deep within Lincoln's soul was galvanized. The Missouri Compromise had set limits on the expansion of slavery along the American frontier. Without it, the practice of slavery could extend into new state and territories. Lincoln had found his purpose- the defense of human rights. Or- more accurately- *the cause of human rights had found Lincoln*. Very modestly, he began traveling though the Illinois countryside, accepting invitations to speak at small political gatherings. He practiced finding the words to speak out against the expansion of slavery. More importantly, he began to advocate for its eventual eradication. For six years he would face into the depths of his depression and overcome several setbacks in his fight against slavery. However, his determination was resolute. He would not give up.

Facing into the Blackness

In the 21st century, many adults feel the same lurking sense of dissatisfaction that plagued Lincoln. Most commonly, we notice it as a lack of initiative and effectiveness that prevents us from doing the things we want in life. This mysterious pull, as if gravity has been amplified, is largely unconscious. It manifests as a vague dissatisfaction and inhibited self-assertion. We can feel in the middle of a huge black ocean, with no points of reference. Every option seems equally meaningless. And yet, in the distance, images of an unfulfilled destiny call like sirens, beckoning us to brighter future. I have had many clients and friends tell me this is "just the way life is." They tell me that the best you can do is to just push away those feelings of despair as best you can- and live with the reality of fading dreams. Lincoln was unwilling to accept such a compromise. The faces of his fellow humans shackled in chains and robbed of their freedom would not let him rest.

Abraham Lincoln's journey during this critical period gives us a new way to understand the nature of human suffering. In this view, the intense episodes of despair and doubt we all experience can be seen as part of the awakening of deeper levels of our instinctual intelligence. Instead of trying to avoid these dreaded feelings, we can begin to probe a little more deeply into the blackness that surrounds them. This is what Lincoln did. Bolstered by his increasing social engagement offered through his political activities, he summoned his courage and faced directly into these feelings of despair. What did he find? While we can never know for sure, we can use our modern knowledge of instinctual intelligence to understand Lincoln's profound instinctual transformation.

Parasympathetic shutdown

As we know, the parasympathetic system acts as a powerful inhibitory force on the nervous system. In children, this parasympathetic inhibition emerges with the shame response that is initially triggered by the disapproving gaze of the mother. As adults, the inhibition of our nervous system often occurs when we are embarrassed in social situations. The response is remarkably similar to the child's- a sudden loss of energy, a narrowing of the perceptual field, and the oppressive feeling that one has done something wrong. We feel like collapsing. By now, you should be suspecting that this instinctual response is being triggered by the activation of a self-image. This is exactly what is happening. If we begin to bring our attention to the feelings and sensations of the collapsed state, the distorted self-image of a small child can be recognized. The feeling of collapse feels like our bones and muscles are like jelly, too wobbly to support us. The internal sensations in our belly and solar plexus can feel constricted and cramped, almost to the point of nausea. A blackness can overwhelm our consciousness, leaving us feeling like we are drowning in a sea of nothingness. These are all signs that a self-image- that was encoded during an intense experience of parasympathetically induced inhibition- has been activated.

The source of inner support

If we examine the neurobiology of the parasympathetic inhibition just a little more closely, we will begin to discover a pathway for transforming this black hole of despair. One of the primary ways individuals can recognize they are experiencing an intense parasympathetic activation is through a sense coldness or the feeling of being chilled. This arises because of the amygdala's activation of the ventrolateral periaqueductal gray (PAG) region, a primary midbrain region involved in producing the freezing response. The freezing response not only inhibits motor activity- which withdraws blood from limbs and thus produces a sense of cold- but produces a feeling of being "chilled" that is unrelated to the ambient temperature. This shift by the PAG into a freezing mode is a form of self-protection. We saw the intelligence behind this inhibitory response when we explored the parasympathetic adaptiveness of young children.

For children, the result of this parasympathetic inhibition is the emotional shutdown of shame. However, for adults it presents an opportunity to unlock a vital source of instinctual intelligence. Here's how: The parasympathetic shame response appears to originate in the orbitofrontal cortex and subsequently activates the neurons in the solitary tract of the medullary caudal reticular formation. Activation of this brainstem area produces motor inhibition. This accounts for feelings of physical fatigue and inadequacy. This parasympathetic activation in the reticular formation is also associated with changes in attentional focus. Parasympathetic information, including visceral afferent information- our gut feelings- biases the individual's perceptual field toward inner sensations. This makes evolutionary sense, because any injury or malfunction of internal organs could be a threat to survival. Our gut feelings act as an *internal warning system*. The bottom line is that parasympathetic activation pulls attention away from the external environment and directs it to inner sensations.

This was the source of Lincoln's inner fortitude. During the years before his presidential bid in 1860, Lincoln twice ran for the senate and suffered crushing defeats. After these losses, he was inconsolable. Yet he did not run from his inner blackness. He found strength in reading, writing, and reciting poetry that spoke openly about feelings of existential meaninglessness and terror. Lincoln was unflinching in his resolve to give voice to the parts of himself that felt utterly helpless and weak. In doing so, he revealed a primordial impression that lies at the heart of our instinctual core. Without embarrassment or shame, Lincoln exposed the self-image of a collapsed child for all the world to see. At the same time, Lincoln constantly kept his adult commitment to end slavery burning in his chest. Intuitively utilizing the nervous system recalibration techniques that would be developed more than a century in the future, Lincoln began to transform his horrible feelings of desperation and isolated wretchedness. The key was his willingness to embrace the intense inner feelings arising from his gut. By consciously acknowledging these feelings, he began to develop a sense of inner support. His willingness to embrace the visceral sensations of his adult body destabilized the self-image of being a small, weak, and isolated boy. Lincoln's example allows us to understand the importance of the intuitive knowledge of the nervous system:

Self-knowledge and inner fortitude are essential components of our instinctual intelligence. These forms of intelligence provide the determination needed to explore the depths of human nature- especially when these depths are filled with despair and doubt. It gives us the objectivity needed to overcome the inertia of the past and embrace the truth about our selves and our potential. It also gives us the confidence that we can align our lives in accord with these truths.

The Hidden Efficiency of Self-Knowledge

Clearly, Abraham Lincoln was an extraordinary human being. However, it is possible to apply his wisdom to our lives in the 21st century. If we dig a little deeper, we can identify the universal principles of instinctual intelligence operating behind the scenes in this epic transformation. Fundamentally, it's important to acknowledge that the more deeply we allow ourselves to be touched by our own suffering, the more readily we find access to sources of determination we never knew were there. This may seem paradoxical at first. However, as Lincoln's life shows us, there seems to be an undeniable eternal truth at work. But how do we translate these eternal truths into practical challenges we face in the modern world?

Let's start with a few obvious facts. Most adults want the economic security of having satisfying and well-paying careers. We also want quality time with our family and friends to relax and connect. However, as the world's economic arena grows more competitive, many of us feel squeezed in both areas. Greater professional challenges demand more and more time at the office or on the computer. There is less time to spend with spouses, children, and friends. Workers end up pushing themselves to the edge of burnout. And beyond. On the other hand, missing too many days at the office to take a relaxing vacation might result in you falling behind at work- and someone else picks up the slack. A few days with the family you suddenly find you're overlooked at promotion time. Workers aren't the only ones feeling the squeeze. The economic costs of burnout are forcing human resource managers to consider new approaches to raise productivity and reduce stress. Both individuals and companies need a more balanced approach to the basic human needs of work and relaxation. This is a perfect case to which we need to apply our knowledge of instinctual intelligence. We can't go back to the old strategies of working harder. Nothing less than an evolutionary shift will cut it.

Beginning with Balance

One of the most important principles of instinctual intelligence is balance. Without question, a degree of nervous system balance is necessary for instinctual intelligence to evolve. We saw how important it is to awaken our courage from the very beginning of this journey. We also saw that without compassion for our selves and others, even the bravest of souls won't make it very far. In order to access the deepest sources of determination, we need a heavy dose of courage and compassion. Here is where we can apply the precise knowledge of instinctual intelligence to help people find new ways of living and working in the world. The new science of nervous system recalibration is helping people achieve *instinctual balance*.

Let's look at the details of how this works. We know that neurobiologically, an amygdala that is no longer dominated by self-images of fear or aggression is better able to produce more precise and efficient self-protective behaviors. This results in less sympathetic overcharge and less nervous system burnout. An orbitofrontal cortex that is no longer filled with memories of threatening interpersonal experiences OFC is better able to maintain a sense of empathy and connection. When these two instinctual centers are free to operate in an unrestricted way, we feel more secure. The PAG can become more settled. We can then go about the daily tasks of working and supporting ourselves in a more relaxed way. But what does instinctual balance look like in the workplace?

Awakening Einstein's Real Genius

Instinctual balance is based on respect for the natural timing and cycles of the human nervous system. Some cutting-edge companies are already beginning to recognize the health- as well as economic- benefits of a more flexible work environment. For example, workers at the outdoor clothing company Patagonia enjoy a "Let My People Go Surfing" flextime policy that allows them to participate in outdoor recreation activities during the workday. Time missed from the office is made up outside the 9 to 5 schedule. Patagonia also encourages children to visit the workplace and provides on-site daycare for its employees. This allows its workers to stay in touch with the natural rhythms of nature and children. Needless to say, morale at the Patagonia campus is pretty high and the level of employee loyalty and productivity are the envy of the industry.

For extremely creative people, brief periods of fatigue and weakness are not seen as a problem. Albert Einstein, Bill Clinton, and Leonardo da Vinci all recognized these waves of fatigue to be sources of inspiration. Many workers are discovering that a 5 to 15 minute nap leaves them refreshed and instinctually invigorated. The momentary loss of productivity is more that made up for by increased efficiency, vitality, and abundant creativity. I suspect that creative geniuses throughout history have been intuitively using this advanced level of instinctual intelligence. Einstein's catnaps must have enhanced his awareness of his intuitive embodied consciousness. The brief periods of stillness recalibrated his nervous system, allowing it to function with optimal clarity and brilliance. His inquisitive mind is characteristic of an aroused but balanced SAM axis. His creative genius is a sure sign of a relaxed and restored PAG that could recognize the abundant possibilities of life.

For this type of instinctual intelligence to become accepted more widely is a cultural change. The cultural work ethic of the modern world often demands that employees work relentlessly, without real respect for the optimal cycles of human efficiency and productivity. Very few bosses would tolerate an employee surrendering to momentary fatigue, much less see the potential value of an episode of doubt and despair. However, in time, the basic principles of instinctual intelligence will become part of the modern economic vocabulary. Companies are finding innovative ways to help employees have more quality time with their families, recognizing that it enhances productivity. Recent studies are confirming that allowing employees to follow the their instinctual rhythms actually yields more productivity in the long run. This new model of instinctual balance offers an alternative to exhaustion and burnout.

Freedom from the Past

Rather than giving up after his second loss for the senate in 1858, Lincoln carried on. He searched relentlessly within himself for the solid unwavering confidence that was needed. He was ready and willing to engage life, confident that he could use his abilities and determination to succeed. The determination Lincoln showed was not like the quick energetic burst of the self-protective instincts. Evolved instinctual perseverance is steadier, focusing on the realistic commitments needed to sustain effort in the long haul. This determination feels consistent, like a smooth slab of solid rock. It is primarily an inner sensation. There is a distinct feeling of fullness in the belly that initially arises from the balanced parasympathetic influx arising in the gut. The feeling of confidence is not flamboyant, but more like a steady humility. We have the sense that our steady commitment is not just our own personal will. Rather, we draw strength from the evolutionary dynamism of our deepest instinctual resources. The grinding, relentless consistency informs our actions and our emotions, infusing us with a quiet fortitude. Lincoln used this fortitude to campaign for president and sustain himself through the horrors of the Civil War.

Explorers of consciousness like Hameed Ali can offer us valuable insights into this evolutionary shift in instinctual intelligence. From the perspective of modern paradigm of the Diamond Approach developed by Ali, we can see that Lincoln went through a transpersonal process of *individuation*. Individuation, for adults, is the separation from the past conditioning encoded in our nervous systems. Although he was often plagued by his own doubts and anxiety, he never let his private fears prevent him from acting on behalf of the highest public good. It would have been easy for him to see the world as a harsh and miserable place. But he refused to see the world through the self-image of a frightened hungry boy that was physically abused by his father. He had achieved a level of independence, where he could act on behalf of truth and justice- regardless of his personal history. He never lost sight of the broader goals of justice and freedom. In this perspective, Lincoln acted with the inner autonomy of a true adult.

Lincoln was able to embrace the vision of freedom and human rights while maintaining a cold practical political sensibility. This balance required an inner resiliency and steadfastness. He could not let the fears or others- or his own inner demons- dictate the course of events that were unfolding during the Civil War. He followed a course of truth- rather than let himself be swayed by fickle political winds.

The capacity to act as an *authentically individuated* adult human being is perhaps the most fundamental attribute needed for evolving our instinctual intelligence. It begins with perceiving the reality of our lives in a more mature way. As we gain a mature acceptance of our instinctual evolution, our cognitive processes become clearer and more realistic. Gone is the incessant chatter of our neurotic, rigid minds that respond only to scarcity and fear. When we are free from these inner fears, we experience conceptual lucidity. We feel we have enough time to make clear, rational decisions. There is a sense that we are not fooling ourselves. This evolved determination carries with it the understanding that being realistic and concrete is better than fantasies and idealizations- and unquestionably better than living a life distorted by the fears of the distant past. This determination allows us to live in the present. When our awareness is embodied in the present moment, we have the capacity to see reality as it is- creative, abundant, and supportive.

A Deeper Surrender

Abraham Lincoln stood poised on the stage, ready to give his speech on that cold night in February 1860. He was speaking at the Cooper Union in New York City. Little did he know that the speech he was about to give would catalyze a change in the instinctual consciousness of humanity. All he knew was that something had to change. Lincoln had written and rewritten his speech on the train ride from Illinois. He knew the words. What shocked him- and totally stunned his audience- was the *gravitas* with which the words emerged. It was as if that that precise moment Lincoln's personal determination aligned with the evolutionary will of the universe. In an address to the New York Republican party, Lincoln took a clear moral stand on slavery, echoing the words of the US constitution that all men are created equal. Those who witnessed the speech recognized something extraordinary had happened. It was as if Lincoln had been divinely ordained to lead the fight against this form of moral and instinctual ignorance. It was a breathtaking moment of instinctual evolution where the highest aspirations of the human soul began to pulse through Lincoln's body. In that moment, Lincoln took on the aura of a true leader, supported by the evolutionary dynamism of all creation. His audience could viscerally feel the shift in momentum. By the end of the year he was elected president. It would take five more years for this momentum to establish a lasting shift in American culture and end a long horrible night of human injustice. Lincoln's determination made it possible for a nation of the people, for the people, and by the people to not perish from the face of the earth.

By surrendering to the larger forces of evolution, Lincoln's own soul became the human focal point of a major turning point in history. He had the awesome responsibility of attempting to change a formidable and deeply engrained instinctual habit. Since the dawn of human history, certain groups of people have sought to use economic, technological, and political power to subjugate other humans. In the most brutal ways, they sought to enslave others to help themselves amass superior wealth and social status. The Darwinian *survival of the fittest* mentality of slavery led to some of the most inhumane oppression and terror ever witnessed on this planet. Slave owners were willing to fight to the death to maintain this power.

The Source of Abundance

The evolving wisdom of instinctual intelligence helps us recognize the true source of Lincoln's resolve to abolish slavery. The ultimate source of human perseverance is not to be found in the usual sources of motivation- greed, lust, power, and control. Lincoln recognized that the institution of slavery was based on the unevolved impulses of greed and abusive power. These personal ambitions draw their energy from the insecurities of our most primal fears of starvation and environmental dangers. They are based on the misperception that resources are scarce and that human beings must fight with each other to survive.

In contrast, a more evolved perception of instinctual reality is that the universe is infinitely creative and abundant. In this view, the more each human helps others to prosper, the greater the total resources available to everyone. This level of instinctual intelligence takes into account the abundant creativity inherent in our instinctual energy. This intelligence is slowly emerging on our planet. A few transnational corporations are starting to embrace the concept of long-term *sustainability*. They are beginning to adopt long-term policies that will support the conservation and sustainable use of material *and* human resources. The enlightened leaders of these corporations recognize the greed of a few individuals has severe limitations. Greed destroys resources through thoughtless consumption and a lack of consideration of long-term consequences. In contrast, there is no limit to the abundance that can be generated by mutual cooperation between humans and the living systems of the environment. This cooperation fosters an appreciation of the mutual interdependence between humans and nature, as well as profound gratitude for the resourcefulness of all creation. By fully embracing our connection to both other living beings and the material universe, we can begin to understand a deep principle of instinctual intelligence:

> The intelligence that directs the evolution of the galaxies, stars, and planets- as well as the miracle of life on Earth- is guided by an inexorable wisdom. In this perspective, each human being is only a small thread in this immense, all-encompassing fabric. The determination inherent in our instinctual intelligence can help us live our lives in balance with the evolving dynamism of the universe. It requires a great deal of fortitude and resiliency to surrender to the ultimate source of evolution- and join forces with this intelligence instead of fighting against it.

Aligning Our Instincts with our Life Goals

It is important that we don't sit back and complacently admire people like Oprah Winfrey and Abraham Lincoln. It would be easy to simply say that *they* are the extraordinary people and *we* are just average folks with no special gifts. We often project the evolved instinctual qualities of determination and confidence onto other people and fail to recognize this capacity in ourselves. In this sense, we are always trying find support outside of ourselves. But remember- what we idealize is exactly what is missing in our own internal sense of support. So, it can be useful to pay attention to your fantasies and daydreams- they often point to qualities of instinctual intelligence that are awakening in ourselves. As our inner support and determination awaken, we become practically focused on *the next step*. When this type of instinctual intelligence is aligned with our life goals, we begin to feel certain that we will do what it takes to support our growth as human beings. This determination will sustain us throughout the long and difficult journey of developing deeper levels of our instinctual intelligence. It allows us to align ourselves with the lifestyle that will truly support our own evolution, as well as that of others.

The story of Abraham Lincoln shows us that it is possible to develop our instinctual intelligence in an organic way. We don't have to run to a psychotherapist or have an extensive knowledge of evolutionary neurobiology. Often, instinctual evolution works intuitively- it is an innate process that is an inherent property of the living universe. The more clearly we recognize and appreciate this pervasive intelligence, the easier it is to surrender to its wisdom.

CHAPTER 16

Passionate Creativity

Narcissistic. Brash. Audacious. Exploitative. Shrewd. Poseur. Exhibitionist.

Madonna doesn't really care what names you call her. As long as people are talking about her- and buying her records- she'll just keep doing what she's doing, thank you very much.

Madonna has displayed a remarkable degree of instinctual intelligence at each stage of her life. Hardly willing to settle for any of the traditional roles offered to women in Pontiac, Michigan where she grew up, Madonna forged her own path. Over the course of her career, she has become an iconic figure, reflecting the aspirations of women- and many men- all over the world. But these aren't your grandmother's aspirations. Madonna has shown us how to express sexuality, experiment with our sense of identity, and engage the fascinating world of passionate creativity. At each step of the way she has had brilliant successes and utter disasters. She has been praised and ridiculed- often in the same breath. Through this whole process, Madonna has provided a template for adults to come to terms with our most passionate instincts. It's been messy, salacious, and often ridiculous. At the same time, she has provoked, inspired, challenged, and aroused us. She has a way of getting under your skin and exposing the secret villains of self-judgment that wither away our more robust impulses. She also shoves the hypocrisy and distortions of modern sexual morality right in our faces. And dares us to lick it.

Whether you like Madonna's music and artistic expression is not the point. Her true genius has been her willingness to develop her instinctual intelligence. It hasn't always been an elegant process. But she has unflinchingly revealed each phase of her exploration with integrity. She has given us a glimpse of how the evolution of instinctual intelligence- of a decidedly erotic flavor- might take form. You might not choose to wear her clothes. But to become instinctually mature, passionate, independent adults we must surely follow her footsteps across a challenging terrain. The path she has walked- overcoming shame and self-judgment, broadening her aesthetic sensibility, and joyfully integrating sexual potency into the complexities of modern life- is an archetypal path of evolving instinctual intelligence.

Over the Borderline

Many people first became aware of Madonna Louise Veronica Ciccone when they saw her crawling around in a thong under her see-through bridal gown at the MTV Music Awards show in 1985. That seemed to get everyone's attention.

Taboo Allure

In the early years of her career, Madonna gradually wielded her instinctual intelligence to gain commercial success. She found that audiences were captivated by a very specific type of sexual exhibitionism. And she quickly realized that she had a particular talent for giving them exactly what they wanted. She knew how to mesmerize audiences by taking them across a line of repression that they did not dare to cross themselves. But how did she develop the confidence to straddle this line so confidently?

It began with building the connection to her own body. From an early age, Madonna was enrolled in one kind of dance class or another. She was always delighted to try out all forms of movement and music. When she got home, she would dance to records. She would even teach boys to dance. All this training gave Madonna a confidence in the expressiveness of her body. She also loved the attention. As a teen, she couldn't help but provoke reactions from her teachers and peers by dressing outrageously. It was just part of her playful nature. However, as she began developing her physical talents, Madonna could feel the restraints of her social environment. Growing up in an Italian Catholic family, she was not allowed to go to concerts, stay out late, or date boys. This made her want these things all the more. She refused to subdue her sexuality and creative passion to conform to the social rules of her community. She left home at 17 and headed for New York City.

At the intersection of her strong instinctual drives and her repressive Catholic background, Madonna began to craft her first artistic breakthrough. With this archetypal form of expression, she could take her listeners across the repressive barrier. And she drew on her own inner conflicts to show us how it's done. In her teen years, she often ached to get free of the responsibilities of school and family. She was forced to babysit and stay at home far more than she wanted. She was acutely aware of how social rules were restraining her passionate desires. She longed for the day where she could be free to pursue her impulses. In many ways, she was tapping into a bedrock reality of American life. For all of our economic success, many adults lead lives of sexual repression. Madonna sensed that it is all too easy to resign one's self to the day-to-day grind of responsibility and work. Many people become so resigned that they feel there is little point in even trying to satisfy the pulsing sexual and creative desire that burns inside. Yet the hope is always there.

Madonna knew how to tap into this longing. So many of her early songs are based on the universal yearning to be free. She has always been honest about the thrill she felt in breaking the rules. She would sneak out at night and go to concerts. She liked crossing the repression barrier. She longed for what was forbidden. It wasn't like Madonna was dangerously promiscuous, sleeping with every boy in town. She claims she was a virgin until the age of 17 and dated her boyfriend for some time before she became sexually active. What excited her was the thrill of allowing her instinctual energy to flow. She had learned to trust that her physical impulses could overcome the inhibitory fears she absorbed from her family, Catholic school nuns, and society as a whole. How did she learn to cross this line that holds so many of us back? Again, our knowledge of instinctual intelligence can reveal her secrets.

Breaking Down the Body Armor

Let's start by being honest and talk about a dirty little secret that no one likes to admit. Despite all the young, beautiful, sexually fulfilled people we see on TV every day, many adults in the modern world experience considerable dissatisfaction, frustration, physical dysfunction, and emotional difficulties with adult sexual intimacy. Seen any ads for *Viagra* or *Levitra* lately? The overwhelming popularity of these drugs gives us some clue that many adults are seeking to boost their sagging sex lives. This is a secret very few friends will tell you: most of their sexual activity is at best compulsive and nowhere near the satisfaction they instinctively know is possible. Many adults who initially come to me for consultations report that their bodies often feel dull and unenergetic. Even those who exercise and actively use their bodies on a regular basis often have areas of contraction and numbness. A great deal of this contraction of our bodily energy centers around the lower pelvis. The roots of these contraction patterns go back to our early childhood experiences. Many women experience pervasive patterns of musculature tension in their pelvis. Often, these unconscious tension patterns were originally needed to ward off unwanted and inappropriate sexual advances during childhood and adolescence. They linger in their adult lives as painful reminders of these early unpleasant social and sexual interactions. These tension patterns affect the adult female's capacity for feeling playful and flirtatious, as well as inhibiting deep instinctual responses to sexual intimacy like lordosis and orgasmic release.

Women aren't alone. Boys learn at an early age that they should hold their bodies in specific ways if they are to stop the social ridicule from other boys or from their fathers. Many fathers play too aggressively with their young boys, hoping to 'toughen them up'. Often, young boys cannot handle the overly aggressive and sometimes abusive physical interaction with their fathers. Older boys can seem intimidating and powerful to young boys. Especially in the locker room. The masculinized genitals of older boys often gives young boys a sense of being inferior. They learn to contract their young bodies in a natural self-protecting fear response of freezing. This freezing distorts the natural supple energy of the child and this body armoring continues into adulthood. Men can become physically and psychologically *hard*, making themselves impermeable to all but the most aggressive of physical pleasures. This predisposes them to become stuck in a rut of chronic sexual arousal, addicted to the fleeting but intense pleasure of repeated ejaculatory discharge. They can experience sexual satisfaction through the visual stimulus of pornography or meaningless sexual encounters. Their armoring makes it difficult for them to experience the pleasures of playful physical touching, cuddling, or other forms of intimate emotional contact with their partners. *Viagra* sells not because men can't get it up- it sells because men have a lot of trouble getting it up in situations of intimacy and vulnerability.

Grooving in the G-Spot

Although it makes a lot of people uncomfortable to admit it, the physical and psychological impressions formed during childhood impact our sexuality in a big way. As we have seen with all instinctually intense experiences, the human nervous system records these experiences by creating inhibitory neural networks. Consciously acknowledging the various levels and depths of sexual inhibition within our adult bodies can be a painful process, both physically and emotionally. A great deal of shame surrounds the slightest implications of sexual inadequacy. Madonna's artistic and instinctual skill was to find a way to push listeners over the line of shame. She does this by making her private shame public. Check out the lyrics from *Into the Groove:*

ONLY WHEN I'M DANCING DO I FEEL THIS FREE
AT NIGHT I LOCK THE DOORS, SO NO ONE ELSE CAN SEE
I'M TIRED OF DANCING HERE ALL BY MYSELF
TONIGHT I WANNA DANCE WITH SOMEONE ELSE

Madonna gracefully implies that she feels some shame about her dancing. She doesn't want anyone to see her, but she also yearns for connection. By disclosing her private inhibitions, she activates the listeners' inhibitory circuits. At the same time, she hits them below the belt with an infectious groove that promotes an immediate awareness of their adult bodies. As the music pumps and our bodies begin to move, years of fear, anxiety, frustration, inhibition, and shame begin to melt. The ancient shamanic technique of letting music and rhythm move our bodies is probably the oldest method of nervous system recalibration known to humans. Her disclosure of secret shame, combined with a rhythm that makes our adult bodies feel muscular and sexual destabilizes the self-image of a frozen child. The neural circuits of this fading self-image hold the residue of being overwhelmed by the intimidating physical presence of adults and older siblings. We vicariously share her desire to obliterate the restrictive presence of others. Supported by a thumping bass, Madonna takes us over the edge and into a fundamental truth about instinctual intelligence:

> The primary way to access our instinctual intelligence is to be in touch with the natural energy and playfulness of our bodies. Actively sensing, listening, and *responding* to the wisdom flowing in our bodies is fundamental to recognizing and developing our instinctual intelligence. The connection to our adult bodies helps us destabilize the inhibitory networks- and fearful self-judgments- that were established during childhood.

After Madonna moved to New York, she worked on and off as a dancer and a nude model for seven years. She lived in a shabby flat and lived on popcorn. And she certainly did not have the confidence that she does now. She has often stated that every new dance or music venue she entered make her feel awkward and fearful- initially. Her knees would tremble. She would criticize herself. But then she would set her mind and body to learning the new steps or the new song. During this seven year process she went through this recalibration process over and over. With each audition, each modeling session, each performance- she burned through another inhibitory self-image. She danced her way through layer after layer of repression, shame, and self-doubt. She had literally lost her inhibitions and broken through the repressive barrier.

Anyone Can Shake Their Ass

I'd be lying if I told you that opening the world of adult creativity and sexuality was as easy as simply breaking trough the repressive barrier. To be sure, it takes a lot of courage and hard work. But in many ways, people have known that dancing to rhythmic music is a great way of developing their instinctual intelligence. Shamans and healers discovered this tens of thousands of years ago. Once you have broken through the repression barrier, what comes next?

What's a Material Girl to Do?

For a creative artist like Madonna, past success can be a deadly trap. Once the public latches on to an image, they resist an artist's attempts to change. Yet if the artist keeps doing what they always did, the work grows stale and people lose interest. An artist can fade quickly, becoming irrelevant overnight. Once she fully crossed the repression barrier, Madonna was a megastar. Her singles were climbing the pop charts. *Like a Virgin. Borderline. Into the Groove.* And who can forget *Material Girl*? Madonna had definitely overcome her shame. She professed her love for hot sweaty dancing, sex, and piles of money. It was with *Material Girl* that the world fully understood that Madonna was not afraid to tell everyone what was on her mind and what she was feeling in her body. But Madonna wasn't satisfied. She had seen other women use their sexuality to fuel a similar meteoric rise- and then become punch lines of late-night TV jokes. She wasn't going to allow this to happen to her. But what was her next move? Think of the dilemma she faced. During the '70s and '80s how many women were there who were sexy, intelligent, confident, and totally in charge of their own economic and creative destiny? Margaret Thatcher was intelligent and confident. But not sexy. Farah Fawcett was sexy. But…well, let's just say she wasn't known for her brilliant insights into the human condition. It wasn't like there were a thousand role models that she could emulate. Until Madonna, women had to be either sexy or smart. We didn't really have a cultural archetype of the combination.

Madonna knew she could not rely on her past success to keep her artistic creativity flowing. In a sense, she had literally exhausted her own personal experiences. She showed everyone how a Catholic girl from Pontiac, Michigan can be very very sexy. And very rich. But how many times could she use the metaphor of overcoming her inhibitions to satisfy instinctual desires? One more foray in that direction would risk her becoming a parody of herself. She had a deep longing to feel the passionate creativity of her initial breakthroughs. This is where we can begin to see a shift in Madonna's sources of creativity. Gradually, we begin to see her drawing on elements of *other people's* experiences. Now this may seem like an obvious source of artistic inspiration. But it represents an important shift in the development of her instinctual intelligence. And it took her career to a new level.

Perspective Taking

One of the ways our passionate creativity matures is through contact with other people. Initially, we learn about playing and fun and excitement by hanging out with our parents and other children. Both our instinctual energy and repressive patterns are shaped these experiences. But until we reach adulthood, these experiences are largely shaped by the *specific cultural attitudes* in the micro-communities in which we grew up. Even our attempts to break free of the prevailing cultural constraints occur within the barriers and opportunities of our familiar cultural settings. Look at Madonna's example. She crossed over the repression barrier that instilled in her through the specific cultural experiences of Catholic families urban Michigan during the 1970s.

Yes, she had broken through. Freeing herself from the constraints of her family and local culture made her feel liberated. Like many of us who have made that leap, she managed to find fresh and authentic ways of engaging life. And yet she longed for something more, something beyond her own experiences. This is a trap many of us fall into. We manage to get free of our initial constraints, only to realize that there is something we still long for. At first we may not recognize what it is. But as we get older- and get a taste of instinctual gratification- another dimension of life begins to awaken. We fall in love. Loved ones die. We have children. All of a sudden, another person's well-being becomes as important- or even more important- than our own. Our instinctual perspective shifts out of its self-centered myopia.

As Madonna evolved into a deeper layer of instinctual maturity, she began to ask herself a profound question: What would it be like to be somebody else?

One of her first experiments with taking on the perspective of another person was her hit single and video *Poppa Don't Preach*. In this song, we enter into the world of a young woman who finds herself pregnant- much to her father's disapproval. The song mixes feelings of anger, fear, vulnerability, and personal redemption. Listeners begin to subjectively identify with this woman's perspective and experiences. Through this musical vehicle, Madonna had found a way to mature as an artist. So many of her previous songs where about breaking free of repression and embracing sexual playfulness. Now we see another side of the story. Here's the key thing Madonna shows us: Breaking through the repression barrier is only one stage of becoming a sexually mature adult. There's a huge onslaught of real world consequences surrounding sexuality. Part of developing our instinctual intelligence is to consider these consequences.

Sex in the Real World

21st century Earth is a complex place. It gets more complex every day. Finding ways to express our embodied creative passion takes a bit of work. When we are children, we are largely sheltered from the more extreme consequences of acting on our instinctual impulses. Our mothers yelling at us is not a life-threatening situation. However, as adults, pregnancy, AIDS, marriage, jealousy, betrayal- the whole slew of real-world consequences- complicate things exponentially. No matter how uninhibited we are, these realities will affect our lives. Sometimes, acting on an instinctual impulse is liberating. Other times it can totally change your life. Forever.

One reaction we can have to this adult reality is to ignore it. We can pretend science doesn't really apply. AIDS is something that happens to someone else. *I* won't get pregnant if he doesn't use a condom. We can feel that being practical and careful when it comes to sex can be a killjoy. Coming to terms with these realities can feel like a retreat back behind the repressive barrier where we were safe. Maybe it's just easier not to get involved. By the time we think through all these consequences, we're just not in the mood anymore. We *really can* end up with a sex-killing headache.

A lot of people were waking up to these realities in the 1990s. AIDS was entering public aware-ness with a vengeance. Madonna was affected by the AIDS epidemic in a very personal way. Many of her colleagues and friends in the dancing community were testing positive for HIV. Several close friends died agonizing deaths. Madonna was caught in no small dilemma. In the first few years of her success, she made a name for herself in dance clubs across the world as an icon of sexual liberation. Now, suddenly, the sexual freedom she had championed was a source of fear and death. Her response? She didn't bury her head in the sand. Nor did she back off repen-tant from her outspoken sexual boldness. Her response to this situation reflected a developmental shift in her instinctual intelligence.

Kaleidoscopic Logic

Madonna didn't pretend that there were simple answers. She began to absorb the personal and global consequences of the AIDS epidemic. She had to open herself to the intense emotional roll-ercoasters on which so many AIDS victims lived. She also had to find a way to remain true to the ideals of sexual liberation and tolerance that fueled the creativity of these physical artists. From this matrix, a new creative style would emerge. Her music, videos, and concert imagery began to reflect the complex perspectives of contemporary sexuality. Flavors of different cultures began to punctuate the groove. She sang songs of heart-wrenching sadness. Postmodern juxtapositions were driven to the edge of absurdity. Scenes of simulated orgies with semi-naked dancers would be followed by a song about losing friends to AIDS. And of course, she continued to bump out her relentless groove. In watching some of her concerts, many people did not know what to think or feel. Her artistry was provocative and confusing- but its net effect was to make audiences figure it out for themselves.

Madonna was making people sweat, both physically and emotionally. She was also making them think. If we were willing to enter into her kaleidoscope, she offered us a schooling on the grow-ing pains of evolving our instinctual intelligence. She took us out of our comfort zones. She showed us that it is hard to get comfortable in unfamiliar situations. When we leave the safety of the familiar, we too might feel our knees wobble. We come face to face with the fact that we have to take risks. As we grow older and have some measure of success, it can be so easy to bury ourselves in our habitual social and cultural circles. Through her artistry, Madonna reveals a very direct insight about the type of intelligence needed for a real instinctual maturity:

Integrating the "non-linear emotional" orientation of the right brain with the "linear organi-zational" orientation of the left brain is critical to cultivating advanced levels of instinctual intelligence. This integration allows us to experience greater instinctual intensity, curiosity, and satisfaction with a necessary degree of common sense, competence, and safety. This level of intelligence allows us to explore more complex and sophisticated realms of sexual, cultural, physical, emotional, and artistic play.

Left Brain-Right Brain Integration

One of the most difficult challenges we face in developing our instinctual intelligence is to integrate our instinctual impulses with our adult cognitive knowledge. Modern neuropsychologists would explain this as the integration of our right-brained emotions with the linear reality rationality of our left brains. Madonna gave us a powerful method for navigating this stage of development. First of all, she showed us that it's OK to be confused. Being uncomfortable, lost, bewildered, wobbly- even dizzy- is a *good* thing. In fact, being dizzy is a sure sign that both sides of our brains are being activated. In the last decade, neuroscientists have established that the certain regions of the right hemisphere produce a motivational state of avoidance. These areas are active when we feel afraid or distressed by the external environment. However, when we feel excited about what is happening around us, certain regions in the left hemisphere become active and we feel like approaching the people and situations that turn us on. So, when the old inhibitory avoidance networks of the right hemisphere are destabilized by the left hemispheric activation- we literally don't know if we are coming or going. This feeling of dizziness means that the old self-images and inhibitory neural networks of our familiar worlds are off balance. But if we don't run from the confusion, they'll start to fall apart.

Next, she showed us a to embrace the confusion. She danced. Her thumping bumping humping groove gave us a way to work out the tension. In her concerts and videos, the sheer variety of perspectives inundated viewers to the point where our rigid linear sensibilities are lost. She adopted personas as quickly as she changed her costumes, giving form and voice to what otherwise might not be seen or heard. It gave our left brains something to chew on, while our bodies keep moving to the music. In peak physical shape, Madonna found new ways to gyrate. She showed us the possibilities of a more flexible and graceful way to move through life. She shows how it's possible navigate the harsh realities of the world and not lose our passion. Her body reflected the change. Lean and muscular, she prowled the stage like a panther in heat. Her adolescent exuberance had morphed into a sophisticated articulate medium without a fixed center of gravity. She showed us how to physically embrace what is alien. At the same time, she utilized her wit, serving up images, lyrics, and wicked banter that forced us to see an unfamiliar slice of life. Instinctually sexy *and* intelligent, she sculpted a dance of many voices, midwifing the birth of a more sophisticated sexual intelligence that was desperately needed.

TantricSexySmart

Even at her relatively young age, Madonna was coming to grips with some fundamental truths that many of us have to face. As we grow older, we begin become aware of a certain longing. We long to reconnect with the innate joy we felt the in glorious moments of our lives when we felt free. It might be memories of the brief moments that we crossed the repression barrier and found the courage to dance. It might be the time we were bold enough to assert ourselves and finally get the professional recognition we deserved. Star athletes and performers feel the longing for success and achievement even more acutely. It's ironic that such happiness can become a source of suffering in later life. This longing can haunt us. We might valiantly plug away with the responsibilities of our adult life, but we know that something is missing. Something gnaws at us, subtle intimations of an absence, evoked by lingering memories of joy and satisfaction. Once we have known the depths of passion, we want it back.

Longing

Passionate joy is the most elusive of instinctual qualities. So ephemeral and precious, it seems to pirouette out of our grasp each time we reach for its delight. We want it so desperately to last, yet it never obeys our commands. So unpredictable, even repeating the exact same circumstances never guarantees its presence. Dulled by repetition and wary of expectations, joy dances unique, independent of our designs. Over the centuries, humans have been maddened by this chase, trying to enslave pleasure through addiction or buy it through power.

It creeps in slowly. Why might find ourselves oddly dissatisfied at times. Things don't seem quite so fresh. Breaking through the same old repression barriers doesn't bring us the joy it once did. Even the discovery of new cultures and breathtaking paradigms of emerging knowledge doesn't excite us the way it once did. We long for something more, but we often don't even know what it is we are missing. Madonna's music in the mid '90s begins to reflect this feeling. Her sound starts to become more ephemeral, as if a subtle vulnerability is emerging. The bravado gives way to a deeper confidence where this longing is given voice.

Ignoring the Call

Within this longing we can see one of the most difficult barriers to evolving our instinctual intelligence. Overcoming this barrier is basically like overcoming an addition.

The nature of this addictive barrier is hard to see at first. Our modern lives are so busy that it is quite easy to ignore the subtle voice of longing. Our careers are compelling. Our plans for the future are entrancing. It can be easy in to give into the seduction of kaleidoscopic knowledge in our ever-growing web-connected world. We can stay one step ahead of our longing by always running to the next new thing.

There's a reason why we ignore the call of longing. It feels lonely.

While we rarely recognize it, most adults spend a considerable amount of time and energy regulating their internal somatic and emotional states. Most of the time we this by pursuing specific instinctual gratifications like food (chocolate), mood altering substances (Starbucks), and sex (I'll leave that to your imagination). For the most part we usually dismiss these addictive behaviors- telling ourselves that we are just meeting our natural needs. However, as we begin to grow into more instinctually mature adults, we have to ask ourselves a difficult question: How do we use social and sexual preoccupations to distract ourselves from inner feelings of longing and emptiness? This is a difficult question, one that takes a lot of instinctual maturity to confront. We already know how eating food or changing our internal state with caffeine or alcohol is one of the most basic ways that we distract ourselves from unwanted feelings. But consider some of the other ways in which we avoid feeling lonely.

The Distraction of Busyness

In the frantic modern world, it is quite easy to keep ourselves so busy that we don't have time to even notice how lonely we really are. In my private practice and in various workshops I conduct, people are always remarking to me that there are few social settings where they feel they can be sincere and honest about their personal experiences and still feel socially included. While many of us put up a good façade, it is painful to me to see how starved people are for real intimate contact. By real intimate contact I do not mean the busy cycle of talking to the clerk at the store or the colleague at work with whom we bitch about the boss or chatting on the cell phone to a friend about a friend while you get your coffee on the way to the store. Nor do I mean intimate sexual contact, which we will discuss next. I mean real intimate heartfelt contact between mature adults. It's pretty rare these days.

It means sitting with a friend with no place to go. It means turning off the cell phone. It means really listening and sharing with authenticity and vulnerability. It means when you finally have to part there are tears of gratitude in your eyes because the contact you just experienced somehow transformed your soul.

We feel a small amount of pleasure in crossing things off our list or completing a project at work. But that quickly fades as the next engaging project arises. All of these incessant compulsive activities give us some instant gratification, but the truth is that they are often used to fill a hole. They engage many of the environmental seeking systems and motivational reward centers of the brain. They also fleetingly stimulate the release of opioids with brief flurries of superficial contact. Once again, these behaviors distort the natural pleasure seeking systems of the brain by dissipating the underlying feelings of a lack of real social connection.

Sexual Discharge

The other way we distract ourselves from feelings of loneliness is through compulsive sexual activity. For many men and women, the feeling of sexual longing is difficult to tolerate. When we feel the pull of sexual desire we either seek out an available partner or we discharge the energy through fantasy and masturbation. Masturbation can be a normal and healthy part of one's overall sexual experience. However, it can become distorted to the point where it severely restricts other essential instinctual needs and behaviors. For example, it can be used to discharge the anxiety and frustration of not having gratifying interpersonal social and sexual experiences. Look at what's happening with the increase in internet pornography. Young men can obtain the instant gratification of sexual discharge with ease. This prevents them from developing the social and communication skills, as well as the cultural knowledge needed to attract potential sexual partners and sustain intimate friendships. It also changes their biological responses to physical touch and intimacy. Of course, there are numerous other ways in which males and females can distort the natural pleasure seeking instinctual systems related to sexual behavior. Many women shop compulsively, exercise, or diet to the point of exhaustion in an attempt to become more attractive. Men can become locked into an intractable behavioral pattern of resource acquisition believing that more wealth and status will help them find the deep satisfaction and love for which they long.

The Depth of Vulnerability

All of these discharging behaviors act as an addictive barrier that can keep us locked in a cycle of instinctual stagnation. But what is the alternative? Why shouldn't we want to avoid these very unpleasant and painful feelings of loneliness? Well, as you may suspect by now, these behaviors *prevent the evolution of our instinctual intelligence*. They prevent us from having deeper and more intimate contact with a profound source of energy and wisdom. However, we must be willing to forgo the instant gratifications of distractions and discharge if we are to gain access to this source. It requires that we break our deeply entrenched fixation on the external world. In exploring the underlying feelings that drive these anxiety-discharging behaviors, we once again find the frozen self-image of a small child. This self-image is comprised of neural impressions of feeling lonely, the complete and utter lack of nourishing energetic social contact. These networks contain memories of a social environment in which there is no hope for fun or pleasure. When this self-image is activated, we feel like there is no one around who wants to engage our playful embodied energy. As children, we all have experiences of feeling lonely and isolated. When these experiences occur in infancy, they form particularly strong impressions of fear and abandonment. When these neural networks are activated they create nearly unbearable feelings of desperate, life-threatening aloneness.

Motherhood

It's not easy to acknowledge these gnawing feelings of emptiness. Once again, Madonna gave us an opportunity to take this journey with her. She had reached a point in her career and her personal life where external satisfactions could no longer obscure the call of a more compelling inner longing. She had no choice but to give it voice through music. We can hear her coming to grips with the reality of this mysterious longing in songs like *Take a Bow* and *Frozen*. The haunting melodies and lyrics draw us into feelings of intense loneliness verging on hopelessness. The atmosphere of the songs is icy, as if cold wind is blowing through a desolate landscape. There are no bold personas or thumping dance beats to pull the listener out of this void. Madonna no longer urges us to overcome self-doubt by bolting through the repression barrier. Nor is there the gratification of a clichéd "girl gets boy" ending. Instead, she focuses our attention on the feeling of longing. She strikes a universal chord we all have for passionate contact with life and love. She challenges us to acknowledge intolerable feelings of reaching out and finding no one there. Through her music, we can face directly into the absence of the lover we secretly long for. If we dare to join her in this vortex of longing and desperate aloneness- tolerating feelings utterly beyond horrible- we might find something quite unexpected.

A Ray of Light

The process of exploring our most vulnerable feelings of loneliness and longing is an incredibly difficult juncture of developing our instinctual intelligence. Fortunately, we can follow in the footsteps of other brave individuals who have walked this path. Over many centuries, some spiritual traditions discovered that this method of inner exploration offered an extraordinary way of utilizing the natural instinctual energy of the human body as a means of spiritual realization.

This approach to integrating the physical with the spiritual is commonly referred to as *Tantra*. Since they were first developed over two thousand years ago, numerous forms of physical and spiritual Tantric practices have emerged. The primary orientation of many modern Tantric disciplines- of which there are many- is to help individuals come into more complete contact with their physical energy, especially their sexual energy. This process uncovers the various ways in which sexual energy becomes blocked, both in our own bodies and in relationships with others. There are a wide variety of specific Tantric-based practices that are widely available throughout the world. Many incorporate physical exercises like yoga in as part of their overall approach to spirituality. Some traditions- like Kabbalah- use music, singing, and dancing as a way of cultivating a deeper inner awareness. There are several traditional Tantric systems developed by ancient Taoist, Buddhist, and Hindu teachers many centuries ago. There are also many modern systems that integrate esoteric knowledge with more contemporary discoveries and methods. Madonna's much publicized practice of yoga and Kabbalah again introduced millions of people to these ancient practices. Once again, she helps her audience find new pathways for personal transformation.

Evolving our instinctual intelligence allows us to access the deepest levels of our visceral energy with sobriety and wisdom. This intelligence helps us align this raw volatile energy with the most sublime aspirations and potentials of the human spirit. It also helps us recognize that the sense of who we are is more flexible than we originally thought and that all human beings are capable of profound inner and outer transformation.

One of the central principles of Tantric practices is to develop the individual's capacity to tolerate extreme levels of instinctual and emotional arousal. They commonly use meditation, yoga, breathing, and other types of nervous system training. These practices recalibrate the functioning of the basic instinctual programs. Perhaps the most important part of this recalibration is to increase the individual's capacity to tolerate arousal. This allows our bodies to experience more pleasure, energy, and excitation without discharging this energy through orgasm. This is done by developing specific pathways within the body through which the powerful energy of life and sexual excitation can circulate. This internal circulation has been used for centuries to cultivate physical, emotional, mental well-being- which, in turn, serves as a gateway for profound spiritual awakening. Developing this knowledge of energy circulation is an extraordinarily powerful method of developing sexual and instinctual intelligence.

There are various methods of exploring and integrating sexual energy available throughout the world. It's possible to explore this path of instinctual wisdom in a monogamous relationship or with multiple sexual partners. One of the most straightforward approaches to cultivating a basic physical understanding of evolved sexual intelligence is found in the work of Mantak Chia. In several very readable books and widely available workshops, Chia's Universal Taoist system provides the basic physical practices of circulating sexual energy within the human body to improve health and energetic well-being. They are widely accessible because they are not based on any religious beliefs or rituals, which many people find out of place in our modern culture.

Tantric Transformation

It all sounds pretty good. Great sex. Well-being. Energy. More great sex. Why isn't everyone all over the world enhancing their sexual and instinctual intelligence through these Tantric practices? Well, here's the other side of the Tantric path: It takes a considerable amount of time and refined awareness to learn to discriminate amongst and consciously control the more subtle dimensions of sexual energy within the body. We have to forgo many of the discharging behaviors we described above to practice becoming more intimate with our own sexual energy. In addition, in order for energy to *really* circulate throughout the body, the various inhibitory neural networks that constrain our instinctual energy need to be destabilized. This means that the different layers of frozen self-images have to be made conscious and dissipated through the various techniques we have been describing. This is hard work. Really hard work. And it's often a very lonely process. It means coming to terms with the fear and anxiety and loneliness and terror that is stored in our nervous systems. It means constant reorienting our attention inwards- away from the lure of external gratification. The good news is that the Tantric methods of energy circulation can help cleanse our nervous systems of these inhibitory self-images. And the more our nervous systems become clear, the easier it becomes to circulate the natural healing energy of life. The most important thing is to relax, have fun, and be curious about the energy of life within our own bodies- and the mysterious dynamism between human beings.

The methods of Tantric transformation developed within the esoteric spiritual traditions are extremely powerful. If we begin to incorporate them, the possibilities for evolving our sexual and instinctual intelligence grow exponentially in ways we never could have imagined. Not only that, it is also quite a lot of fun. These techniques can literally change the way we experience ourselves and the way we experience the world. Briefly, let's look at two ways in which the use of Tantric practices can change the nature of both men's and women's instinctual consciousness:

1) Predatory Sweetness in males. As we saw in chapter 4, testosterone and arginine vassopressin (AVP) account for many of the male-typical attributes of sexual behavior, including persistence, inter-male aggression, attentional focus, and memory formation relating to sexual experiences and partners. AVP can be seen as the overall arousal inducing hormone that accounts for the *predatory* quality of male sexual motivation. In males, the pleasure inducing neruopeptide oxytocin is released during orgasm. The effects of oxytocin are easily recognized as the afterglow of sexual satisfaction. Certain Tantric sexual practices involve extended periods of intercourse without male ejaculation. With sufficient experience, men can experience high levels of oxytocin-based orgasmic pleasure without ejaculation. These techniques appear to involve high levels of predatory assertiveness via AVP release, while simultaneously inducing the sweet softening orgasmic effects of oxytocin. At advanced levels of this practice, it is possible to direct the flow of vital energies throughout the body with great precision. The combination of neurophysiological balance, emotional suppleness, and energy control remain active in the man even when he is not sexually aroused. This instinctual balance will impact several areas of a man's world, including his competitive engagement with other males.

2) Receptive Nurturance in females. There are several evolutionary and neurobiological systems that induce deep levels of instinctual satisfaction when a female surrenders fully to her receptive urges. The pattern of the female orgasmic cycles allows higher and higher concentrations of oxytocin to be circulate in the nervous system. In certain Tantric practices, women develop the capacity for multiple orgasmic plateaus of increasing intensity and pleasure. Similar to men, women also have the ability to direct vital bodily energies throughout the body. This energy facilitates the evolution of profound capacities for nurturance. Nurturance is not a submissive role. It is the active and often highly assertive flow of energy that supports the family unit and larger community. This evolved capacity for nurturance integrates the estrogen and progesterone-mediated cycles of interpersonal attunement and environmental resourcefulness. It also promotes a deepening commitment to a woman's sexual partner and her offspring. At a fundamental level, the woman's receptivity facilitates a flow of nurturing energy that supports an instinctually vigorous life for herself and others on many levels.

Feeling Like You Just Got Home

Both of these qualities extend far beyond the bedroom. These integrating sexual practices actually help bring about the synergistic functioning of all the evolved forms of instinctual intelligence we have been exploring. *Predatory sweetness* and *receptive nurturance* help refine our assertiveness and our capacities for interpersonal connection, as well as promoting an embodied sense of confident determination. They also support the evolution of our personal power and contentment, as we will see in the final chapters. Ultimately, the evolution of our passionate creativity awakens a deep curiosity to know ourselves as completely as possible. It gives us the embodied energy to reach into our awareness and explore the depth of our souls. It also allows us to articulate what we find within ourselves completely and fully. We come home to ourselves. In this process we evolve into a fully mature innocence- wide-eyed with wonder at the extraordinary delights of creation.

CHAPTER 17

Peaceful Power

In the world of professional golf, the difference between winning and losing is often no more than a nervous twitch.

Based on his performance, Tiger Woods doesn't seem to twitch very often.

Clearly, Tiger has enormous physical talent. But so does every other professional golfer. What sets him apart is his instinctual intelligence. It is the hidden factor in his unprecedented athletic- and financial- success. But it didn't happen by accident. Nor can it be attributed to his legendary commitment to practice. Throughout his life, Tiger has utilized specific nervous system recalibration techniques to help him achieve the highest levels of excellence.

Unlocking the secrets of Tiger's excellence provides us with a blueprint for evolving some of our most primitive instinctual programs. In studying Tiger's training techniques, we'll discover how we can refine the most aggressive and violent of human impulses into an elegant power. Harnessing the potent survival energy that spawns hatred and unleashes the unspeakable horrors of warfare is not child's play. Tiger had to subject himself to some pretty unorthodox- and often brutal- methods to attain this level of nervous system intelligence. He learned to take himself to the mysterious edge between aggression and inner tranquility. With this intimate knowledge, he found a way to evolve beyond violence, and tap into the true source of power. It's easy to feel admiration for Tiger and chalk it all up to his superior talent. But I think the impact of his instinctual intelligence goes way beyond the golf course. It awakens something in all of us. As the world grows more violent each day, the necessity of using our instinctual intelligence to transform our most primitive impulses becomes more pressing. The choice is clear: We can sit back and say Tiger has the magic- or we can learn to harness it for ourselves.

Unleashing the Tiger

It takes more than talent to achieve excellence. This is something Tiger's father, Earl, had known all his life. As soon as baby Tiger came home from the hospital, Earl began handling clubs and hitting golf balls right in front his infant son. Earl was well aware that Tiger watched every move he made. Back then, no one really knew about mirror neurons and intersubjective instinctual

- 179 -

resonance. However, Earl intuitively grasped that he was Tiger's teacher, physically modeling for him a body-based intelligence that Tiger absorbed directly into his nervous system. As soon as Tiger could hold a club, he seemed to know exactly what to do with it.

In Earl Woods, we can begin to see the original blueprint for Tiger's instinctual intelligence. Earl was a Lieutenant Colonel Green Beret that served in Vietnam. His keen mind for military strategy trained him to exploit an opponent's weakness. But Lt. Col. Woods would pass something more than strategic thinking to his son. He would be the primary influence on Tiger's instinctual prowess. All elite professional golfers can think strategically in ultra-competitive situations. Tiger's superior instinctual intelligence is what allows him to *physically execute* his strategy. That's the critical difference. It's what gives him the edge.

How did Earl help develop and refine Tiger's instinctual intelligence? Well, the first thing we need to understand is that the cultivation of this level of instinctual intelligence is a *long-term process*. It doesn't happen overnight. It began before Tiger was even born. In Vietnam, Earl formed a deep friendship with a South Vietnamese military colleague. His soldier was known by friends- and respected by enemies- for having an extremely intense competitive drive and military instincts. In working with him on Special Forces missions, Earl was in awe of his capacity to maintain his nervous system composure under the most horrifically stressful conditions. He absorbed his friend's instinctual wisdom, compiling an organic set of mental notes that he would use later. Earl so respected this gentleman that he would pass his nickname on to his son.

Staying in the Zone

Earl Woods would be the first to tell you that he did not "create" Tiger's competitive drive. However, it is clear that he had a unique ability to *encourage the development* of his child's innate abilities. Earl's genius was to use the knowledge he had learned in the Special Forces- and from his Vietnamese friend Tiger- to guide his son's developing instinctual capacities. From an early age, Earl recognized his son's competitive nature. He encouraged it by competing with Tiger in a way that was appropriate for his age and level of development. For example, when they played golf, young Tiger had his own par. They called it Tiger Par. This gave him a few extra strokes on the longer holes to compensate for his lack of adult strength. By measuring their scores on an age-adjusted level, it was possible for Tiger to engage in direct, head-to-head competition with his father. These adjustments allowed Tiger to play to the best of his ability without being discouraged or overwhelmed. In neurobiological terms, this competitive scenario kept Tiger's autonomic nervous system operating at optimal levels. Because his father was not overbearing or abusive, his sympathetic nervous system did not become hyper aroused. And because the age-adjusted scoring system allowed Tiger to beat his father about half the time, Tiger's parasympathetic nervous system was not subjected to repeated experiences of failure that precipitates inhibitory shame. Earl knew just how to maintain Tiger's nervous system in the zone between the charge of winning and the sting of defeat. When Tiger won, the victory enhanced his confidence in his ability. When he lost, Earl helped Tiger find ways to improve his game. Each month, as Tiger improved, they had to lower the Tiger Par. Soon they were playing as equals, with no scoring adjustments. By the time he was 11, Tiger was beating his father straight up- with no scoring adjustments. But that wasn't the end of it. Earl knew this day would come- and he would have to find more sophisticated ways of challenging his son.

Both of his parents had a knack for putting Tiger in situations that would allow his nervous system to adjust to increasingly intense physical and emotional challenges. When he was only a few years old, Earl arranged for Tiger to demonstrate is budding golf skills on the *Tonight Show* with Johnny Carson. While Earl often served as the coach and psychologist, Tiger's mother, Thea, was the real taskmaster. She would often get up early to drive Tiger to practices and tournaments. She would instill in him a particular form of grace that he would need in a variety of situations, not only golf. As a child, Tiger was not always able to mange his emotions. As his competitive drive became more honed, he sometimes found it hard to treat others with kindness and respect. One time, after he played poorly in a local tournament, young Tiger threw his clubs around and refused to congratulate the winner- or even thank the tournament sponsors. His mother was appalled at his instinctual outburst and lack of social grace. She immediately forced him to apologize and make amends. Like Earl, Thea realized that instinctual intelligence always operates in a balance between arousal and relaxation. Without grace, competitive intensity can easily devolve into aggression and violence. This competitive grace was deeply instilled into Tiger's consciousness.

Grace Under Pressure

As Tiger became a teenager and began playing in more and more tournaments in Southern California, he began competing against other talented golfers. In some cases, he was competing against older teens with more experience. Tiger was feeling that he could not quite focus at the level he needed to- that here was some competitive toughness that he lacked. He felt distracted at key moments. He intuitively knew his instinctual intelligence had to evolve to the next level. Naturally, he turned to his father for guidance. He asked Earl to make him tougher so he could compete with the older kids. In Earl's training techniques, we can observe the first principle of cultivating true power:

> Developing the most powerful and potentially volatile aspects of our instinctual intelligence requires a sophisticated knowledge of how to regulate one's nervous system in stressful conditions. This type of intelligence helps us recognize the *optimal amount* of stress that our nervous systems can handle. An optimal amount of stress effectively recalibrates the nervous system by training it to cope with competitive and hostile conditions without falling into a state of collapse.

Drawing on his Green Beret training and the instinctual toughness he had imbibed from his military friend Tiger, Earl set about to recalibrate his son's nervous system. The training was relentless, on and off the golf course. Even before the round began, Earl would begin harassing Tiger, getting in his face about being weak and soft. This would recalibrate Tiger's parasympathetic system so that a shame response would not be triggered after a disapproving gaze from a parent. But that was just the beginning of a deeper transformation. As Tiger would be teeing off,

Earl would break the cardinal rule of golf and make noises just when Tiger was swinging at the ball. Earl would drop his clubs when Tiger was putting. He would cough, yell, and insult Tiger throughout the round. As Tiger initially grew used to Earl's tactics, Earl would have to resort to even more fiendish measures to provoke anger and frustration in his son. He would throw golf balls at Tiger while he was hitting his shots. Then he would criticize Tiger for taking too much time. Tiger would get so mad that his face would shake and his teeth would gnarl, seething in hatred and frustration. Earl would then torment him even more.

The key part of this training was that Tiger could not say a word. Obviously, this taught Tiger how to deal with pressure. Tiger is now regarded as having the most highly developed instinctual intelligence among elite performance competitors. He dominates a field of highly skilled, well-conditioned, and fiercely competitive athletes through his mastery of predatory aggression. As such, he demonstrates an evolution of a particular kind of instinctual intelligence. If we want to incorporate this wisdom into our own lives, we need to take a closer look at the nervous system recalibration techniques behind Tiger's excellence.

Embracing Extreme Agitation

For many adults, the central barrier to developing an instinctually intelligent level of predatory aggression is tolerating the extreme levels of nervous system arousal that arise in the course of this kind of provocative training. When someone provokes in this way, our survival instinctual programs are automatically activated. Deep down in the amygdala, we feel the threat of attack. Emotionally, this response is full of hatred and escalating impulses of violence. In a very basic way, it is hard for most of us to acknowledge, much less embrace, feelings of extreme nervous system arousal. There are two primary reasons for this. First, our own internal sense of inhibition- held in place by self-judgments and a desire to conform to social rules- often tells us that we should not feel extremely powerful emotions like hatred and violence. Culturally, these feelings are often marginalized. Due to various moral and religious beliefs, these natural impulses are repressed so efficiently that we rarely even recognize that they exist. Part of the changing culture of a more evolved instinctual intelligence will be to acknowledge these feelings with greater maturity and sophistication. Lt. Col. Woods recognized their value. He did not make the mistake of dismissing feelings of hatred and violence as "bad" or "wrong". Just like Navy SEALS, Green Berets are trained to embrace these powerful currents of instinctual energy and use them with intelligence.

The second reason why it is so difficult to tolerate feelings of extreme agitation, hatred, and violence can be found deep in our nervous systems. As always, we can see the roots of our instinctual tendencies in infancy. During the first year of life, all infants will inevitably experience episodes of extreme anxiety and painful physical feelings. In most circumstances, these intolerable sensations arise when parental caregivers cannot meet the infant's immediate instinctual needs. The mother's rejection of the infant can stem from unavoidable physical absence or incapacity, a lack of parenting experience, or the mother's psychological/emotional difficulties. Even children with the most loving and caring parents will experience periods of extreme nervous system arousal. An urgent phone call keeps a hungry infant waiting. An older child's injury will need immediate attention before the newborn's diaper can be changed. Children with abusive or neglectful parents will experience these extreme states more often. Regardless of its frequency, the frustration experienced by infants when their needs are unmet is *far beyond the capacity* of their immature nervous systems to tolerate.

Splitting

In order to survive these episodes of intense arousal, infants will attempt to discharge their nervous system agitation through their polyvagal regulating systems. At first they will yell and cry. This helps, but it cannot completely eliminate the inner sensations of pain and discomfort. If there is no parental response, the extreme nervous system dysregualtion will elicit a more primitive polyvagal response. Just as in the traumatic response of adults, the primitive dorsal vagal region of the midbrain is activated, resulting in a disassociative freezing response. Even a partial activation of the dorsal vagal region will block the conscious awareness of pain. This dissociative response will allow intolerable affects to be *split off* from the flow of the infant's self-awareness. As with all instinctually intense traumatic experiences, a self-image will be formed. These types of self-images will be comprised of neural networks that will trigger a dissociative response whenever the possibility of extreme frustration and agitation are perceived. They exert a powerful influence on the nervous system. As adults, we still use this primitive self-defense mechanism every time we avoid dangerous situations that might result in harm or call for a hostile response. Our inhibitory self-judgments tell us it is "wrong" to feel hatred. We try to maintain a self-image of being "good". Very few people deliberately set out each day to aggravate themselves to the point of violence. Except for a master polyvagal regulators like Earl Woods and his pupil.

At the core of this self-image is a young child trying to protect itself. In a deep sense, blocking the awareness of intense agitation gives the young child a sense of *power*. As infants, it is the only type of power we have. However, as adults, this dissociative nervous system response is a very limited and immature source of power. When we are caught in a dissociative loop, we cannot access deeper sources of instinctual energy. Further, there are very strong inhibitory barriers that we learn as children against expressing violent energy against our parents. To get past these barriers, we have to be willing to experience our feelings of agitation, hatred, and violence in a very conscious and deliberate manner. This is exactly what Earl Woods was training Tiger to do. Fortunately for Tiger, his father knew a thing or two about polyvagal regulation and optimal stress. A trainer needs to have an intimate knowledge of polyvagal regulation to help someone learn to tolerate this level of agitation. It also calls for a deft touch to place just the right amount of the optimal amount of stress on an individual's nervous system. Too little stress maintains the status quo. Too much stress sends in nervous system into frozen shock.

By forcing Tiger to consciously embrace the full intensity of his hatred, Earl helped him disrupt the deep dissociative tendencies imprinted in Tiger's nervous system during infancy. Earl was a brilliant instinctual teacher. He was intuitively utilizing many of the leading edge polyvagal regulating techniques that are being used by clinical psychologists today. Notice how he activated the primitive dissociative freezing responses while Tiger was actually hitting the ball. This forced Tiger to be aware of the frozen self-image while *simultaneously* being aware of his adult body. This is the same approach used by Levine and Ali in their advanced nervous system recalibration techniques. By forcing Tiger to remain silent- yet totally mindful- Earl prevented Tiger from simply discharging the energy. *Notice that the energy was not inhibited.* Embracing this unrelenting instinctual surge in every cell of his body, Tiger learned to access the secret source of authentic power known to martial artists, great athletes, and noble warriors throughout history. His father did not fear Tiger's emerging aggression. In Tiger's snarl, he recognized the predatory wisdom of his old Vietnamese brother in arms.

Yet, as Earl peered deeper into this mysterious power, he could sense that there was one more piece of instinctual intelligence his son would need in order to achieve true mastery.

The Elegance of Power

The human nervous system- right down to the molecules of its DNA- has an innate orientation that seeks to obliterate anything that threatens the continuation of its existence. For our human ancestors, this basic survival response helped them defend themselves and hunt down small game. However, his physical destructive power was no match for the overwhelming physical power and aggressiveness of some of the larger animals which would prey upon these groups of protohumans. One day, that all changed.

One day, about a hundred thousand year ago, on the edge of a forest in Africa, a small young human male picked up a branch that had fallen from a tree. Has he felt it in his hands, he felt a tingle in his gut. Something about it felt compelling. It was perhaps a meter long. Maybe a couple of inches round. It felt *just right* in his hands. The wood was hard and knotted. It had a density to it that made it strong. Without knowing why, the young man carried it with him as he continued to look for edible roots. Holding the club made in feel more relaxed. Suddenly, he heard a rustle in the bush. A small wildebeest darted out. Reflexively, the young man grabbed the end of his stick with both hands. Ordinarily, he would have run off. Now he held his ground. His stick was now a club. In his gut, he no longer felt afraid and weak. The tables had turned- now the wildebeest was his *prey*. The instinct of predatory aggression had undergone an evolutionary advance.

The First Relaxation Response

While not everyone might see a turn toward violence as an evolutionary advance, from the perspective of instinctual intelligence there is something important about this shift. The evolutionary development of the human brain allowed humans to use tools and create weapons. We no longer had to use our bare hands to defend ourselves. It became possible to exert control over the environment in new ways. Walking through the grasslands was way less scary if you were wielding a club or a spear. These early humans no longer had to cringe in fear that the rustling of leaves or the things that went bump in the night. From the perspective of the nervous system, this is a huge change.

The simple act of holding a club in one's hands changes our neurobiological state. If you don't believe me, pick up a baseball bat or a big stick the next time you get a chance. Find one that's not too heavy or too light. Swing it through the air a few times. Don't let some pesky old self-judgments make you feel ashamed or tell you it's wrong. We're all descended from ancestors who survived at one point or another by swinging a club in aggression or self-defense. The truth is that this type of weapon arouses our predatory aggression circuits. This is the basis of the advance in our instinctual intelligence that occurred during the last hundred thousand years. If you're wondering how violence is an evolutionary advance, hold on to your club and be patient. The answer may surprise you.

Imagine what it was like for infants back then. Mothers had only their most basic instincts to guide them. Famine, disease, predators, and basic ignorance all took their toll. Survival was always in question. Under these brutal conditions, the emotional well-being of infants was probably not a high priority. Those that did survive were probably pretty neurotic by today's standards. The combination of early nervous system trauma and overwhelming environmental conditions must have incessantly triggered the inhibitory freezing response in these early weaponless humans. When the first *Homo sapiens* started swinging their clubs, the boost in the predatory aggression circuits was substantial. In neurobiological terms, holding a weapon changes the threshold at which the dorsal vagal freezing response is triggered. Feeling one's adult body (and the muscles invigorated by swinging the club) disrupts the self-image of being small, powerless, and at the mercy of overwhelming forces. It is a very primitive- but effective- form of polyvagal regulation. In a very primal way, the development of weapons afforded these early humans a chance to relax.

Predatory Relaxation

Fast forward about one hundred thousand years, to the early spring of 2004 on the grassy plains of Georgia in the southeast United States. Tiger Woods is poised over his golf ball, about twenty meters from the hole. The shot he faces looks impossible. Between him and the cup is a huge sloped depression that makes it impossible for him to aim directly at the hole. Instead, to get it anywhere close, he needs to aim about seven or eight meters to the left of the hole and then hope that the ball will trickle down a bump on the other side of the green- ending up somewhere close to the pin. Having surveyed the way the ball will roll and visualized the shot he wants to hit, he steps up to hit the ball. He has the strategy, now it is time for execution. What's going through Tiger's mind right now?

Almost nothing. That's the source of Tiger's power.

Let me explain. For those of you who have ever played golf, you will know exactly what I'm talking about. The slightest noise is jarring to the nervous system, and will often result in a poor shot if we are startled in mid-swing. But our internal distractions are even more jarring. Every golfer knows that just as you finish raising the golf club and start into your swing to hit the ball, all sorts of things flash into your mind. It can be an irrelevant thought like "What will I have for dinner?" Or "What club shall I use to tee off on the next hole?" If we really focus in, see can see that the source of the distraction is actually a cascade of fleeting mental images that suddenly flash into our consciousness. Golfers will tell you that as the stakes increase, the more distracting the thoughts and images become. For professional golfers playing for millions of dollars in front of millions of viewers each week, the intensity of the mental distractions is excruciating. They have a disproportionate ability to wreak havoc with the players' emotions. When this image flashes, they briefly lose touch with the sensations and perceptions that are occurring in the present moment. In clinical terms, they *dissociate*. This causes them to lose control over their muscles to for just a split second- sending the ball minutely, but maddeningly, off target. This reveals one of the most paradoxical and elusive truths behind the development of instinctual intelligence:

The ability to utilize the power inherent in our instinctual intelligence comes from the knowledge of how to unlock the potent instinctual impulses of hatred and violence. Actually accomplishing this is a rare skill that requires advanced levels of neurobiological knowledge, compassion, integrity, and clarity of purpose.

So how does Tiger do it? Why does he seem impervious to these mental distractions? The answer lies deep within Tiger's nervous system. Neurobiologically, we could say that he does not dissociate when he is about to hit the ball. He does not experience the momentary activation of the inhibitory dorsal vagal region of the midbrain. Remember that swinging a club- or anything that feels like a weapon- automatically activates the neurobiological networks that regulate the predatory aggression response. The problem for most of us is that whenever this deep instinctual response is activated, it will also trigger the inhibitory neural networks of the dorsal vagal region. These inhibitory networks were first established as a result of the dissociative splitting responses that occur in infancy. The feeling of aggressive hatred is deeply associated with the activation of the inhibitory networks. It's completely automatic and unconscious. In adults- just as with infants- the activation of the predatory aggression circuits will often be accompanied by a dissociative inhibitory response. For individuals that experienced some kind of trauma during infancy the inhibitory response can cause the nervous system to slip into a state of frozen shock. In most other cases, the inhibitory effect will be more subtle. For professional athletes with years of high intensity training, the inhibitory freezing response sent to the limbs causes no more than an infinitesimal twinge of shakiness. In most situations, no one would ever even notice it. Back in the day, if a starving protohumanoid felt a little nervous twinge while he was planting his club into the head of a saber-tooth tiger- it just didn't matter. But in the high-stakes world of professional athletics, this microsecond dissociation and jolt of motor inhibition can alter the path of the ball ever so slightly. It's this fraction of an inch that separates Tiger from the rest of the pack.

The Cleanse of Peace

Why doesn't Tiger dissociate like everyone else? Here we can appreciate the instinctual intelligence of Lt. Col. Woods. He knew that the predatory aggression of a seasoned warrior is fueled by a cold deliberate stillness that is based on precise parasympathetic activation. Without this stillness, it is impossible to apply one's power in a precise and elegant fashion. Golf- like so many of life's challenges- cannot be played well when our rage is boiling. It requires a great deal of inner stillness to focus the elegant and precise application of power. We know that Earl would relentlessly push Tiger to the point of hatred and violence. This would activate the predatory aggression circuits. Arousing his survival circuits was easy. Focusing them was the hard part. The key element of Tiger's polyvagal training was that he had to keep silent. He couldn't whine or complain- nor could he discharge the energy that was boiling up by attacking his father. His predatory aggression circuits were in overdrive. Just as we saw in the Navy SEALS training, not crying or violently lashing out modulates the parasympathetic system- enhancing the flow of vagal sensory inputs from the stomach, intestines, and rest of the body in conscious awareness. The key is to focus one's attention on the flow of inner sensations. Focusing on the sensations of one's adult body- while simultaneously feeling the silent rage imprinted into the nervous system during infancy- disrupts the unconscious self-images of being a small helpless, instinctually frozen infant. As his father went through this instinctual training cycle with Tiger over and over, they systematically dissolved deeper and deeper layers of these dissociative inhibitory networks. Nothing was left in Tiger's consciousness except the sensations of his adult body. Within this deep inner awareness is a profound sense of calm and stillness. On the golf course, the outside world may be noisy and chaotic. But inside, the sensation in his consciousness is one of complete peace.

The Evolutionary Possibilities

Few of us are Navy SEALS or professional golfers. How can we make use of this profound instinctual knowledge in our everyday lives? We can begin by acknowledging that it takes a lot of courage and determination to come to grips with our deepest fears. Many of the inhibitory freezing responses that stand in the way of our true power are deeply engrained in our nervous systems. Disrupting their restrictive influences won't happen overnight. Even Tiger Woods had to undergo years of training to find the deeper sources of inner peace.

Responsibility and Honesty

It is easy to feel overwhelmed by the dark instinctual forces that still dominate our world. Our evolutionary past is full of epic, violent struggles for domination and power. How do we even begin to turn the tide? We can't really expect the world to overcome its deepest fears and grow out of its violent tendencies unless we are willing to do it ourselves. There are leaders in today's world who refuse to submit to the forces of ignorance and violence. Nelson Mandela comes to mind. The Dalai Lama. Leaders that have cultivated an instinctually intelligent power are not interested in exploitation and dominance. They feel an inner power that is not enhanced by making others weak. Rather, their refined sense of power impels them with a sense of responsibility. One doesn't have to be a world leader to make a difference in the instinctual evolution of humanity. Like Earl Woods, an instinctually intelligent father never seeks to overpower his children. He empowers them by sharing his knowledge and wisdom.

Taking responsibility for the world we live in becomes imbued with power when we make a commitment to face our fears more openly and honestly. Accessing our inner sources of power begins by *being honest with ourselves*. A lot of times we avoid being honest about the things that scare us. We don't drive to certain parts of town because they're unfamiliar or we are afraid. We avoid being in nature because we don't like the bugs and other creepy things. And let's face it- we're all experts at avoiding the fears that surround intimate relationships. Sometimes we're afraid to ask somebody on a date. Sometimes we're afraid to tell a friend that his drinking is creating problems. If we simply acknowledge the situations and conflicts that we usually run away from, we can begin to turn the tide on our subconscious dissociative tendencies. Most of the time, we avoid threatening situations without ever really examining if they are really as overwhelming as they seem. Truth be told, we make a lot of assumptions about reality and our own capacities-and more often then not we sell ourselves short. We surrender our power to imaginary fears.

The Illusion of Limitation

When we are aligned with our true instinctual power, our consciousness is transformed by a quiet, unsuspected force. We commonly associate power with dramatic, large-scale physical force. However, the true power within our instinctual intelligence is more subtle. Its power is derived from the capacity to eliminate the influence of all past impressions within our instinctual consciousness. Following the Woods' example, the more we can open ourselves to feeling the intensity of our hatred and predatory aggression- without acting on it- the more we can begin to sense the quiet annihilating power. Maybe we don't want someone to hurl golf balls at us or subject ourselves to verbal abuse the way Tiger Woods did. But we can all begin to enhance our polyvagal regulation. The real world offers plenty of opportunities for us to feel our frustration. We just have to have the mindset to enter in to those situations with a peaceful, open mind. Most of the time we avoid them like the plague. However, armed with our newfound instinctual intelligence, we might slow down and investigate the reality of the situation- and our feelings- a little more closely. If this chapter has shown you anything, I hope it is the simple recognition that feeling a little frustration, agitation- even hatred- is not a bad thing. It can be a doorway to an instinctually empowered life.

Authentic power acts like a dissolving agent, effectively causing the object of our hate- as well as the hate itself- to disappear. This dissolving power reveals something stunning: *The target of our hatred was actually just an image in our minds*. Our efforts to push it out of existence, to obliterate it, to kill it- were an attempt to exclude something from our instinctual awareness. When the mental image of the object is dissolved, there is nothing to exclude, nothing there we need to hate. Without the object of our hatred, the sense of power can flow freely. It feels like an overwhelming oppressive force has suddenly been lifted. No longer restrained or threatened by the hated object, there is a sense we can do whatever we wish. There is no one to fight against. Our actions feel swift, powerful, and decisive. We feel totally free to put as much force or intensity into our actions as is needed. There is no perception that someone will oppose or restrict us. This true power has annihilated the fundamental dichotomy that inhibits our instinctual capacity. The basic oppositional dichotomy of *me* vs. *my enemy* is no longer the unquestioned polarity of our instinctual consciousness. This strict dichotomy is the vestige of our need to split off intolerable frustration when we are infants. This division underlies the most powerful distortions of our instinctual emotions. This form of instinctual intelligence helps us see reality more clearly by dissolving the illusion of opposition and limitation. In its place, we are left with an open field of possibilities. Our power flows from a sense of freedom, not from violence and subjugation. This freedom is more powerful- and far more real- than our imaginary oppressors.

Pervasive Peace

If we allow our awareness to settle into the reality of the unrestricted openness of power, we can begin to observe a subtle quality dawning in our instinctual consciousness. It is a pervasive feeling of peace. We can perceive this quality most directly when we notice the smooth, velvety dissolving action of the power. This smoothness feels like an elegant black fabric that softly drapes our consciousness. Within the receding blackness, there is stillness. We feel this in our bodies as a sense of calm. Our minds are clear and bright, our thought patterns free from opposition and doubt. It literally makes us more intelligent by imbuing our minds with sharpness and precision, vividly comprehending reality without obscuration. It is as if the power has annihilated all the false distortions that twist our perceptions. The only experience that arises is what is objectively true. We are at peace in our minds and in our actions. We feel uncluttered, serene, and fluid- eminently capable of taking any action we need at a moment's notice. We feel the sensation of peace in our bellies, where a stillness is arising from a lack of unnecessary activity. If we extend our perception, we feel the stillness outside of our bodies. It pervades everything we are aware of, helping us to see one of the profound truths of instinctual intelligence:

> The subtle wisdom inherent in this form of instinctual intelligence is the recognition that the ultimate source of true power is not in the individual. It arises from a mysterious source that requires a great deal of inner calm to perceive. The intelligence that flows from humility and stillness allows us to align our embodied instincts with this source of indestructible power.

Tiger has described the experience of elegant power as a heightened state of awareness. It is the complete opposite of dissociation. His focus is totally absorbed. As he enters into his 40-second pre-shot routine, time begins to slow down. In this state of evolved predatory aggression, Tiger's nervous system is totally at peace. Thanks to Earl's training, when he feels the predatory energy of intense competition, there is no self-image of a weak, helpless infant that needs to freeze its instinctual impulses. His polyvagal training dissolved the inhibitory networks that activate the dorsal vagal region. Not only that, but Tiger doesn't boil over with sympathetic arousal. And there's no trace of the inhibiting shame of an overblown parasympathetic response. His nervous system responds in a balanced and elegant manner, characterized by efficient nervous system adjustments flowing from the ventral vagal complex. The feeling of raw power in his adult body calms him down. His mind is free of distracting thoughts. Totally aligned with elegant instinctual power of the universe, he is totally in the present moment.

He can feel the pressure of his hands on the club, and make micro-adjustments to get the right feel. He can sense each blade of grass, the way it leans and how that will affect the roll of the ball. He can feel his arms and legs, making sure they are balanced and responsive. Because time is moving so slowly, all of these perceptions- inner and outer- can be flow seamlessly through his awareness. With no self-image to interfere, the instinctual intelligence of the universe can flow. Through the club, through the grass, through the ball- through the fans watching. In that moment, when it all comes together, Tiger- along with the rest of us- *participates* in something mysterious.

Standing on the timeless grasslands of Augusta, Georgia- utterly relaxed but totally participating in his body, the environment, and the eternity of *this* moment- the ball is struck. At first, it seems headed in the opposite direction from the flag. It rolls up a large mound...pauses...and slowly completes an arc, pulled back toward the cup following a precise line of gravity inexplicably opened in the fabric of space and time. The ball finds a new groove, and heads directly into the hole.

The next time you see Tiger swinging a club, perhaps you might pause with respect for the evolutionary elegance- and profound mystery- behind it.

CHAPTER 18

Contentment

The deepest instinctual nature of every human being is exposed when they are placed under conditions of extreme stress and brutality. In these situations, the most primal impulses of selfishness and violence are revealed. Only someone who has developed the highest levels of instinctual intelligence would be able to maintain their rationality, integrity, and compassion under the most hostile of conditions.

The Dalai Lama, the spiritual and political leader of Tibet, has experienced some of the most horrific mistreatment of his people that any world leader has ever been forced to endure. Beginning in 1950, the Communist Chinese began to systematically invade Tibet. In 1959, he and Tibet's government were forced to flee their homeland and set up a government in exile in India. Since then, it is estimated that over 6 million Tibetans have been killed or died as a direct result of the Chinese invasion. The Chinese have systematically raped the Tibetan plateau, ruthlessly extracting its natural resources and using it as a nuclear waste dump. They have outlawed religion and mercilessly persecuted Buddhist monks and nuns for practicing their religion. It is even illegal for a Tibetan to possess a picture of their beloved leader, whom they refer to as *Yeshi Norbu*- the Wish Fulfilling Jewel. For nearly fifty years, the Dalai Lama has worked tirelessly on behalf of the Tibetan people, trying to stop the violent oppression by the Chinese. He has also sought to restore some measure of political, social, and religious autonomy for Tibetan society. During this entire time, the Dalai Lama has never expressed anger towards the Chinese, nor has he called for any kind of violent retaliation. Despite the misery and profound mistreatment of his people-many relatives and close friends of the Dalai Lama have been tortured and killed by the Chinese- the Dalai Lama remains as optimistic and kind as ever.

Overcoming Self-Centeredness

Many people wonder how the Dalai Lama can continue to be so warm and genuinely compassionate in the face of the barbaric conditions in Tibet. Almost everyone who meets him remarks that he exudes a genuine loving radiance that never seems to waver. What makes him different? How has he evolved his instinctual wisdom to such a profound level?

To answer this question, we have to examine his lifelong training as a Tibetan Buddhist monk. This training- which includes a variety of highly complex meditation practices- profoundly alters the nervous systems of the individuals who undertake this path of intellectual, emotional, and spiritual development. We're going to examine how these practices actually change the human nervous system by reviewing some of the state-of-the-art research that has emerged in the last few years. For several decades, scientists have known that certain meditation practices can increase concentration and other *cognitive* capacities. However, this new research revealed some startling findings. It is demonstrating that meditative practices like those found in Tibetan Buddhism can actually alter the functioning of primitive *instinctual dispositions*. To see how this is possible, we'll take a closer look at the meditation practices of the Dalai Lama and other Tibetan Buddhist monks. This exploration will help us uncover the highly evolved intelligence of these extraordinary spiritual- and instinctual- masters.

Expanding Compassion

Part of the Dalai Lama's daily meditation routine consists of extending his empathetic awareness to all living beings. This practice- known in Tibetan as *tonglen*- involves breathing into one's self the suffering of all living beings and then breathing out to them all of one's positive feelings and intentions. This taking and giving practice is an extraordinarily powerful means of breaking down one's self-centered preoccupations. As such, it is a central practice of all devout Tibetan Buddhists who continually seek to cultivate compassion as a central means of attaining spiritual enlightenment. If practiced with sufficient intensity, meditations that focus on compassion can literally change the way one thinks and feels. It can help an individual consider the perspective of others more easily, thereby increasing tolerance. Empathetically responding to the suffering of others with competency and wisdom becomes possible, thereby increasing the basis of human moral intelligence. Neurobiologically, tonglen recalibrates nervous system responses to situations that would normally leave the individual frightened, discouraged, or completely unnerved.

To understand how this is possible, we have to consider the basic evolutionary orientation of the human instincts. Recall the definition of *instinct* from the introduction:

1) An enduring disposition or tendency of an organism to act in an organized and biologically adaptive manner characteristic of the species. 2) An unreasoning impulse to perform some purposeful action without an immediate consciousness of the end to which that action may lead. 3) In psychoanalytic theory, the forces assumed to exist behind the tension caused by the needs of the id.

Implicit in this definition is that the adaptive intelligence of the instincts promotes the survival of the *individual organism*. This makes a lot of sense. As we have seen, the intelligence of our instinctual systems has been honed by millions of years of evolution to maximize our chances of survival and the successful reproduction of our genetic material. But as we examine this definition from the perspective of an instinctual intelligence that changes and evolves, this conventional understanding of the instincts is inadequate. It's not that it's wrong- just incomplete. There's something more that must be included. Our instincts, especially as they develop and evolve into their full intelligence, can include a concern for others, as well as ourselves. This concern for the well-being of others, when experienced with its full instinctual intensity, can become a force of nature. In fact, it can become *exponentially* more powerful that the survival instincts that are based on the exclusive concern for one's self alone.

Now, of course, we often have a passionate concern for our loved ones. But often, this concern for others is usually limited to those for whom we have vested interest in protecting and enhancing the odds of their survival and reproductive capacities. In other words, our concern is *genetically* driven. This type of concern obviously focuses on offspring, sexual mates, siblings, and other genetic relatives. This concern can often extend to tribal affiliations that protect these genetic interests by enhancing economic wealth, security, and social resources. Friends, companies, communities, and other organizations all fit into this category. However, as the instincts begin to evolve beyond their basic functions of ensuring survival and reproduction for ourselves and our loved ones, new capacities and intelligences emerge. This does not mean we lose all interest in protecting our genetic interests- it means that we begin to include the larger field of humanity and other living beings in our protective sphere of love and empathy.

The erosion of self-centeredness is the basis for *aligning* our embodied instinctual energy with the higher aspirations of the human soul:

Within the most evolved expression of our instinctual intelligence is the ability to overcome the self-centered orientation of our instinctual consciousness. This other-centered orientation makes us more open, curious, and determined about improving the state of humanity. When our heart and minds are truly invested in the well-being of others, our natural cooperative and efficient intelligence takes over and guides our actions. This cooperative intelligence also changes our inner feelings by activating areas of the brain that are associated with happiness and contentment.

The Joy of Compassion

Some very sophisticated research by Richard Davidson and his colleagues is helping us understand the neurobiological basis for this compassionate intelligence. Davidson is a professor of psychology and psychiatry at the University of Wisconsin- Madison, where he serves as Director of the Laboratory of Neuroscience for Affective Neuroscience. He, along with many other scientists, has been collaborating for several years with the Dalai Lama and other Tibetan Buddhist monks to investigate the neurobiological dimensions of long-term meditation practice. This new field of research is called *contemplative neuroscience*. Under Davidson's guidance, a team of scientists recently performed EEG tests on a Buddhist monk who has trained in Tibetan meditation practices for most of his adult life. They designed a series of experiments to record his brain waves while he engaged in specific meditation practices. In one experiment in particular, the monk was instructed to engage in a form of meditation that specifically focused on the generation of compassion. This practice is similar to the practice of tonglen described above, except that the meditator focuses more on the pure feeling of compassion rather than performing the taking and giving visualization found in the traditional tonglen practice.

The results of this experiment were stunning: Davidson and his colleagues found that the monk displayed a considerable level of gamma activity in the left middle gyrus- a region of neurons within the left prefrontal cortex. The level of gamma activity in the left prefrontal area of this Buddhist monk was not only above the norm- it was the highest ever recorded in a human being. Why is this important? Davidson's previous research has shown that this region of the left prefrontal cortex subserves positive emotional feelings. Moreover, Davidson has found that the corresponding region of the middle gyrus in the right hemisphere is directly associated with distressing feelings and avoidance behaviors. It appears that this meditation practice alters brain functioning by laterally shifting the locus of neuronal activity to a specific region in the left hemisphere. This reduces the potential distressing feelings associated with excessive right hemispheric activation. This research is helping Western scientists confirm something that Tibetan Buddhists have known for centuries- that the most immediate benefits of meditating on compassion are bestowed on the person doing the meditation!

The Intelligence of Compassion

However, from the perspective of the Tibetan Buddhists, the benefits to one's self are secondary. It is obvious to them that meditating on compassion infuses one with a sense of optimism and confidence. The primary goal of this practice is to reduce the self-centered focus of our concern and direct it toward others. In their experience, meditating on compassion not only reduces the concern with one's own welfare, it also makes individuals more capable of helping others. Western scientists are beginning to understand the neurobiological basis of how this practice generates intense feelings of happiness and bliss within the person meditating- but how does it produce *intelligent* responses to the suffering of others?

A variety of research over the last few years has shown that many Tibetan Buddhist meditation practices- as well as the meditative practices of other spiritual traditions- produce high levels of activity in the prefrontal cortex. Decades of experimental research have conclusively demonstrated that the prefrontal cortex is the central brain region that subserves specific cognitive processes known as *executive functions*. Executive functions are the basic mental capacities that allow us to make sense of the world in an orderly way. They are the cognitive capacities that organize images, words, and thoughts into logically coherent sequences and patterns. In the prefrontal cortex in the right hemisphere, executive functions help us organize sensory perceptions and images in a coherent spatial field. They give our minds the capacity to move images forward and back, up and down, and side-to-side to form organized patterns. These executive functions allow us to visualize what the furniture in our living rooms will look like before we move it- so we don't have to rearrange each piece over and over. These visual-spatial executive functions help us interact with other humans in an intelligent way that incorporates the realities of three-dimensional *space*.

The left side of the prefrontal cortex specializes in organizing thoughts and words into logical sequences. The left side of the brain mediates most of the human linguistic functions and the prefrontal cortex has multiple interconnected networks throughout this hemisphere. These networks help us communicate with other humans in a logical way that reflects the sequential realities of *time*. Thus, we can understand how executive functions of both hemispheres help humans organize the images and thoughts within the logical parameters of space and time. The prefrontal cortex is also the central brain region that controls attention. Current research indicates that it is directly involved in the selection of which sensations, perceptions, memories, images, and thoughts are brought into the spatial and temporal organizational matrix for further executive attentional processing.

Clearly, meditation practices that focus on compassion have obvious benefits on an individual's executive functions. This is one of the things about the Dalai Lama that impresses the scientists he works with the most. He seems to have an unlimited capacity to direct his concentration to the intricacies of what is being discussed. He can follow the most complex discussions of neuroscience, quantum physics, and psychology with ease, despite his lack of formal training. Not only is he capable of precisely ordered spatiotemporal cognition, but he also seems to have an unbreakable concentrative focus. He can literally keep his mind focused on a topic for several hours, with no sign of mental fatigue or distraction. In addition to his penetrating scientific mind, the Dalai Lama has a vigorous enthusiasm to find practical applications that will benefit humanity. The neuroscientists he works with could describe the extraordinary development of his executive functions in great biological detail. While he would appreciate the scientific explanation, the Dalai Lama would doubtlessly emphasize a simpler and more immediate reality that arises from his compassion outlook: The contentment of compassion makes us smarter. Without the incessant preoccupation with selfish impulses, it is easier to focus attention and organized thought processes on the welfare of others.

Meditation and Instinctual Plasticity

Any meditation practice that involves the visualization of interactions with other human beings will involve the orbitofrontal cortex (OFC). We know that the OFC is the primary brain region where the impressions of instinctually intense interpersonal experiences are stored. We also know that the networks centered in the OFC regulate the activity of the amygdala, as well as other limbic, brainstem, and autonomic responses. The OFC shares extensive interconnections with the prefrontal cortex, as these two brain regions are located adjacent to each other and comprise the majority of the frontal lobes. Could it be that meditation practices that focus on cultivating compassion can rewrite dsyregulating networks encoded in the orbitofrontal cortex and it associated networks? This is exactly what Davidson and his colleagues are trying to find out. They are utilizing new technology that will allow researchers to observe the activation patterns of neural networks. This will help them pinpoint the interactions between the interconnected networks of the OFC, prefrontal cortex, amygdala, and lower brain regions. This research has enormous implications for the continuing evolution of instinctual intelligence. The research of Davidson and many other scientists will continue to help us understand the neurobiological basis for the cognitive, emotional, and instinctual mastery demonstrated by these Tibetan Buddhist practitioners. It will also explain the precise mechanisms that utilize the plasticity of the brain to recalibrate the functioning of our instinctual systems. As we begin to analyze these formerly secret meditation practices more closely, we can not help but be struck by their implicit- yet highly evolved- instinctual sophistication.

Cleansing of the Void

Humans that have developed high levels of instinctual wisdom don't appear overnight. Mastery of this nature requires many years of dedicated practice. The Dalai Lama's training began when he was just a young novice monk. From an early age, Tibetan Buddhist monks like the Dalai Lama are required to study complex philosophical texts that analyze the nature of reality. This study- which includes, reading, memorization, and debate of key points- helps them develop the analytical, logical, and cognitive skills needed to scale the heights of the most complex philosophical tradition in world history. But this intellectual training isn't intended to just produce smarter monks. It's actually designed to prepare the nervous systems of these young monks for the profoundly challenging meditation practices that they will undertake when become fully mature adults. In short, this training is the beginning of a long-term training in instinctual intelligence.

Embodying Emptiness

The study of philosophy is a central part of Buddhist contemplative training as well as being central to Tibetan Buddhist culture in general. The central philosophical doctrines of Tibetan Buddhism are derived from the insights of the Buddha, who had originally introduced the concept of selflessness during the 5th or 6th century BCE. The central notion of *selflessness* as taught by the Buddha is that things- including people, objects, concepts, categories- do not exist inherently in and of themselves. Rather, things arise as a result of causes and conditions that arise as a result of other causes and conditions. In other words, everything we perceive, feel, and think about arises in dependence on an infinite matrix of changing causes and conditions. They are empty of any inherent self-sustaining basis of existence. This understanding of reality is now finding scientific confirmation, as the field of quantum physics has come to similar conclusions regarding the insubstantial nature of elementary particles.

Within the Buddhist system, there are many ways of understanding emptiness. In the 25 centuries since the Buddha's original teachings, several Buddhist masters have elaborated on the original words of the Buddha, creating a rich tapestry of philosophical and contemplative thought. However, to really understand how this type of philosophical training helps recalibrate the nervous systems of these monks at an instinctual level, we have to consider how the knowledge of these texts is applied. The study of these complex philosophical texts is accompanied by an equally rigorous system of debate, contemplation, and meditation. Part of the monastic training of Tibetan Buddhist monks is the participation in formal debating exercises. The monks are required to take turns defending or critiquing various tenants of Buddhist philosophy. This debate practice can go on for hours. The monk who is critiquing the position of his partner tries to force his colleague into illogical or inconsistent philosophical views that would contradict the understanding of emptiness as it is expressed by the Buddha and other Buddhist sages.

If you ever have the chance to see this debating exercise in person, you'll quickly realize how playful it is. It's much like a sporting event in other cultures. The rest of the monks will gather around the two debaters and encourage them with wild cheers and gestures. As we know, human societies all over the world use play as a means of integrating instinctual energy with the behavioral rules of a culture. Here, Tibetan Buddhist monastic training is utilizing this basic form of instinctual intelligence to help monks develop an emotional and embodied understanding of emptiness. Neurobiologically, it appears that this is accomplished by the intense activation of the prefrontal and orbitofrontal corticies. The use of logic and sequential reasoning required in these debates clearly activates the prefrontal cortex. And because these debates are carried out in an interpersonal social context, the orbitofrontal cortex is also active. In order to maintain the fine-tuned functioning of their executive cognitive capacities (and thereby win the debate), the monks must develop the capacity to regulate their levels of instinctual arousal. If the intensity and excitement of the debate over-arouse a monk's amygdala, it is likely that his concentration will be disrupted by the activation of the HPA stress response. On the other hand, if he slips into an inhibited or dissociative state, he would lack sufficient nervous system arousal to maintain his mental acuity. There can be little doubt that the intense activation of these two brain regions help build robust and highly balanced instinctual regulating capacities via their interconnected networks with the amygdala and other limbic/brainstem regions. As we'll see below, the capacity to regulate one's instinctual impulses with the utmost refinement is needed for monks to engage the sophisticated meditative practices of Vajrayana Buddhism. The practices of Vajrayana system- which is translated as the *Diamond Vehicle* in English- are considered to be the most advanced of all Buddhist meditation techniques.

Entering into the Void

The Dalai Lama is acknowledged by many as one of the foremost scholars of Buddhist philosophy, especially the extraordinarily complex analysis of emptiness. He was acknowledged as a fully fledged master of this philosophical debating practice by the time he was 16 years old- an unprecedented achievement in the history of Tibetan Buddhist culture. But that was only the beginning of this training. The understanding of emptiness is brought even deeper into the nervous system by sustained meditation practice. By focusing their minds unwaveringly on the lack of inherent existence of all things, Tibetan Buddhist practitioners develop an intense and penetrating level of insight into the nature of reality:

Meditating on emptiness is a direct means of accessing the natural cleansing properties of instinctual intelligence. Through this practice, we gain an unmediated experience of the inherent nonexistence of all things- including the self-images that sustain our sense of self. The cleansing action of this wisdom allows us to perceive the nature of reality more clearly by dissolving the neural networks that sustain our habitual sense of self. When *selflessness* is comprehended at a visceral level, instinctual agitation is reduced, facilitating extraordinary levels of inner quietude and contentment.

How does this meditation practice of emptiness actually affect the instinctual consciousness of the practitioner? We have seen that one of the basic properties of the instinctual intelligence of the universe is the capacity to cleanse the nervous system of living beings. It is a priceless yet mysterious gift that seems to exude from the ineffable Void from which all creation arises. Mysterious as it may seem, its effects on human consciousness are quite discernable. Let's see how it effects our self-experience.

Self-images and Boundaries

As we have discussed throughout this book, inhibitory self-images actively shape the cognitive, emotional, and physical expression of instinctual consciousness. The restrictive influences of self-images can be understood in terms of *boundary* creation and maintenance. We can observe two general modes in which boundaries are experienced.

1) Psychological Boundaries.

These are boundaries that are related to our capacities to behave, express and feel emotions, perceive, and think. Psychological boundaries are often experienced as internal limitations. They tell us what we can and cannot feel or experience. At other times, psychological boundaries are also experienced as limitations imposed by our surrounding social environment. Most individuals are so deeply embedded in the self-images and relational schemas that maintain these boundaries that they are taken to be an unalterable way of experiencing the world. The constrained feeling of these psychological boundaries and the suffering they engender are often what leads an individual to seek out avenues of personal evolution and growth.

2) Spatial Boundaries.

These are boundaries that are related to our embodied existence in the physical world. Externally, boundaries can be experienced as a constraint imposed on our physical movement by the surrounding environment. This can manifest as a feeling of being closed in, unable to move freely or in an expansive manner. Internally, boundaries can manifest as tension or fatigue, when we feel 'cut off' from our energy. The felt sense of spatial boundaries is the *physical sensation* (as opposed to the cognitive or psychological awareness) of inhibitory self-images.

The understanding of emptiness actually helps dissolve the perception and sensations of these boundaries. In a very direct and immediate way, meditating on the inherent non-existence of the self systematically challenges the reality of the inhibitory self-images. Most of the time, our self-images are the basis for our implicit sense of self. As we meditate on emptiness, we begin to realize that these self-images are not who we are. Of course, since there are many types and layers of self-images, simply meditating on emptiness a few times will have only a small effect. Rather, it is a slow and systematic process of allowing emptiness to penetrate more deeply into our consciousness. The realization of emptiness- especially the realization of the inherent non-existence of the self- emerges gradually. At first, we might begin to experience a sensation of *inner spaciousness*. This can allow us to feel that something has simply vanished or melted away. Psychologically, one feels less restricted, less confined by thoughts and beliefs about what other people think. Physically, it feels as if the constraints around one's body have been dissolved. There is a felt capacity of being able to move about freely with no thought that anyone or anything will interfere or restrict these movements.

As individuals become more deeply absorbed into the meditative awareness of emptiness, it begins to pervade every aspect and dimension of experience. At this stage, the direct perception and sensation of spacious emptiness feels like a clarity and openness that pervades both inner and outer domains of experience. The objects that once served as the basis of instinctual gratification no longer seem so solid and alluring. In the most personal way, inner spaciousness is experienced as the lack of restriction in human consciousness. In contrast to the familiar boundaries and limitations, inner spaciousness feels like a cool breeze of unencumbered possibility. There is no intuition, physical or psychological, that anyone or anything is opposing the natural expression of our being. Meditating on emptiness and inner spaciousness literally cleanses our sense of physical space. This has been confirmed by recent functional magnetic resonance imagery studies. These studies examined the neural activation and deactivation patterns of meditation practices among several different spiritual traditions. The practices that emphasized the dissolution of the normal self-defining boundaries displayed interesting commonalties. In both Buddhist and Christian traditions, meditators were shown to have a *decreased* blood flow in the superior parietal lobe. It is thought that the superior parietal lobe is the primary brain region involved in creating a sense of spatial awareness and maintaining self/not-self boundaries. The study and contemplation of emptiness- when intensified by focused meditation- has powerful and immediate benefits for our instinctual intelligence. It's hard to imagine the sense of freedom and liberation unless one has actually experienced this directly. The sense of freedom expands into our bodies as a feeling of complete contentment. It penetrates the seemingly solid objects of the external world, making it easier to maintain a balanced inner state. Our instinctual consciousness now includes the capacity to remain still, completely unagitated by even the most provocative stimuli.

The Loss of Self

Tibetan Buddhist monks meditate many hours a day, seeking to stabilize and deepen their understanding of emptiness. Often, they will meditate in isolated retreats for several years, sitting in absorbed contemplation for as many as ten to twelve hours a day. Some even learn to meditate around the clock, maintaining their meditative focus as they slip into a light state of sleep. However, as the deeper perception of emptiness continues to erode the familiar sense of self, feelings of encroaching terror and intense anxiety may arise. This is only natural, as the feeling of emptiness can begin to dissolve the sensations of solidity and permanence that are associated with the body. At a fundamental level, our sense of existence is derived from the awareness of visceral sensations. These inner body sensations are so familiar that they become an automatic, implicit background of our consciousness. In the course of the most refined contemplations of emptiness and selflessness, these inner body sensations may start to disappear. When this happens, the primary source of self-awareness is lost. Deep within our instinctual reflexes, this can only mean one thing: *imminent death*. The innate reaction of the human nervous system is to activate the core survival responses.

From the perspective of Tibetan Buddhism, the activation of instinctual survival responses indicates that the understanding of emptiness has not yet penetrated into the deepest levels of consciousness. It also means that the fullest potentials of our instinctual intelligence have not been realized. Why is it important that the inherent nonexistence of the self be embraced at this visceral level? This question brings us to the final frontiers of instinctual intelligence and deeper into the profound secrets of Vajrayana Buddhism.

The Ultimate Frontier

Every day, the Dalai Lama wakes up at 4am and begins his daily practice of prayer and meditation. Few Westerners have any real notion of a highly accomplished Buddhist master like the Dalai Lama might be doing as he sits quietly meditating. It may look like he is going into a deep state of relaxation or meditative bliss. And that is partially true. But there's a lot more to the story. While sitting silently, the Dalai Lama is actually engaged in an extremely sophisticated set of Vajrayana Buddhist mediation systems known in Sanskrit as the *mahaunuttarayoga*. In the West, these meditation systems are referred to as *Highest Yoga Tantra* or the *Unexcelled Tantric Yogas*. These advanced meditation practices have a profound effect on those who practice them. As is abundantly evident with the Dalai Lama, these practices can help individuals cultivate extraordinary levels of compassion, patience, concentration, and happiness. Anyone who has spent even a moment with a great Buddhist master like the Dalai Lama instantly recognizes that his nervous system operates on a different level from you and me. You can viscerally feel how his instincts are completely *aligned* with heart and mind. His body literally oozes intelligence and compassion. By exploring the neurobiological basis of these practices, we can gain insight into how the Dalai Lama became one of the foremost masters of instinctual wisdom on the planet.

Beginning with Respect

Right from the start, I want to emphasize that the level of instinctual intelligence utilized in the Unexcelled Tantra Yoga systems requires a great deal of knowledge, guidance, practice, and maturity to even understand- much less practice. Out of respect for the Tibetan Buddhist tradition, it is essential to keep in mind that the practice of the Tantric meditations is restricted to those who have had proper preparatory training. In addition, it is necessary to have received an initiation conferred by a recognized lineage holder of that particular practice. I am discussing a tiny snapshot of these practices here to demonstrate the extraordinary knowledge of instinctual wisdom encoded within Buddhist meditation techniques. As such, these examples are intended to be a source of inspiration, helping us to consider the evolutionary *potentials* of instinctual intelligence. Individuals wishing to study and practice Tibetan Buddhism- or any other authentic spiritual tradition- should follow the guidelines for preparation, initiation, and practice set forth by the customs of the specific lineage they wish to study. This is not only respectful of the cultural standards of these traditions- but it's also wise in terms of one's own personal development. The most advanced practices of any sophisticated contemplative tradition are always situated in a developmental hierarchy that supports the individual's long-term growth. It is never wise to adopt a highly advanced practice without a thorough understanding of its role in the overall developmental training approaches of that tradition.

Destabilizing the Self Habit

There is a reason that Tibetan Buddhists require a great deal of training before entering into the esoteric practices of the Unexcelled Tantric Yogas. These practices *radically destabilize* the deepest instinctual attachments to our habitual sense of self. We have seen how the practice of compassion gradually erodes our self-centered tendencies. We have also seen how the meditative contemplation of emptiness can dissolve the restrictions of psychological and spatial boundaries. The practices of the Unexcelled Tantric Yogas take this one step further. It is stunning to recognize the precision and elegance with which these practices recalibrate the ways in which humans habitually perceive their bodies. Many of the Unexcelled Tantric Yoga meditation systems are divided into two stages of practice, the *generation stage* and the *completion stage*. In the generation stage practices, practitioners perform complex visualizations. Each meditative session, or *sadhana* as they are referred to in Sanskrit, takes the individual on a journey through the complete potentials of the human awareness.

The practices of the generation stage begin to disrupt the *procedural memories* that comprise the core sense of self. These procedural memory (often called implicit memory) systems are the motor patterns and other nervous system responses that are established when we engage in new tasks. The brain and spinal cord record the sequences of movements and micro-adjustments involved at a subconscious level. Later, when we wish to do these activities again, our nervous systems recall these complex movement patterns with little or no conscious effort. We use these procedural memories so we can walk, talk, ride bikes, drive cars, and wash dishes- all without having to think about how to move our bodies. Procedural memories are different from auto-biographical memories, which are called *explicit* or *narrative* forms of memory. These are the memories associated with the thoughts and images related to one's life- specific events, conversations, friends, objects, etc.

The specific visualizations of the generation stage destabilize the procedural memories associated with habitual body consciousness by altering the basic sense of self as a two-armed, two-legged being that moves through time and space. This is achieved in multiple ways. First, the practitioner visualizes his or herself as Buddhist deity, in sexual union with a consort of the opposite sex who is also visualized as a Buddhist deity. These two deities are surrounded by an entire retinue of deities, all situated in an elaborate three-dimensional palace. The entire palace, along with the principal and surrounding deities, is referred to as the *mandala*. The principle deity in most of the Tantric systems has as many as 24 arms and legs and at least four faces. Repeated visualization of one's self as this deity actively disrupts the habitual sensory and perceptual networks that have become habituated to the ongoing perception of having one face, two arms, and two legs.

Generating Divine Pride

Ordinarily, the disruption of the usual sense of self caused by the perceptual alteration of our arms, legs, and face would cause an ordinary person to panic. The normal movement and functioning of one's limbs is vital to almost all of the procedural memories involved in day-to-day survival. The loss of this sense of self is normally interpreted by the instinctual centers of the brain as a direct threat to one's life. How can the Dalai Lama go through this process every morning and remain so calm? Most likely, the answer can be found in his prefrontal and orbitofrontal corticies. The visualization of the deities and the entire mandala requires the activation of the executive functions. It requires tremendous focus to maintain a steady mental image of this entire mandala. Try it for yourself. Try to visualize your house in vivid detail and hold it in your mind-uninterrupted- for ten seconds. Not that easy- is it? Now imagine what the Dalai Lama and other highly accomplished Buddhist practitioners do: They can visualize themselves as multiple armed and multiple legged deities, having multiple faces, wearing elaborate costumes and holding as many as 24 symbolic implements in each of their many hands. While doing this, they silently recite mantras- short sets of words with symbolic meaning- that are repeated over and over. As they recite the mantras, they also visualize three-dimensional symbolic shapes and letters of the mantras circulating in between and through the bodies of the two principal deities. At the same time, they are visualizing the surrounding deities - of which there can be as many as 722- that inhabit several floors of the richly decorated mandala complex. And they can perform this entire visualization- uninterrupted- for *four* hours at a time. It takes years of practice to assemble this visualization so each element can arise in their internal awareness simultaneously with clarity and vibrancy.

To understand the significance of this practice- and its profound implications for cultivating the highest levels of instinctual intelligence- we have to examine what is happening at a neurobiological level. It is well established that the visualization of three-dimensional spatial objects requires the activation of several areas within the right prefrontal cortex. The recitation of mantras also activates the left prefrontal cortex, as the repetition of mantras requires the verbal and sequential executive capacities of the left hemisphere. The visualization of complex three-dimensional rotation of letters and geometric figures further activates additional areas of the prefrontal cortex in both hemispheres. In addition, the visualization of the deep instinctual connection between the two principal deities- remember they are in sexual union- undoubtedly activates the orbitofrontal cortex. It is important to realize that this entire visualization is done with a very high degree of emotional and instinctual intensity. Meditators are instructed to generate a consistent inner feeling of *divine pride* while performing the visualization. Divine pride is often described as a feeling of unshakable inner confidence arising from the direct realization of one's eternally divine nature.

Modulating Instinctual Identity

The primary physical sense of self as a two armed, two legged physical entity is mapped out in the region of the midbrain called the *superior colliculus*. Within this region, somatosensory, vestibular, and visual information interfaces with the mesencephalic locomotor region, which integrates some of the basic neural functions required for coherent action sequences like walking, talking, eating, and standing- in short, most of our procedural memories. It cannot be emphasized enough the degree to which these basic motor systems orient the body in a very fixed and predictable sense of spatial/tactile perception. They are so basic to our ongoing sense of self they we rarely notice them. Unless, of course, they are disturbed.

Any disruption of this implicit internal stability will provoke intense responses of anxiety, stress, and vomiting. How do Tibetan Buddhist meditators prevent these responses during their visualization practices? The generation of divine pride appears to be the key to the remarkable instinctual regulation behind this practice. Maintaining the vibrant clarity and emotional intensity of this visualization, meditators like the Dalai Lama most likely enhances the capacity of their *corticolimbic* neural networks to modulate the activation of instinctual survival systems that are activated in response to any perceived threat to the physical body. The corticolimbic networks are the interconnected networks between the prefrontal cortex, orbitofrontal cortex, amygdala, hypothalamus, midbrain, and brainstem regions. In order for these instinctual responses of anxiety, stress, and vomiting *not* to arise, the brain regions that regulate these responses must be sending out messages neural impulses that signal high levels of profound contentment. There is no impulse to panic despite the loss of a familiar sense of one's body. This is exactly what must be occurring in the corticolimbic circuits that are steadily activated with a stable sense of divine pride. The prefrontal and orbitorfrontal corticies are modulating the activity of the amygdala and the PAG (which is directly adjacent to the superior colliculus)- averting potential panic by generating feelings of pride and confidence. We could say that the *affective sensation* of "pride" replaces the habitual sense of identity held in place by the inner identification with the procedural memories of limbs that move in time and space. It may be years before contemplative neuroscience researchers understand the precise neuobiological basis for these extraordinary types of instinctual regulation displayed by these Buddhist practitioners. But clearly the ability of these practitioners to cultivate deep levels of contentment should motivate scientists to study these meditation techniques more fully.

Cleansing our Perception

Why would the Dalai Lama and other Tibetan Buddhists want to destabilize their habitual sense of self as a two-armed and two-legged human being? The experience of one's self as a body that exists in three-dimensional space is a primary source of identity for human beings. It's how we recognize ourselves. But there's the key thing: The experience of ourselves as physical beings is primarily a *mental image*. You can check this out yourself. Close your eyes. Now imagine yourself in your kitchen, standing at your sink. Imagine you turn on the water to wash a dish. Keeping your eyes closed, turn off the water and walk over to the refrigerator. You'll notice that you can actually feel the sensations of warm water and the solid floor. Most importantly, you can see how your body knows exactly how to move your arms and legs in three-dimensional space to perform these tasks. Recent research has confirmed that the superior colliculus contains three-dimensional maps of the physical space around the body and a map of the motor movements needed to physically navigate in this space. Once learned, we rely on these networks of procedural memories to do almost all of our daily tasks. The maps and movements operate automatically at a subconscious level, guiding each small movement. This shows us that, in neurobiological reality, our primary experience of our physical bodies is *not a direct sensory perception of what is occurring in the present moment*. The vast majority of our moment-to-moment experience as physical beings is actually filtered though the sensorimotor maps constructed by the superior colliculus. In short, the usual experience of our bodies- and our inner sense of identity- is mostly a memory.

As we have seen over and over, the dissolution of self-images enhances the direct conscious awareness of the body as it exists in the present moment. We are no longer experiencing our bodies through an image of the past. We become directly aware of the somatosensory, vestibular, and visual integration that is taking place in the mesencephalic locomotor region and the superior colliculus.

The dissolution of our habitual physical sense of self does not mean our bodies *disappear*. I just saw the Dalai Lama a few weeks ago. His body looks as healthy and vibrant as ever. What actually dissolves are the *mental images* of our body as it was in the past. Without a restrictive image in the way, the experience of the movement and sensations becomes an exquisitely integrated expression of instinctual consciousness. This expression can take many forms. Some people report an awakening of their musical and artistic capacities. Others experience a stunning clarity and expressiveness in their communication and contact with other people. Freed from the physical impressions of our history, our facial gestures are not habitual or stereotypical. Our awareness is rich with the pure sensation of smooth coordinated facial gestures and responses. In other words, our movements and gestures are fresh, sincere, and spontaneous. The Dalai Lama radiates this sense of immediacy and presence to everyone he encounters.

The disruption of the habitual mental images of our physical bodies is a powerful way to develop advanced levels of instinctual intelligence. When the restrictive influence of these self-images dissolves, we notice that the usual boundaries between our bodies and the environment are not present. These boundaries are revealed to be *empty* of any inherent existence. The innate instinctual intelligence of creation dances effortlessly through the vehicle of the human body. Free from old beliefs about the nature of physicality, it is no longer possible to consider any particular sensation or perception as belonging to our "selves" or our "bodies". Without a clear inside or outside, there is no distinct substrate that any perception or sensation can "belong" to or be "identified" with. There are simply movement without a mover, sensations without a senser, perception without a perceiver, and thoughts without a thinker. It is possible to become so in touch with physical reality that there is no intervention of thoughts and self-doubt. Being knows itself directly.

The Transformation of Death

Every morning, the Dalai Lama practices dying. The most important element of the Unexcelled Tantric Yogas is the visualization- and physical reenactment- of the dissolution of consciousness that occurs during physical death. While this dissolution is visualized during the generation stage practices, it is enacted *physically* during the completion stage practices. The practice involves the systematic dissolution of the fundamental inner body sensations that give us a sense of existence. The Tibetan Buddhist completion stage yogic practices found in tantric systems like Guhyasamaja and Chakrasamvara are designed to help the practitioner gain an experiential familiarity with the dissolution of the inner body images and sensations. These esoteric meditation systems are the pinnacle of the most advanced Tibetan Buddhist practices. It requires a profound level of maturity and discipline to maintain these practices. From a neurobiological point of view, the sequence of dissolution can be seen as the systematic withdrawal of conscious awareness from these domains of inner sensation:

1) **The Presence of Inner Visceral Sensations.** These are the sensations received by the medulla including the gastric vagal sensory neurons of the stomach, intestines, and surrounding musculature. It also includes the direct somatic awareness of the genitals, bladder, and anus, as well as the somatosensory information from the nerves in our skin and muscles, particularly information about sensations of temperature and pressure.

2) **Direct Sensory Input from Gustatory, Oral, and Nasal systems.** These are the sensations of the neural substrates of the cranial nerve systems and the neurobiological basis for reflexes such as sneezing, coughing, and other responses that prevent airway or esophagus obstruction.

3) **Respiratory Consciousness.** These are the sensations of the nervous system input into the medullary brainstem. This region is the center of the sensory monitoring of the lungs, diaphragm, and the surrounding musculature and connective tissue. The absence of inner sensations of respiratory consciousness would normally evoke a suffocation response.

4) Heart consciousness. These are the sensations associated with the primary vagal regulating pathway and an intricate network of secondary regulating systems. In the completion stage yogas of the Tibetan Buddhist tradition, the subtle consciousness in the heart area is considered the absolute core of our physical instinctual existence. The pumping of the heart and the maintenance of an internal vascular pressure is the ultimate source of physical life. The absence of inner sensations of the heart consciousness would feel like one has physically died.

All of these basic domains of instinctual consciousness are mediated by specific regions of the brainstem. As such, in order to practice the dissolution of consciousness techniques of these meditation disciplines, the practitioner must be able to modulate neurophysiological survival responses that arise in response to the absence of the inner sensations mediated by the brainstem. This is the final frontier of instinctual intelligence. The ultimate fear of the instinctual regulating systems of the body is the dissolution of our inner body sensations. The absence of sensation is the subjective experience of death- the complete loss of our embodied identity. And as far as our primitive reflexes are concerned, it is impossible to distinguish it from actual physical death.

The Dissolution of Sensation

From the perspective of the Tibetan Buddhist tradition, the realization of Buddhahood cannot be attained without experiencing the dissolution of death. In fact, it has to be experienced over and over, to dissolve the subtlest instinctual tendencies that can obscure the pristine nature of Buddha consciousness. This is exactly what the Dalai Lama is doing every morning, as he sits in meditation. The highest levels of mastery in the completion stage practices like Guhyasamaja or Charkrasamvara involve the systematic withdrawal of conscious awareness from the four types of inner sensations described above. The initial emphasis in most completion stage yogas is to withdraw the inner visceral, muscular, and skin sensations. Tibetans refer to all of these sensations as the *all-pervading wind*. At subtler levels, it includes the internal sense of vascular pressure that comes from the blood pumping through our veins, arteries, and capillaries. The all-pervading wind is drawn into the center channel, which is visualized as a long thin tube that runs from the genitals to the top of the head just in front of the spine. Clearly, without extensive meditative training, the disruption of these inner sensations would cause the autonomic centers of the brainstem to go into a state of panic. The cardiovascular centers of the brainstem might also respond to the perceived loss of vascular pressure by shutting down conscious awareness. In other words, one would simply faint.

How do the practitioners of these yogas modulate brainstem responses to prevent panic and the loss of consciousness? Again, the instinctual wisdom that is designed into these practices is quite profound. In order to modulate the brainstem responses to the potential life-threatening conditions, most of the completion stage sadhanas of the Unexcelled Tantric Yoga systems begin with the practice of *inner heat* meditation. The practice of inner heat, referred to as *tummo* in Tibetan, is done by visualizing an intense sensation of melting warmth inside the center channel at the level of the navel. Western scientists have documented considerable changes in the internal temperature of tummo practitioners. They have also documented the traditional test of tummo meditators, a final exam of sorts. During the coldest parts of winter, tummo practitioners are brought outside totally naked. The meditation instructor then drenches bedsheets in ice water and drapes them over the shoulders of the naked trainees. The test becomes a competition to see who can dry the most sheets in one hour through the generation of internal body heat.

Now this is an extraordinary feat of instinctual control by any standard. But what is the purpose of this practice? It was originally thought that the monks were just trying to stay warm in the Tibetan winter. We now know there is far more to it that that. First of all, the practice of tummo is said to aid in the dissolution of the all-pervading wind into the central channel. It also appears to have an essential neurobiological function as well. The generation of inner heat likely recalibrates the functioning of the periaqueductal grey region (PAG). It may do so by modifying the instinctual responses to the temperature dysregulation, loss of environmental security, and social isolation associated with physical death. The inner heat generated by tummo is the basis for the cultivation of extraordinary levels of bliss within the central channel that is said to be a thousand times more powerful than an ordinary sexual orgasm. These inner sensations of warmth and bliss must somehow signal deep levels of contentment to the PAG- so there is no reason to panic. The loss of sensation in the body is not interpreted as a threat and the activation of the HPA axis and dorsal vagal freezing responses are averted. The feeling of bliss accumulates and increases in the center channel, further facilitating the remaining stages of the dissolution process.

The Dissolution of Consciousness

As the internal sensory awareness of the practitioner dissolves, the basis of the subjective experience also begins to fade. The neural basis for conscious awareness is located within the medial zone of the brainstem. This region is the primary neurons of the ascending reticular activating system (ARAS). Starting in the pons and midbrain, the ARAS has ascending pathways to the thalamus and hypothalamus. This is the primary physiological substrate of conscious awareness and attention. The activation of the ARAS is the experience of waking consciousness. When it is not active, we are asleep or in a coma. In the absence of any sensation, the absence of activity in ARAS would be experienced as being asleep.

Within the Tibetan Buddhist completion stage yogas, there is a well-developed and intricate understanding of this final stage of the dissolution process. As the other domains of consciousness awareness are dissolved, awareness becomes increasingly subtle and difficult to perceive. The systematic withdrawal of the sensations from the gustatory, oral, and nasal systems, as well as the respiratory consciousness and heart consciousness, all lead to the complete cessation of awareness. At this stage, which is called *black near-attainment*, awareness is devoid of sensation, like the darkest part of the night. It feels like one is fainting or falling into the deepest unconscious sleep. Profound levels of meditative stability and refinement are required to navigate this last stage of the dissolution process. It is the *absence* of all sensation- the experience of nothingness. There is no sensation of anything, not even a dimensional space in which nothing exists.

Gaining experiential familiarity with the dissolution process is the ultimate frontier of instinctual intelligence. In these practices, one can experience complete cessation of inner body images and sensations. The complete cessation of consciousness that is attainted is even thought to relax the suffocation and cardiac responses in the medulla, the most primitive survival reflexes in our instinctual makeup. Western science has not yet discovered the complex neurobiological regulating mechanisms at work in this extraordinary spiritual practice. Obviously, several instinctual reflexes such as the suffocation response, various cardiopulmonary responses, and the activity of the ARAS must somehow be modulated. Up until now, the modification of these reflexes was thought to be impervious to any kind of conscious control. However, an experiment conducted by Paul Ekman a professor of Psychology and Director of the Human Interaction Laboratory at the University of California Medical School in San Francisco has dramatically changed this understanding.

He conducted a fascinating test on the same Tibetan Buddhist monk who generated the highest levels of gamma activity in the left prefrontal cortex ever recorded. In this experiment, he exposed the monk to a very loud sudden noise (as loud as a gun going off right by your ear). Ordinarily, the human nervous system will produce a *startle reflex* in response to this sudden loud noise, which is a cascade of muscle contractions in the face and head generated within the brainstem. It arises automatically. In decades of scientific testing, no human being has ever demonstrated the ability to suppress this reflex via conscious intent. Ekman, however, surmised that the advanced Tibetan Buddhist meditation practices facilitate the development of conscious control over brainstem responses. Therefore, he asked the monk to suppress the startle reflex when he heard the noise. He was able to do it. Ekman was amazed. So was the entire scientific community. Although we are probably decades away from a complete neurobiological understanding of the long-term effects of these advanced Vajrayana meditation practices, experiments like this will generate interest (and the necessary funding) for further exploration.

The Dalai Lama probably isn't surprised by any of this. He was just waiting for the rest of us to figure it out. In time, the evolution of our instinctual intelligence many help more and more humans understand these mysteries scientifically- and experientially. But until we have it figured out, all we can do is simply bow in awe to the amazing instinctual wisdom implicit in these profound spiritual practices. But at least we now have some clue as to how this great political and spiritual leader can maintain his infinitely optimistic disposition in the face of the ongoing tragedy in Tibet.

Beyond Existence and Non-Existence

It is said that the great yogis like the Dalai Lama can enter into a state of suspended animation during meditation, where their life processes are sustained at the most minimal levels. When we are free from the attachment to the existence of inner sensations, we can experience a profound freedom within our consciousness. The experiential range of our awareness is expanded. No longer instinctually afraid of the dissolution of inner sensation, our consciousness is freed from the constraint of the human form. In the Tibetan tradition, it is said that the *clear light* of awareness arises spontaneously from the dark depths of the black near-attainment. This clear light is the most subtle form of awareness. Because it arises spontaneously from nothingness, it has no physical substrate to limit it or influence it in any way. This subtle awareness is literally beyond any conception of life or death. This is why it is also referred to as *primordial awareness*. We could say that this level of awareness represents the ultimate liberation of instinctual consciousness.

The integration of death allows instinctual intelligence to be absolutely free- beyond all clinging to existence or fears of nonexistence. As this freedom pervades all experience, our instinctual energies appear to emerge from a mysterious void of open potential. Freed from the limitations of the past and expectations of the future, boundless innate dynamism is experienced with exquisite sensitivity and purity. At this depth, we can perceive the ultimate nature of instinctual consciousness, pure and complete absence of restrictive boundaries of any kind. There is no sense of self that could restrict the spontaneous play of our instinctual nature. Free from all restriction, reality is experienced openly, as the complete absence of any thought, structure, or boundary. In this field of open awareness, instinctual intelligence is completely spontaneous, totally participating in the reality of here and now:

> The evolution of our instinctual intelligence nears fulfillment when there is a true and lasting alignment between the human body and the evolutionary wisdom of all creation. At this stage of development, one's sense of self is no longer limited to one's physical body. Instinctual energy is totally in service of the greater evolutionary needs of all beings. Within this realization, one feels contentment from the gradual instinctual evolution of all of humanity- the tiniest movement of even one soul is experienced with a joy and satisfaction far beyond any thought of one's own well-being. That is the ultimate contentment of the instinctual intelligence of the universe- the true source of all life.

Letting Go

Some unknown part of our instinctual consciousness will subtly resist the total embrace of freedom. I know for myself, I fear the loss of what is most precious to me- my loved ones and the delicate beauty of this earthly life. It is not only a concern for my personal loss of this miraculous beauty- but more the silent fear that that my loved ones and even the earth will somehow cease living also. This attachment to the presence of life itself is perhaps the most difficult aspect of letting go. Physically, it can be traced back to the most primitive substrates of our brain, an evolutionary holdover from the reptilian instincts that creates attachments to our physical environment. But this subtle longing for life itself goes beyond our own personal sphere, it is concern for the evolution of life on our planet. Letting go at this level feels like surrendering our home and giving up what is most personal and valuable to us. I think each one of us recognizes- deep down- that we are the personal expression of eternal life. We have embodied it, taken responsibility for it, and participated fully in its expression. Now, in the end, we must let go of our attachment to life in the human form.

Union with the Way of the Ten Thousand Things

All things that are born must die. That is the way of all physical life on this earth. It miraculously springs into organized existence and eventually dissipates. Every human is part of this cycle. More correctly, this cycle is a part of every human. As we relax into this reality, we realize that this has been the case all along. We have always been part of the larger dynamics of this earth, this solar system, and the entire universe. Realizing our true identity, contentment becomes boundless. Recognizing that we have always been inseparable from the effortless outpouring of intelligence and guidance is the quintessential hallmark of an evolved instinctual wisdom. This wisdom was there when our parents conceived us. It was there when we pushed our way out of the birth canal. It was there when we were playing as children. It was there when we went on our first date. It was there when we finally got the job we wanted. It will be there when we say goodbye for the final time.

It is right here, always, as we continuously draw the first breath of the last days of our lives.

Absolute Life

All things unborn must live. That is the nature of the mysterious void from which all things spontaneously arise. As I look back to the ultimate source of life and our instinctual consciousness, I wonder- how is it all possible? How could life arise from an outburst of energy that occurred 14 billion years ago? How did I come from the Big Bang? What did the Big Bang come from? As I consider these questions, I am aware that my conceptual mind will never know the answers. However, there is a deeper part of our consciousness that can embrace the mystery of our origins. It is- by its very nature- eternally quiet and completely content. This part of our awareness arises from the eternally dissolving edge between existence and nonexistence. The final practice of letting go is relaxing into this mysterious unknowable edge between life and nothingness. Never taking either extreme to be final, we become the contentment itself.

Absolute Freedom

We are, as we have always been, completely nonexistent yet forever imminently manifesting the myriad appearances we call life. It is said that the moment just before the Buddha attained enlightenment that he remembered each and every one of his previous lives. This allowed him to extinguish the final karmic imprints that stood between him and complete freedom. From our modern perspective, we might see this as the liberation from the imprints that restrict the absolute freedom of our instinctual consciousness. Throughout this book, we have illuminated all the major restrictive imprints, from the most obvious to the most subtle. With no imprints, no habits, and no tendencies to fall into, we can be totally free. Even the preference for existence over nonexistence can make no claims on our primordial awareness. The source of consciousness is not bounded by life or death. The wave of evolutionary intelligence that illuminated our lives and gives form to our instinctual consciousness was never ours to begin with, nor do we have to let go of it.

All that is left is its eternal expression, in this moment, right now.

Notes

Introduction

The definition of instinct was taken from *Steadman's Medical Dictionary, 26th Ed*. (Baltimore, MD: Williams & Wilkins, 1995).

For more on Freud's theories of instinctual drives and how they evolved throughout the history of psychoanalysis, see Gedo, J. *The history of psychoanalysis*. NY: Other Press (1999).

Affective Neuroscience is a growing field with many researchers and theorists. One of the major pioneers in this discipline is Jaak Panksapp. A comprehensive introduction to his work can be found in Panksepp, J. (1998). *Affective Neuroscience: Foundations of Human and Animal Emotions*. (NY: Oxford University Press, 1998).

Experience dependant maturation is a well-established concept in developmental neurobiology. Allan Schore's *Affect Regulation and the Repair of the Self* (NY: W.W. Norton, 2003) and *Affect Dysregulation and the Disorders of the Self*. (NY: W.W. Norton, 2003) provide a thorough overview.

The repercussions of the World Trade Center terrorist attacks on mental health in the US were considerable. See Neria, Y., Gross, R., & Marshall, R. (Eds.) *9/11: Mental Health in Wake of Terrorist Attacks*. (NY: Cambridge University Press, 2006) for a full description.

For a comprehensive overview of the latest theory and techniques in treating PTSD, see the state-of-the art work of Pat Ogden, Kekuni Minton, and Clare Pain in their *Trauma and the Body* (NY: Norton, 2006).

An excellent overview of how instinctual responses are recalibrated in psychotherapy, see Cozolino, L. *The Neuroscience of Psychotherapy: Building and Rebuilding the Human Brain*. (NY: Norton, 2002).

The Dalai Lama has participated in many conferences on the intersection of spiritual practice and neuroscience. Check out www.mindandlife.org for a full overview and a complete list of publications.

Chapter One

A great introduction to Joseph LeDoux's work on the stress response and the role of the amygdala, see Joseph LeDoux's *The Emotional Brain* (NY: Simon & Shuster, 1996).

The core mammalian amygdala/hypothalamus/PAG network is described in Panksepp, J. (1998). *Affective Neuroscience: Foundations of Human and Animal Emotions*. (NY: Oxford University Press, 1998).

For the neurobiological basis of the differences in activation of the sympathetic-adrenomedullary (SAM) axis the hypothalamo-pituitary-adrenocortical (HPA) axis, see Malarkey, W., Lipkus, I., & Cacioppo, J. (1995) The dissociation of catecholamine and hypothalamatic-pituitary-adrenal responses to daily stressors using dexamethasone. *Journal of Clinical Endocrinology and Metabolism, 80*, 2458-2463.

For more on the gut as a source of intelligence, see Michael Gershon's *The Second Brain* (San Francisco: Harper, 1999).

Chapter Two

Jaak Panksepp has written extensively on distress vocalizations. See Panksepp, J., Nelson, E., & Bekkedal, M. (1997). Brain Systems for the mediation of social separation- distress and social reward. *Ann. N.Y. Acad. Sci.* 807: 78-100.

Limbic resonance is a term popularized by Thomas Lewis, Fari Amini and Richard Lannon's *A General Theory of Love*. (NY: Random House, 2000).

Allan Schore likes to say that the mother serves as an auxillary cortex that regulates the infant's emotional and instinctual states. See his *Affect Regulation and the Repair of the Self* (NY: W.W. Norton, 2003) for more.

The pleasure of connection is described neurobiologically in Panksepp, J. (1998). *Affective Neuroscience: Foundations of Human and Animal Emotions*. (NY: Oxford University Press, 1998).

For more on how social interaction shapes the child's brain, see Louis Cozolino's *The Neuroscience of Human Relationships: Attachment and the Developing Social Brain*. (NY: Norton, 2006).

For details on the storage of interpersonal experiences and the central role of the orbitofrontal cortex social interaction, in the brain, see Allan Schore's *Affect Dysregulation and the Disorders of the Self*. (NY: W.W. Norton, 2003).

Dan Goleman's *Social Intelligence* (NY: Bantam Dell, 2006) provides a comprehensive resource for the research on the brain and social interaction.

A detailed exploration of the role of the orbitofrontal cortex in eating and other reward-based behaviors can be found in Rolls, E. (1998) The orbitofrontal cortex. In Roberts, A., Robbins, T., & Weiskrantz, L. (Eds.) *The Prefrontal Cortex: Executive and Cognitive Functions* Oxford: Oxford University Press, pp. 67-86.

An account of the brainstem's role in gustatory functioning can be found in William Blessing's *The Lower Brainstem and Bodily Homeostasis*. (NY: Oxford University Press, 1997).

The impact of early feeding experiences is often overlooked in modern developmental psychology see Linda Smith's and Mary Kroeger's *Impact of Birthing Practices on Breastfeeding* (Sudbury, MA: Jones and Bartlett, 2004) for more on the neurobiological implications of early breastfeeding experiences.

David Stern has described how the sense of agency is essential the development of the infant's emerging sense of self in *The Interpersonal World of the Infant*. (NY: Basic Books, 1985).

Chapter Three

The underlying neurobiology of seeking behaviors is detailed extensively in Panksepp, J. (1998). *Affective Neuroscience: Foundations of Human and Animal Emotions*. (NY: Oxford University Press, 1998).

The basis of reward seeking impulses- and addictive behaviors- and modern consumer advertising is explained in Gad Sadd's *The Evolutionary Bases of Consumption*. (Mahwah, NJ: Lawrence Erlbaum Associates, 2007).

The discovery of how children internalize and activate stored memories of parental interactions is presented in Robert Karen's *Becoming attached: First relationships and how they shape our capacity to love*. (NY: Oxford University Press, 1994).

Chapter Four

For more on the evolutionary importance of rough and tumble play, see Panksepp, J. (1993) Rough and tumble play: A fundamental brain process. In *Parent-Child Play: Descriptions and Implications*. (K. MacDonald, Ed.) pp. 147-184. NY: SUNY Press.

The pleasure of play is described more fully in Panksepp, J. (1998). *Affective Neuroscience: Foundations of Human and Animal Emotions*. NY: Oxford University Press.

The pleasures of social interaction in childhood are detailed in Louis Cozolino's *The Neuroscience of Human Relationships: Attachment and the Developing Social Brain*. (NY: Norton, 2006).

For an overview of the neurobiology of human sexual motivation, see Donald Pfaff's *Drive: Neurobiological and Molecular Mechanisms of Sexual Motivation.* (Cambridge, MA: MIT Press, 1999).

For an introductory primer on evolutionary psychology, go to http://www.psych.ucsb.edu/research/cep/primer.html

David Buss' homepage at the University of Texas at Austin provides a complete list of his publications and current research http://homepage.psy.utexas.edu/homepage/Group/BussLAB/

For more on the role of AVP in male sexual and aggressive behaviors, see Farris. C. (1992). Role of vasopressin in aggressive and dominant/subordinate behaviors. *Ann. N.Y. Acad. Sci.* 652: 212-226.

On the differences in sexual cognition between men and women, see David Geary's *Male, Female; The Evolution of Human Sex Differences* (Washington: APA, 1998).

Chapter Five

For an inside look at Navy SEAL training, see Dick Couch's mesmerizing *The Warrior Elite* (NY: Random House/Three Rivers Press, 2003).

Stephen Porges' articles include his original 1995 breakthrough article Orienting in a Defensive World. *Psychophysiology, 32*, 301-318. For further context, see Porges, S. (2001). The polyvagal theory: Phylogenetic substrates of a social nervous system. *International Journal of Psychopathology, 42*, 123-146.

For a more precise description of predatory attack as a sub-type of aggressive responses, see Weinshenker, N. & Siegel, A. (2002). Bimodal classification of aggression: Affective defense and predatory attack. *Aggression and Violent Behavior, 7*, 237-250.

For more on maternal aggression and rage, as well as predatory aggression in males, see Allan Siegal's *The Neurobiology of Aggression and Rage.* (NY: Informa Health Care, 2004.)

For more on the internal warning system, see Janig W. & Habler, H. (2000) Specificity in the organization of the autonomic nervous system: a basis for precise neural regulation of homeostatic and protective body functions. *Progress in Brain Research* 122: 351-367.

For a list of Bruce Perry's research and publications, go to http://www.traumacentral.net/TC_brucedperry.htm

An introduction to Perry's research can be found in Perry, B., Pollard, R., Blakly, T., Baker, W., & Vigilante, D. (1995) Childhood trauma, the neurobiology of adaptation, and "use-dependent" development of the brain. How "states" become "traits". *Infant Mental Health Journal, 16*, 271-291.

Chapter Six

For a comprehensive review of autonomic nervous system anatomy and functioning, see Vinken, P., Appenzeller, O., & Bruyn, G. (1999). *The autonomic nervous system*. NY: Elsevier Health Sciences.

Allan Schore is again the authoritative source for understanding how early childhood experiences affect the development of the autonomic nervous system. Much of this information can be found in these two articles:

Schore, A. (2001) The effects of a secure attachment on right brain development, affect regulation, and infant mental health. *Journal of Infant Mental Health, 22*, 7-66.

Schore, A. (2001) The effects of early relational trauma on secure attachment on right brain development, affect regulation, and infant mental health. *Journal of Infant Mental Health, 22*, 201-269.

The psychological impacts of early separation experiences were originally developed by Margret Mahler and her colleagues.. See Mahler, M., Pine, F., & Bergman, A. (1975). *The psychological birth of the human infant*. NY: Basic Books, for a description of this process. It remains a classic piece of psychological literature.

Chapter Seven

For a detailed examination of the neurobiological, evolutionary, and psychological dynamics of inhibitory shame, see Schore, A. (1998) Early shame experiences and infant brain development. In P. Gilbert & B. Andrews (Eds.) *Shame: Interpersonal Behavior, Psychopathology, and Culture*. NY: Oxford University Press. pp. 57-77.

The importance of emotional regulating mutual gaze transactions are described at length in Trevarthen, C. & Aitken, K. (2001) Infant intersubjectivity: Research, theory and clinical applications. *Journal of Child Psychology and Psychiatry, 42*, 3-48.

Chapter Eight

For a review of the evolutionary significance of inhibiting actions of executive functions, see Barkley, R. (2001). The executive functions and self-regulation: An evolutionary neuropsychological perspective. *Neuropsychology Review, 11*, 1-29.

For a more detailed discussion of the neurobiological basis of inhibition see, Knight, R., Staines, W., Swick, D., & Chao, L. (1999) Prefrontal cortex regulates inhibition and excitation of distributed neural networks. *Acta Psychologica* 101: 159-178.

For more on how inhibitory self-regulation develops during childhood, see Ryan, R., Kuhl, J., & Deci, E. (1997) Nature and autonomy: An organizational view of social and neurobiological aspects of self-regulation in behavior and development. *Development and Psychopathology* 9: 701-728. Dan Siegal's excellent *The Developing Mind: Toward a Neurobiology of Interpersonal Experience*. (NY: The Guilford Press, 1999) also offers a description of how emotional and instinctual self-regulation develops in early childhood.

On the social inhibition of sexual energy, see Zoldbrod, A. *Sex smart: How your childhood shaped your sexual life and what to do about it*. (San Francisco, CA: New Harbinger Publishing, 1998).

For discussions on how internal guides for being "good" and "right" contribute to life-long emotional and behavioral dispositions, see Strauman, T. (1992). Self-guides, autobiographical memory, and anxiety and dysphoria: Toward a cognitive model of vulnerability to emotional distress. *Journal of Abnormal Psychology, 101*, 87-95; and Strauman, T. (1995) Psychopathology from a self-regulation perspective. *Journal of Psychotherapy Integration 5*, 313-321.

An overview of the cross-cultural dimensions of emotional regulation can be found in Trommsdorff, G., & Rothbaum, F. (2008). Development of emotion regulation in cultural context. In S. Ismer, S. Jung, S. Kronast, C.Scheve & M. Vandekerckhove (Eds.), *Regulating emotions: Social necessity and biological inheritance*. (pp. 85-120). NY: Blackwell.

For a scholarly perspective on how children and teens develop increasingly complex forms of social self-regulation, see Higgins, E. (1989) Continuities and discontinuities in self-regulatory and self-evaluative processes: A developmental theory relating self and affect. *Journal of Personality, 57*, 407-444.

Byron Brown has written a useful guide to recognizing and reducing the barrier of self-judgment in his *Soul without Shame: A Guide to Liberating Yourself from the Judge Within*. (Boston: Shambhala, 1999).

Chapter Nine

For clinical perspectives on the negative effects of self-evaluation, see Strauman, T. (1996) Self-beliefs, self-evaluation, and depression: A Perspective on Emotional Vulnerability. In L. Martin & A. Tesser (Eds.), *Striving and feeling: The interaction between goals and affect*. Hillsdale, NJ: Erlbaum; and Strauman, T., Lemieux, A., & Coe, C. (1993). Self-discrepancy and natural killer cell activity: Immunological consequences of negative self-evaluation. *Journal of Personality and Social Psychology, 64*, 1042-1052.

Chapter Ten

The basic model of the Spectrum of Consciousness can be found in Wilber, K., Engler, J. & Brown, D. (Eds.). (1986). *Transformations of Consciousness: Conventional and Contemplative Perspectives on Development*. Boston: Shambhala.

A complete description of holarchical development and the Integral Model can be found in Wilber, K. (1995). *Sex, Ecology, Spirituality* Boston: Shambhala. For more recent updates and applications, go to http://in.integralinstitute.org/

Deepak Chopra has written several popular books on the mind/body connection. An introduction can be found in his *Quantum Healing: Exploring the Frontiers of Mind/Body Medicine*. (NY: Bantam, 1990).

Dan Goleman's bestselling *Emotional Intelligence* (NY: Bantam, 1995) helped people conceive of a more evolved mind/body functioning.

Michael Washburn provides a clear description of working with repression at various levels of human spiritual development in his *Embodied Spirituality in a Sacred World*. (Albany, NY: SUNY Press, 2003).

For an account of the importance of emotional regulation for cognitive development, see Greenspan, S. (1997) *The Growth of the Mind* Reading, MA: Addison/Wesley.

Research on the emotional and psychological benefits of meditation is still in its early stages. See B. Allan Wallace's *Contemplative Science: Where Buddhism and Neuroscience Converge*. (NY: Columbia University Press, 2006) for a review of the latest findings.

Wilber continues to refine and apply his work in new directions. For the latest updates, see his website www.kenwilber.com

Chapter Eleven

For a review of the evolutionary development of the human cortex, see Goldberg, E. (2001). *The executive brain: Frontal lobes and the civilized mind*. NY: Oxford University Press.

For an account of traumatic memory storage and its effects on neurocognitive processes, see Van der Kolk, B. (1996). Trauma and memory. In B. van der Kolk, A. McFarlane, & L. Weisaeth (eds). *Traumatic stress*. (pp. 279-302). NY: Guilford Press.

A comprehensive review of Bessel van der Kolk's research can be found in van der Kolk, B, McFarlane, A., & Weisaeth, L. (Eds.) (1996). *Traumatic stress*. NY: Guilford Press.

Louis Cozolino provides an excellent summary of the research concerning the role of the hippocampus in inhibiting amygdala hyperactivation in *The Neuroscience of Psychotherapy: Building and Rebuilding the Human Brain*. (NY: Norton, 2002).

Peter Levine's 1997 *Waking the Tiger: Healing Trauma* (Berkeley, CA: North Atlantic Press) is a great introduction to his work.

I cannot recommend Pat Ogden's work enough. Her 2006 *Trauma and the body: A sensorimotor approach to psychotherapy*. (NY: Norton) (co-authored with Kekuni Minton and Claire Pain) is the most sophisticated approach to working with trauma I have seen. For therapists, her training programs are also outstanding. For more information on these trainings, go to http://www.sensorimotorpsychotherapy.org/home/index.html

Chapter Twelve

Introductions to the work of A.H. Almaas (Hameed Ali) can be found in Almaas, A. (1984). *Essence: The Diamond Approach to Inner Realization*. York Beach, ME: Samuel Weiser; Almaas, A. (1987). *Diamond Heart Book 1: Elements of the Real in Man*. Berkeley, CA: Diamond Books.

For a comprehensive account of the transformation of emotional conflicts on the spiritual path, see Almaas, A. (1988). *The pearl beyond price: The integration of personality into being: An object relations approach*. Berkeley, CA: Diamond Books.

For a broad overview of the Diamond Approach, see Almaas, A. (2004). *The inner journey home*. Boston: Shambhala. For more on the work of A.H. Almaas, go to www.ahalmaas.com. For more on the spiritual teachings of the Diamond Approach, go to www.ridhwan.org

The storage and retrieval of traumatic memories is described in Perry, B. (1999) The memories of states: How the brain stores and retrieves traumatic experience. In J. Goodwin & R. Attias (Eds.) *Splintered Reflections: Images of the Body in Trauma*. (pp. 9-32). NY: Basic Books.

For more on self-images in the Diamond Approach, see Almaas, A. (1986) *The Void: Inner Spaciousness and Ego Structure* Berkeley, CA: Diamond Books.

A description of Pat Ogden's Sensorimotor Psychotherapy technique of dual processing can be found in Ogden, P., Minton, K., & Pain, C. *Trauma and the Body* (NY: Norton, 2006).

The importance of interpersonal connection in psychotherapy and its role in modulating amygdala function is detailed in Cozolino, L. (2002). *The Neuroscience of Psychotherapy: Building and Rebuilding the Human Brain*. NY: Norton; and Siegel, D. (2006). *The mindful brain in psychotherapy: How neural plasticity and mirror neurons contribute to emotional well-being*. NY: Norton. Both of these books provide a review of the recent neuroimaging studies.

A comprehensive account of how the accumulation of self-images affect personality development can be found in Almaas, A. (1986). *The Void: Inner Spaciousness and Ego Structure*. Berkeley, CA: Diamond Books; and Almaas, A. (1988). *The pearl beyond price: The integration of personality into being: An object relations approach*. Berkeley, CA: Diamond Books.

Self-images also form the basis of ego-identity, as described in Almaas, A. (1996). *The Point of Existence: Transformations of Narcissism in Self-Realization*. Berkeley, CA: Diamond Books.

Chapter Thirteen

For an overview of Howard Gardner's work, see his original *Frames of Mind: The Theory of Multiple Intelligences* (NY: Basic Books, 1993) and his recent *Multiple Intelligences: New Horizons in Theory and Practice* (NY: Basic Books, 2006)

The story of the purse snatching appeared in the *Syracuse Post-Standard*, December 20, 2005. Delen Goldberg was the reporter.

A recent study of optimal autonomic arousal and cognitive function can be found in Duschek, S., Muckenthaler, M., Werner, N. and Reyes del Paso, G. (2009). Relationships between features of autonomic cardiovascular control and cognitive performance. *Biological Psychology, 81, 2,* 110-117.

Flow is a term popularized by Mihaly Csikszentmihalyi in his work *Flow: The Psychology of Optimal Experience*. (NY: Harper & Row, 1990).

See Almaas, A.H. (2004). *The inner journey home*. Boston: Shambhala for a rich discussion of presence, awareness, and discrimination as inherent aspects of reality.

Chapter Fourteen

A well-balanced portrait of Oprah's life can be found in Helen Garson's *Oprah Winfrey: A Biography*. (Westport, CT: Greenwood Press, 2005).

For a scholarly analysis of Oprah's effect on race, psychology, and spirituality in the US, see Harris, J. & Watson, E. (2007). *The Oprah Phenomenon*. Lexington, KY: University of Kentucky Press.

For more on addictive cravings, see Ronald Ruden's *The Craving Brain: A Bold New Approach to Breaking from Drug Addiction, Overeating, Alcoholism, and Gambling* (NY: Harper, 2000).

For more on the impacts of connection and bonding on adult interpersonal connections, see Daniel Siegels's *The Developing Mind: How Relationships and the Brain Interact to Shape Who We Are*. (NY: The Guilford Press, 1999).

The exploration of frustration and craving as part of the deeper journey of adult spiritual development is discussed in Almaas, A.H. (2004). *The inner journey home*. Boston: Shambhala.

For a readable account of the research on mirror neurons, see Giacomo Rizzolatti & Corrado Sinigaglia's *Mirrors in the Brain: How Our Minds Share Actions, Emotions, and Experience*. (NY: Oxford University Press, 2008).

For more on Dr. Phil McGraw and his relationship to Oprah during the American Beef Association trail, see Sophia Dembling and Lisa Gutierrez's *The making of Dr. Phil: The straight-talking true story of everyone's favorite therapist*. (NY: John Wiley and Sons, 2003).

Google's innovative management strategies are discussed in Bernard Girard's *The Google Way*. (San Francisco: No Starch Press, 2009). For an analysis on how Google is changing modern cultural commerce see, Jeff Jarvis' *What Would Google Do?* (NY: Harper Collins, 2009). For more on Google's latest projects, see David Vise's *The Google Story* (NY: Delacorte Press/Bantam, 2008).

Chapter Fifteen

A comprehensive portrait of Lincoln's life can be found in Ronald White's *A. Lincoln: A Biography.* (NY: Random House, 2009).

For more on the effects of parasympathetic inhibition see Allan Schore's *Affect Dysregulation and the Disorders of the Self*. (NY: WW. Norton, 2003).

The flow of vagal parasympathetic inputs is described in Heilman, K. & Gilmore, R. (1998). Cortical influences in emotion. *Journal of Clinical Neurophysiology, 15*, 409-423. The override of external perception for inner sensations (the *internal warning system*) is discussed in detail in Janig, W., Khasar, S., Levine, J., & Miao, F. (2000) The role of vagal visceral afferents in the control of nociception. *Progress in Brain Research* 122: 273- 286.

For more on Patagonia's work policies, see Chouinard, Y. (2005). *Let my people go surfing*. NY: Penguin.

The science of mid-day naps is described in Rossi, E. & Nimmons, D. (1991) *The 20 minute break. The new science of ultradian rhythms*. (LA: Thrarcher, 1991); and Maas, J. (1998). *Power sleep*. NY: Villard.

For more on the process of adult individuation in spiritual development, see Almaas, A.H. (1988). *The pearl beyond price: The integration of personality into being: An object relations approach*. Berkeley, CA: Diamond Books.

Chapter Sixteen

Randy Taraborrelli's *Madonna: An Intimate Biography.* (NY: Simon & Schuster, 2001) provides detailed examination of Madonna's sexual relationships- as well as her transformation into motherhood.

The notion of *kaleidoscopic logic* is derived from Ken Wilber's description of vision-logic discussed extensively in his *Sex, Ecology & Spirituality,* (1995). Boston: Shambhala.

For more on left/right brain integration and its importance for continuing brain development, see Daniel Siegels's *The Developing Mind: How Relationships and the Brain Interact to Shape Who We Are*. (NY: The Guilford Press, 1999).

For more on Taoist sexual practices, Mantak Chia's original classic, *Awaken Healing Energy Through the Tao* (Santa Fe, NM: Aurora Press, 1983) is an excellent place to start. Learn more about his work at www.universal-tao.com

Chapter Seventeen

For more details on Tiger Woods' early training, see Lawrence Londino's 2006 *Tiger Woods: A Biography* (Westport, CT: Greenwood Press). A DVD with interviews of Tiger and his father discussing his training methods can be found in *Tiger: The Authorized DVD Collection*. (Beuna Vista Home Entertainment, 2004).

A number of researchers have described this fundamental inhibitory mechanism of splitting. Perry and his colleagues describe a *dissociative response* that is activated by extreme levels of hypermetabolic arousal in the infant's nervous system. See Perry, B., Pollard, R., Blakly, T., Baker, W., & Vigilante, D. (1995) Childhood trauma, the neurobiology of adaptation, and "use-dependent" development of the brain. How "states" become "traits". *Infant Mental Health Journal, 16*, 271-291 for detailed information.

For more on the role of parasympathetic nervous system in optimal nervous system performance, see John Doulillard's *Body Mind and Sport (Revised Ed.)* (NY: Three Rivers Press, 2001); see also David Coulter's *Anatomy of Hatha Yoga* (Homesdale, PA: Body and Breath, 2001) for more on the role of parasympathetic regulation, breathing, and yoga.

Chapter Eighteen

For an autobiographical portrait of the 14th Dalai Lama (Tenzin Gyatso) see *Freedom in Exile* (NY: Harper Collins, 1991).

For a close look at the Dalai Lama's practice of toglen, see his *Path to Bliss* (Ithaca, NY: Snow Lion, 1991) for detailed instructions.

For more on the evolutionary biological basis of morality, see Marc Hauser's *Moral Minds: How Nature Designed our Universal Sense of Right and Wrong*. (NY: Harper Collins, 2006).

For the research on meditation and left prefrontal cortex activation, see Lutz, A., Greischar, L. L., Rawlings, N. B., Ricard, M., & Davidson, R. J. (2004). Long-term meditators self-induce high-amplitude gamma synchrony during mental practice. *Proceedings of the National Academy of Sciences,* 101, 16369-16373.

For the latest on Richard Davidson's research at the Lab for Affective Neuroscience, go to http://psyphz.psych.wisc.edu/.

For an overview of executive functions and the frontal lobes, see Miller, B. & Cummings, J. (Eds.) (2007). *The Human Frontal Lobes: Functions and Disorders*. NY: The Guilford Press.

An introduction to the philosophy of emptiness in Tibetan Buddhism can be found in Guy Newland's *Introduction to Emptiness: As Taught in Tsong Khapa's Great Treatise on the Stages of the Path*. (Ithaca, NY: Snow Lion, 2008).

Inner spaciousness is described extensively in Almaas, A. (1986) *The Void: Inner Spaciousness and Ego Structure*. Berkeley, CA: Diamond Books.

Research on the loss of self boundaries is described in Laureys, S. (2006). *The boundaries of consciousness: Neurobiology and neuropathology*. NY: Elsevier.

For an introduction to Vajrayana Buddhism as it is practiced in the Tibetan tradition, see Daniel Cozort's *Highest Yoga Tantra* (Ithaca, NY: Snow Lion, 2005).

The importance of divine pride is described in The Dalai Lama's *The Union of Bliss and Emptiness: A Commentary on Guru Yoga Practice*. (Ithaca, NY: Snow Lion, 1988).

The role of the superior colliculus in multisensory integration is described in Stein, B., Wallace, M., & Stanford, T. (2000). Merging sensory signals in the brain: The development of multisensory integration in the superior colliculus. In M Gazzaniga, (Ed.) *The new cognitive neuroscience* 2nd Ed. pp. 55-72. Cambridge, MA: MIT Press.

The neural basis for cortical modulation of limbic and instinctual reactions is detailed in Davidson, R. J. (2004). Well-being and affective style: Neural substrates and biobehavioural correlates. *Philosophical Transactions of the Royal Society of London B, 359,* 1395-1411.

For a detailed explanation of the autonomic dynamics of the generation stage practices, go to www.instinctualintelligence.org to read my 2009 paper *Cessation and the Instinctual Attachments to Physical Sensation: Contributions of Neuroautonomic Physiology and Tibetan Buddhist Vajrayana Practices*.

A detailed review of the dynamics of death and dissolution in Highest Yoga tantra practices (especially Guhyasamaja) can be found in Lati Rinpoche & Hopkins, J. (1979). *Death, intermediate state and rebirth in Tibetan Buddhism*. Ithaca, NY: Snow Lion.

A detailed explanation of inner heat (tummo) meditation is found in Mullin, G. (1996). *Tsong Khapa's six yogas of Naropa*. Ithaca, NY: Snow Lion.

An account of Ekman's experiments from a Tibetan Buddhist perspective can be found in Matthieu Ricard's *Happiness: A Guide to Developing Life's Most Important Skill*. (Boston: Little, Brown & Co., 2006).

For more on the absolute nature of reality beyond the extremes of life and death, see Almaas, A. (2004). *The inner journey home*. Boston: Shambhala.

Index

Abuse, 45, 47-49, 55, 56, 62, 98, 105-107, 132, 142, 146, 188

abusive power, 162

acetylcholine, 31

addictive behaviors, 24, 146-149, 173-174

addictive patterns, 147, 173

adolescence, 32, 71-74, 86, 118, 122-123, 142, 167, 181

adrenaline, 6, 43, 47, 55

advertising, 24

affective neuroscience, 27-28, 193

affect regulation, 15

aggression, 40-47, 50, 70, 76, 79, 83, 86, 98, 99, 110, 127-128, 133, 142, 160, 177, 179, 181, 182, 188-189

    controlled, 42-46, 184-186

    self-protective, 4, 8-9

    sexual, 35, 38

aggressive energy, 5, 45, 133

AIDS, 170-171

Ali, Hameed (A.H. Almaas), 113-120, 122-124, 133, 161, 183

all-pervading wind, 205-206

aloneness, 25

amygdala, 3-9, 19, 20, 22, 24, 27, 28, 36-37, 158, 160, 182, 195, 197, 202

    arousal, 12-14, 20

    assertive strength, role in, 132-133

    instinctually intense memories, 104-108

    modulation by OFC 19-22, 121-122, 202

    predatory arousal, 44-45, 47-49

    response to threats, 3-9

amygdala/hypothalamus/PAG network, 4, 12, 107-108, 142

anger, 8-9, 44, 47, 56, 62, 67, 81, 83-84, 86, 99, 116-117, 125, 128, 132-134, 142-143, 170, 182, 191

animal intelligence, 105

annihilating power, 188

anxiety, 8, 9, 18, 26, 43, 52, 56, 82-83, 95-97, 105, 107-110, 119-120, 129, 142-143, 146, 161, 168, 174-175, 177, 182, 199, 202

anxiety disorders, 8-9, 52

appraisal, 17, 34, 39, 108

ARAS (ascending reticular activating system), 206, 207

archetypes, 169

arginine vassopressin (AVP), 35-36, 45, 177

artistic expression, 52, 74, 89, 99, 120, 148, 165-166, 168-169, 171, 203

assertive strength, 127-136

attachment, 97, 123, 207, 20
    interpersonal, 12-14, 90

attention processing, 7, 135, 158, 177, 195

authentic power, 184

autonomic nervous system, 6, 14, 16, 19, 52, 57, 59, 64-65, 68-69, 80, 107-108, 180
    development, 51-65

autonomy, 25-26, 53, 62-63, 85, 94, 154, 156, 161, 191

avoidance, 172

Basal ganglia, 22, 27

beastfeeding, 16

big bang, 125, 209

bisexuality, 38-39

black near-attainment, 206-207

blame, 85-86

body armoring, 167

bottom-up integration, 130

brainstem, 5-6, 12, 16, 17, 24, 27, 43, 48, 84, 106, 132, 158, 195, 197, 202, 204- 205, 207

breathing, 109, 120, 176, 192

brilliance, 15, 22, 125, 160

Brin, Sergey, 150

Buddha, 114, 196, 205, 209

Buddhism, 96, 123-125, 176, 191-207

burnout, 52, 56, 59, 64-65, 77, 82, 84, 134-135, 159, 160

Buss, David, 33-34, 39-40

Cardiovascular regulation, 205

Carson, Johnny, 181

catecholamines, 6, 43, 47

Catholic Church, 98

caudal reticular formation of medulla, 158

central channel, 206

cerebral cortex
    evolution of, 104

Chakrasamvara Tantra, 204

Chia, Mantak, 176

Chinese government, 191

Chopra, Deepak, 93

Christian contemplative practices, 96, 199

Christian mysticism, 96

cingulate cortex, 35, 107

Civil War, 154, 161

clear light, 207

Index

Clinton, Bill, 81, 160

cognitive control, 68

cognitive inhibition, 67-77, 94, 98

cognitive psychology, 90

compassion, 19, 87, 89, 99, 103, 115, 123, 125, 144-146, 149, 151, 159, 186, 191, 192-195, 200

competition, 32, 38, 159, 177, 180-182

competitiveness, 29

completion stage yogas, 200, 204-206

compulsiveness, 110

concern for offspring, 193

consciousness, 6, 9, 19-20, 26-28, 30, 33, 40, 47, 49, 50, 60, 65, 85-86, 107, 111, 136-137, 143, 146, 149-151, 154, 157, 160-162, 177, 181, 185, 187-188, 192-193,
     development of, 90-101, 103-104
     spiritual development, 113-125
     Tibetan Buddhist training, 197-209

contemplative neuroscience, 193, 203

contemplative practice, 96, 124

contemplative training, 98, 196

contentment, 18, 178, 193, 195, 197, 199, 202-209

contraction patterns, 167

copulation, 37

core survival responses, 199

corpus collosum, 38

cortex, cerebral, 6, 8, 13, 16, 23-24, 26, 28, 32, 35, 47, 49, 53, 60, 104, 105-108, 118, 121, 122, 148, 155,158, 160, 194, 195, 197, 202, 207

corticolimbic neural networks, 202

corticotrophin releasing factor (CRF), 55

cortisol, 7, 134

courage, 76, 125, 128, 130-131, 136, 142, 143, 145, 149, 151, 153, 156-157, 159, 169, 172, 187

cranial nerves, 204

craving, 23 -24, 114, 146-149

creativity, 62, 86, 89, 103, 113-114, 117, 125, 150, 160, 162, 165, 169, 171, 178

cross-hemispheric interaction, 38, 201-202

cuddling, 167

cultural constraints, 170

Da Vinci, Leonardo, 160

Dalai Lama, 43, 187, 191-193, 195-197, 199-205, 207

dancing, 33-34, 36, 38-39, 59, 83, 128, 166, 168, 171-172, 175

Davidson, Richard, 193-195

death, 4, 22, 41-42, 45-48, 54, 63, 91, 95, 97, 105, 145, 154-155, 162, 171, 199, 204-209

debate practice,Tibetan Buddhist, 196-197

defecation, 69

defensiveness, 142-143

delayed gratification strategy, 23

depression, 52, 59, 65, 82, 154, 157, 185

determination, 22, 123, 153, 156-159, 161-163, 178, 187

developmental hierarchy, 200

developmental neuropsychology, 14-15

developmental psychology, 14-15, 25, 90, 95, 99

Diamond Approach, 113, 116-120, 122-124

diaphragm, 204

disapproving gaze, 61, 69-70, 157, 181

discharge cycle, 110

dissociation, 48-49, 111, 118-119, 121-122, 143-144, 183-189, 197
    and trauma, 107-108

dissociative response, 49, 107-108 183

distinct ego states, 107, 118-119, 122

distress vocalizations, 12-13, 44-46, 48

divine pride, 202

dizziness, 172

DNA, 29, 81, 150, 153, 184

dopamine, 6, 16, 22, 27, 36, 43, 47, 147

dopaminergic circuits, 22, 24, 27

dopaminergic motivational circuits, 26

dorsal vagal complex, 43, 48-49, 105-106, 183, 185-186, 189, 206

dual processing technique, 120

Eastern spirituality, 90-93, 124

ego structures, 94, 96-97, 107, 118-119, 122-125

Einstein, Albert, 160

ejaculation, 177

ejaculatory discharge, 167

Ekman, Paul, 207

embodied energy, 69-70, 75, 86, 175, 178

emotional attunement, 140

emotional memories, 96, 105

emotional regulation, 15, 123

empathetic intelligence, 137

empathetic resonance, 139-140

empathy, 11-12, 137, 139-140, 146, 160, 193

emptiness, 123-125, 146-148, 173, 175, 196-200

energetic refueling, 60

Engler, Jack, 99

enlightened social action, 137

environmental adaptation, 21, 104

environmental cues, 21, 24-25, 106

environmental recognition, 12

envy, 29, 125, 160

Erikson, Erik, 91

esoteric spiritual traditions, 98, 101, 177

essential aspects, 116-117

estrogen, 35, 39, 178

evolutionary development, 42, 110, 184

evolutionary psychology, 33-34, 40

evolutionary will, 162

executive functions, 194-195, 201

existential realities, 95-96

existentialism, 91-92

extreme nervous system arousal, 182

Fawcett, Farah, 169

feeding, 14, 16-18

female nervous system, 16

female sexual attractiveness, 37

female sexuality, 37

fight or flight response, 6, 7, 56, 106

flashbacks, 107

flexible expression, 67

flirting, 37, 39

flow, 135

forgiveness, 124, 145

freezing response, 41, 48, 84, 105-110, 118-124, 129, 143, 145, 158, 183, 185-187, 206

Freud, Sigmund, 77, 90-92, 153

frontal lobes, 13-17, 19, 37, 56, 104, 132, 195

frozen self-images, 119-120, 122, 130, 132, 141-144, 149, 154, 175, 183

frozen shock, 105-106, 183, 186

Gambling, 30-33

gamma activity, 194, 207

Gardner, Howard, 127

gastrointestinal system, 48, 106

gaze transactions, 60

generation stage yogas, 200-201, 204

genitals, 39, 70, 167, 204-205

glutamate, 31, 55

goal-seeking, 22

Goleman, Dan, 14, 93

Google, 150-151

grandiosity, 61

greed, 29, 162, 163

Green Berets, 182

grief, 27, 138, 144-145

Guhyasamaja Tantra, 204, 205

guilt, 62, 81, 124, 140

gustatory satiation, 17

Hatred, 47, 50,
  transformation of, 179, 182-183, 186, 188
healing, 120-121, 145, 155, 177
Hell Week, 41-42, 47-48
hierarchy, 36
Hinduism, 96, 176
hippocampus, 8, 105, 107-108, 121, 132
HIV, 171
holarchical development, 93
Homo sapiens, 3, 104, 125, 185
human evolution, 20, 26, 42, 52, 77, 87, 89, 90, 99, 105, 124
hunger, 13, 17, 19, 71, 79
hyper-autonomy, 84
hypermetabolic arousal, 49
hypervigilance, 118
hypothalamo-pituitary-adrenocortical axis (HPA), 7, 8, 134-135, 197, 206
hypothalamus, 4-6, 8, 12, 16, 19, 22-24, 35-36, 39, 44, 47, 108, 121-122, 132, 133, 202, 206

Id, 77, 192
idealization, 71, 74-76, 82, 115
immune system, 84
implicit memory, 201
impulse control, 19
incomplete satisfaction, 147
individuating energy, 136
infancy, 4, 11, 14-19, 55, 69, 85, 91, 92, 94, 98, 108, 122, 123, 140, 147-149, 175, 182-183, 186-187
inhibition, 54, 56, 67, 69, 70, 72-75
inhibitory responses, 48, 61, 68-76, 96, 105-110, 121-122, 129, 130-132, 143, 144, 148, 157-158, 167, 168, 172, 177, 180, 183-187, 189, 198
inner heat meditation (tummo), 205-206
inner spaciousness, 198-199
instinct for freedom, 113
instinctual agency, 18
instinctual alignment, 99, 193
instinctual balance, 159-160, 177
instinctual development
  stages, 94
instinctual evolution, 25, 27, 80, 89, 136, 153, 161-163, 187, 208
instinctual gratification, 17, 95, 97, 170, 198
instinctual maturity, 123
instinctual memories
  recording, 4, 105-110, 118
instinctual modulation, 104
instinctual precision, 6, 9, 12, 80, 113, 125, 131-135, 144, 177, 189, 200
instinctual regulation, 13, 15, 69-74, 99, 202, 203
instinctual stagnation, 77, 81-86, 94, 96, 117, 124, 175

instinctual transformation, 157

instinctually significant interpersonal exchanges, 12-19, 118

Integral Theory, 100

intelligences,
 multiple, 89, 127, 193

interconnectivity, 13, 151

interdependence, 163

inter-male aggression, 35-36, 177

internal guardians, 77

internal warning system, 47, 158

internalization, 69-74, 76, 94

internet dating, 23

intersubjective intelligence, 12

intersubjectivity, 12

intestinal tract, 48, 106

intimacy, 15, 47, 54, 74, 139, 148, 154, 156, 167, 174

intuitive knowledge, 13, 18, 33, 44, 158

isolated memories, 107

isolated neural networks, 118

Jealousy, 40, 125, 170

Jesus, 114

Kabbalah, 96, 176

kaleidoscopic knowledge, 173

kaleidoscopic logic, 171

Lateral hypothalamatic gateway, 16

LeDoux, Joseph, 5-6, 8-9

left brain, 172

left hemisphere, 172, 194, 202

left middle gyrus of prefrontal cortex, 194

lesbian relationships, 39

Levine, Peter, 108-111, 118, 120, 122, 133, 183

Lewinsky, Monica, 81

limbic resonance, 12-13, 35

limbic system, 4, 24, 44, 105

Lincoln, Abraham, 91, 153-159, 161-163

linguistic processing, 194

linguistic skills, 89

loneliness, 130, 145-148, 151, 174-175, 177

longing, 85, 147, 166, 169, 172-175, 208

lordosis, 39, 167

loving grace, 150

Madonna, 165-173, 175-176

mahaunuttarayoga, 200

maladaptive responses, 122

male sexuality, 35-36, 45, 177

mandalas, 201

Mandela, Nelson, 187

mantra recitation, 201-202

masturbation, 174

mate selection, 34, 104

maternal responsiveness, 11-20

mating, 21, 23-24, 31, 33-34, 39-40

maturation, 15, 34, 53, 60, 69, 73, 89, 118

McGraw, Phil, 141-145, 153

meaninglessness, 95, 157, 158

medial strata, 22

meditation, 90, 92, 96-101, 114, 176,
    in Tibetan Buddhism 192-200, 203-207

medulla, 48, 105, 106, 204, 206

memory formation, 104

mental distractions, 185-186

mental representations, 69, 72-74, 90

mesencephalic locomotor region, 202-203

midbrain, 4, 6, 12, 27, 32, 43-44, 48, 61, 106, 132, 139, 158, 183, 186, 202, 206

mirror neurons, 140, 179

monastic training, 101, 114, 191-193, 196- 197, 199, 206

mood altering substances, 147

moral intelligence, 18, 20, 139, 151, 192

moral restrictions, 114

Moses, 40

motivational instincts, 22, 25

motor inhibition, 48, 158, 186

multiple orgasms, 178

murder, 40

Napping, 31, 85, 160

natural selection, 22, 33-34

nausea, 48, 106, 157

Navy SEALs, 41, 43-49, 105, 182, 186

neocortex, 27, 32

nervous system cleansing, 124

nervous system composure, 180

nervous system exhaustion, 51

nervous system recalibration, 120-122, 124, 128-129, 159, 168, 179, 182-183

nervous system regulation, 43, 99

neural plasticity, 195

neuroarchitectural design, 5, 132

neurosis, 77, 91-92, 98-99, 161, 185

nonexistence, 97, 197, 199, 208, 209

noradrenaline, 55

norepinephrine, 6, 43, 47

nourishment, 16-18, 24, 37, 148

nucleus accumbens, 24, 27

nucleus of the solitary tract, 47

nurturance, 11, 85, 137, 178

nurturing response, 11

Object relations, 90

objective truth, 189

Ogden, Pat, 111, 120, 122

opioids, 13, 15-16, 32-33, 35, 38, 53, 140, 147, 174

optimal arousal, 135, 180

optimal stress, 181, 183

orbitofrontal cortex (OFC), 49, 53, 56, 107, 108, 110, 121-122, 130, 132, 148, 155, 158, 160, 195, 197, 201, 202

    bottom-up networks, 130, 132

    failure to regulate amygdala, 108, 110

    interpersonal interactions, 13-20, 23-26, 121-122

    meditation, 201-202

    motivation, 25-26, 28

orgasm, 37, 176, 177, 206

orgasmic release, 167

orienting response, 145

overwhelming threat, 48, 105, 121, 122

oxytocin, 13, 16, 32-33, 37-39, 53, 140, 177, 178

Page, Larry, 150

pain, 4, 41, 42-48, 52, 84-85, 105, 154, 155, 183, 204

    assertive strength, 131-134

    childhood responses to, 138-140, 143-148

    infant responses to, 11-14

pain avoidance, 12

panic, 46, 48, 201-202, 205, 206

Panksepp, Jaak, 27, 28, 31

paradigmatic shifts, 90

parasympathetic system, 12-13, 44, 45, 47, 48, 52, 57, 59-64, 69, 73, 106, 154, 157, 158, 161, 180-181, 186, 189

    development, 59-64

    disapproving gaze, 60-63

    inhibitory response, 60-63, 69

    predatory aggression, 44-45, 47-48

parental interaction, 25, 68-72

parental responses, 52, 54, 56, 62-64, 68-71, 128, 147, 182, 183

passion, 15, 39, 40, 68, 75, 81, 113-115, 125, 166, 170, 172-173

passionate creativity, 165-178

passionate joy, 173

peaceful power, 179-190

periaqueductal gray region (PAG), 49, 61, 132-133, 139, 155, 158, 160

    distress vocalizations, 12, 44-46

    infant frustration, 12, 14

    motivation, 24, 27-28

    regulation of, 202, 206

    self-protection, 4-6, 8

Perry, Bruce, 49

perseverance, 21-22, 94, 154, 161-162

persevering drive, 21

persevering intelligence, 27

personal phase, 94

physical isolation, 13

physical play, 34

physical prowess, 36

Piaget, Jean, 91

pituitary gonadal axis, 34

play, 32-34, 37-38, 82, 125, 166-167, 175, 180, 196

pleasure, 17, 25, 31-32, 37, 53, 70

polar bears, 103-104, 109, 111, 113

polyvagal regulation, 42-44, 48-49, 183, 185, 188

Porges, Stephen, 42-43, 48-49

pornography, 167, 174

power, 40, 44-50, 76, 80-81, 117, 123-127, 150, 162, 173, 178, 179-189

predatory aggression, 37, 44-47, 50, 177, 178, 182, 184-186, 185, 188-189

predatory glow, 37

predatory sweetness, 177

prefrontal cortex, 8, 19, 23, 47, 53, 56, 60, 132, 194-195, 197, 201, 202, 207

preoptic area, 36

pre-personal stage, 93-96, 98

primates, 38

primitive survival systems, 48

primordial awareness, 207, 209

procedural memories, 201-203

progesterone, 35, 39, 178

protective intelligence, 127

psychological boundaries, 198

psychological conflicts, 51, 117

psychosexual development, 91

psychotherapy, 90, 99, 114, 116, 119, 121

PTSD (post traumatic stress disorder), 8, 107, 109, 118, 121-122, 124

puberty, 34, 72

Reality testing, 108, 123, 155

receptive nurturance, 16, 178

refined qualities, 87, 116-117

regulating mechanisms, 19, 42
relaxation, 12, 18, 32, 42, 51-52, 57, 62, 64, 140, 147-148, 159, 181, 200
repression, 74-76, 86, 98-99, 125, 166, 168-170, 172-173, 175
repressive barrier, 166, 168-170
reproduction, 21, 31, 37, 39, 73, 105, 192, 193
resiliency, 46, 161, 163
responsibility, 85, 125, 162, 166, 187, 208
restrictive force, 111, 113, 123-125
reward centers, 174
right brain, 172
right hemisphere, 15, 172, 194
rough and tumble play, 31
rule learning, 95

Sadhana, 201
scarcity, 23, 25, 155, 161
Schore, Allan, 15, 18, 19, 49
security, 28, 74, 131, 139, 155, 159, 193, 206
seeking behaviors, 21-22, 26, 35
seeking systems, neural, 22-27, 36, 156, 174
self-concept, 70
self-criticism, 82
self-deception, 81
self-destructive behaviors, 146
self-doubt, 62, 75, 76, 168, 175, 204
self-images, 119-125, 128-130, 132, 136, 142, 149, 160, 172, 177, 183, 187, 197, 198, 203-204
self-inhibition, 67-77
self-judgments, 76-77, 82-83, 86, 131, 139, 156, 165, 168, 182-184
selflessness, 196-197, 199
self-organizing systems, 100
self-protective instinct, 3-9, 19, 125-132, 134, 136, 142, 161
self-regulation, 17-18, 26, 71, 94, 107, 120
sensorimotor maps, 203
Sensorimotor Psychotherapy, 111, 120
sensoriphysical stage, 94
sensual touching, 38
septal area, 35
sequential reasoning, 197
sexual addictions, 95, 174
sexual arousal, 33-39, 166-170
sexual attraction, 33-39, 59
sexual behavior, 33-39, 174, 177
sexual confidence, 29, 67, 165-168, 176-178
sexual desire, 29, 33, 37, 74, 174
sexual energy, 38, 69-71, 75, 176-177
sexual exhibitionism, 166

sexual identity, 71

sexual intelligence, 34-35, 37, 74, 172, 176

sexual intercourse, 39, 177

sexual motivation, 34-35, 177

sexual orientation fluidity, 38

sexual persistence, male, 36

sexual pleasure, 35, 37, 176-178

sexual potency, 165, 177

sexual receptivity, 39, 178

sexual satisfaction, 37, 167, 176-177

sexuality, 33-39, 62, 64, 73, 74, 89, 90, 117, 165-171, 174-178

shamanism, 168, 169

shame, 45, 59-62, 64-65, 69, 75, 77, 81, 85-86, 110, 124, 140, 157-158, 165, 168-169, 180-181, 189

simultaneous awareness technique, 120-122, 133, 144, 168, 183

social acceptance, 73, 95, 140

social adaptation, 73, 105

social bonding, 12-19, 31, 38, 44, 138-139, 147-148

social confidence, 32

social dominance, 29

social hierarchies, 40

social instincts, 11, 30, 125

social intelligence, 14-15, 19, 38-39, 108, 137-140

social isolation, 61, 63, 130, 143-144, 147, 149, 155, 206

social status, 36, 38, 95, 162

somatic dysregualtion, 48, 106

Somatic Experiencing, 109-110

somatosensory cortex, 32, 35, 140, 202, 203, 204

soul, 11, 40-41, 72, 75, 86, 113, 124, 126, 144-145, 153, 156, 162, 174, 193, 208

spatial boundaries, 198, 200

spatiotemporal cognition, 195

Spectrum of Consciousness model, 91-97, 99-100

spiritual development, 80, 98-99, 113, 116, 123, 127, 192

spiritual intelligence, 97

spiritual realization, 98, 116-117, 119, 123, 175, 192-209

spiritual traditions, 40, 92-93, 96, 98-99, 101, 114, 123-124, 144-145, 175, 177, 194, 199

splitting, 98, 183, 186, 188

stages of development, 60, 70, 74, 92-98, 123, 172, 208

startle reflex, 207

starvation, 162

stillness, 160, 186-189

stress, 51, 107

stress response, 3, 43, 48, 106, 135, 197

subcortical regions, 16

suckling reflex, 18

suffocation, 42, 46, 204, 206-207

superego, 77

superior colliculus, 202-203
superior parietal lobe, 199
suppression, 84, 95, 98
survival mechanisms, 105
survival of the fittest, 54, 162
sustainability, 162
sympathetic nervous system, 60, 62, 130, 134-135, 180
    activation, 3-8, 12, 43-44, 53-57, 132, 134
    adaptation, 54-57
    arousal, 3-8, 43, 55, 62, 134, 189
    development, 54
sympathetic signature, 56, 130, 133
sympathetic-adrenomedullary axis (SAM), 6, 7, 135, 160
synergistic functioning, 178

Tantric practices, 176-178, 200-201, 204-207
Taoism, 96, 123, 176
temperature dysregulation, 43, 46, 206
temperature regulation, 22, 139
terror, 41, 95, 97, 107, 110, 158, 162, 177, 199
testosterone, 35-37, 177
thalamus, 5, 17, 24, 32, 206
Thatcher, Margaret, 169
The Void, 97, 123-124, 196-197
thermal regulation, 12
three-dimensional rotating visualization, 202
Tibet, 191, 207
Tibetan Buddhism, 123, 191-207
toilet training, 69
tonglen meditation, 192-193
transpersonal development, 93-99, 117, 119, 123, 161
trauma, 8, 48, 106-111, 118-121, 129, 133, 143, 183
traumatic memory activation, 105-111
tribal affiliations, 193
true power, 181

Unexcelled Tantric Yogas, 200-207
Universal Taoist system, 176
urination, 69

Vagal brake, 43
vagal complex, 43
vagal sensory neurons, 204
Vajrayana Buddhism, 197-207
value, 70
van der Kolk, Bessel, 106-111, 118-120, 122

vascular pressure, 205

vengeance, 45, 47, 84, 171

ventral tegmental networks, 24, 27, 35-36

ventral vagal complex, 43, 189

ventromedial hypothalamus, 39

vestibular systems, 202-203

vicarious traumatization, 105

visualization practices, 193, 195, 201-202, 204

visual-spatial processing, 194

vomiting, 202

vulnerability, 12, 138-139, 142, 145, 156, 167, 170, 173-174

Wealth displays, 36

Wilber, Ken, 91-94, 115

    developmental models, 91-101, 111,

    transpersonal development, 96-99, 117, 123

Winfrey, Oprah, 137-146, 149, 151, 153, 163

Woods, Earl, 179-184, 186-187, 189

Woods, Thea, 181

Woods, Tiger, 43, 179-190

    polyvagal regulation, 183, 185, 188

World Trade Center, 105

Yoga, 96, 176

About the Author

Theodore Usatynski earned Master's degrees from Harvard University and Naropa University. After a few years in private practice in Boulder, he discovered that he could serve clients more effectively using the education and training techniques that were emerging through the paradigm of Instinctual Intelligence. He relocated his consulting practice, *Instinctual Intelligence, LLC* to the San Francisco Bay Area in 2007.

As founder and director of Instinctual Intelligence LLC, Theodore has served a variety of clients in the US and across the globe. Its educational services provide lectures, demonstrations, and in-house training programs to individuals, as well as educational and professional organizations. Introductory training programs introduce the embodied principles of Instinctual Intelligence. More comprehensive and advanced training in nervous system regulation is offered though customized programs. *www.instinctualintelligence.org*

Theodore lives in Berkeley, California where he is a long-time student of the Ridhwan Diamond Approach. The Diamond Approach is contemporary school of spiritual development that uses modern psychological knowledge along with traditional meditation practices to systematically uncover the essential nature of the human soul. *www.Ridhwan.com*

Theodore has also been a long time student of yoga, Chi Gung, and other Tantric Disciplines from the Master Teachers in Tibet, Europe, and the US. He works within a growing network of knowledge and skill offered by the wide range of extraordinary gifted healers, guides, and spiritual teachings available in the SF Bay Area and throughout the world.

4902104

Made in the USA
Lexington, KY
13 March 2010